This book begins by asking, How could it be that under the Deng regime, when the People's Republic of China experienced its greatest economic prosperity, the largest and most tragically concluded popular protest took place? To answer this question the author examines, from the viewpoint of a participant, the relations between the Communist political elite and the largely anti-Communist intellectual elite during the decade of reform (1977–89). He shows how the Deng Xiaoping regime precipitated a legitimacy crisis by encouraging economic reform while preventing political reform: By departing from the economic guidelines of Maoism, the leadership undermined the basis of its own authority. Justifying this policy in the eyes of both the ruling political elite and the increasingly powerful intellectual elite proved increasingly difficult.

In addition to demonstrating the role intellectuals played in shaking Communist-party rule, the book offers a theoretical model to explain how they were able to do so. The author's concept of "institutional parasitism" depicts how, rather than developing separate institutions, resistance to the ruling political elite occupied state structures from which oppositional activity was carried out. In challenging the state versus civil society model, this book makes an important contribution to understanding changing state–society relations in late communism, and the dynamics of the transition from communism. It will be of interest to both scholars of China and students of comparative communism.

The decline of communism in China

The decline of communism in China

Legitimacy crisis, 1977–1989

X. L. Ding

CAMBRIDGE
UNIVERSITY PRESS

Published by the Press Syndicate of the University of Cambridge
The Pitt Building, Trumpington Street, Cambridge CB2 1RP
40 West 20th Street, New York, NY 10011-4211, USA
10 Stamford Road, Oakleigh, Melbourne 3166, Australia

First published 1994

Printed in the United States of America

Library of Congress Cataloging-in-Publication Data
Ding, X. L.
The decline of communism in China: legitimacy crisis, 1977–1989 /
X. L. Ding.
p.   cm.
Originally presented as the author's thesis (doctoral)
Includes bibliographical references and index.
ISBN 0-521-45138-8
1. Communism – China. 2. China – Politics and government – 1976–
3. China – Intellectual life – 20th century. I. Title.
HX418.5.D56   1991
335.43′45 – dc20   93-11270
                          CIP

A catalog record for this book is available from the British Library.

ISBN 0-521-45138-8 hardback

For my children,
in the hope that they will see a more civil China

Contents

Tables and figure

Preface

If someone were to ask me, What is the most agonizing intellectual experience you have ever had? without hesitation my response would be: Writing a book in a foreign language. Finding the precise words to express even simple, familiar thoughts can sometimes be laborious. Rending complex or subtle ideas using a relatively meager vocabulary feels as painful to me as one would imagine it to be for a long-starving Somali mother squeezing milk for her baby from wizened breasts. Every sentence compels a compromise. What I write down is never exactly what I want to say. I can only select from the narrow choices available to approximate, from a far distance, what I am trying to say. The vivid, the sophisticated, the subtle, and the personal style are all sifted away, leaving only the dry, the rough, and the basic. I feel myself in a constant process of self-distortion.

The basic difference between what one writes in one's native language and what one writes in a strange foreign language is that, in the former, one's thoughts command words that, in turn, penetrate and stimulate one's mind. But in the latter, words dictate one's thoughts and only float on one's mind.

In any case, I and my manuscript survived, but not without help from many of the following people, who deserve thanks but who are in no way responsible for whatever I said and whatever flaws I left in the output.

I am grateful

to my doctoral thesis committee – Daniel Bell, Roderick MacFarquhar, Ezra F. Vogel, and Andrew G. Walder – for their years of instruction and advice that led to the completion of my thesis, on which the present book is based;

to Gilbert Rozman for his comments and suggestions at almost every stage of this study;

to Andrew J. Nathan, Michel Oksenberg, Richard Madsen, and Mark Field for their comments on an earlier outline of this project;

to Ellin Sarot, Kalman Applbaum, Anna Seleny, Blanford Parker, Karl Eschbach, Joseph Soares, and Consuelo Cruz for their encouragement and friendship, which helped me endure the most trying moments during the creation of this work;

to Carol Lee Hamrin, Ken Jowitt, Liah Greenfield, Arthur Stinchcombe, Aldon Morris, and Leslie Cintron for their comments on different parts of this study;

to the three anonymous readers for their comments and suggestions, which helped me enormously in improving the manuscript;

to Rachael Winfree of the Cambridge University Press for her judgment and experience, which led me through the final stage of this production;

to Brian R. MacDonald for his careful editing of the manuscript;

to Nancy Hearst of the Fairbank Center Library at Harvard University for her always efficient assistance;

to the United Daily Cultural Foundation for its support allowing me to study political and social developments in Taiwan and their impact on the Chinese mainland;

to the Division of Social Science at the Hong Kong University of Science and Technology for the logistic support it provided during the editing of this book;

to Helen F. Siu and Zelda Stern for their permission to quote from "Pan Xiao's letter," translated in their book *Mao's Harvest: Voices from China's New Generation,* edited by Helen F. Siu and Zelda Stern (New York: Oxford University Press, 1983);

to M. E. Sharpe, Inc., for its permission to quote from the translated materials "Changing Attitudes among Chinese Youths: Letters to Zhongguo Qingnian," edited by David Ownby (*Chinese Sociology and Anthropology* 1985, No. 4), and "The Chinese Debate on the New Authoritarianism," edited by Stanley Rosen and Gary Zou (*Chinese Sociology and Anthropology* 1990–91, Nos. 2–4);

to all the Chinese informants who provided valuable data for this study; and

to my wife for her understanding and support during the long and arduous journey of this work.

Abbreviations

CAS	Chinese Academy of Sciences
CASS	Chinese Academy of Social Sciences
CCP	Chinese Communist Party
CYL	Communist Youth League
FBIS	Foreign Broadcast Information Service
IRESR	Institute for Research on the Economic System Reform (under the State Council)
KMT	Kuomintang (Nationalist party)
PCPD	Party Central Propaganda Department
PLA	People's Liberation Army
PRC	People's Republic of China
SEZ	Special Economic Zone
USSR	Union of Soviet Socialist Republics
CI	cultural intellectual
MI	marginal intellectual
OI	official intellectual
TI	technical intellectual

Introduction

In the spring of 1989, the world witnessed massive antigovernment demonstrations in major Chinese cities, followed by a military crackdown by the People's Liberation Army. Since then, a question raised again and again in scholarly circles has been: How could it be that under the Deng Xiaoping regime, when the People's Republic had experienced its greatest prosperity, there could occur the largest popular protest in the PRC's history?

In fact, it is not unique for a regime like the Chinese one under Deng to face popular protests. Since Tocqueville published *The Old Regime and the French Revolution*, scholars have been familiar with the paradox that unrest and revolutions break out more often when things go from bad to better than when they go from bad to worse. What the Deng regime experienced is but the latest example of the famous "Tocqueville effect" – the inability of a group in power to control change.

In the late 1970s, when Deng and his allies had just returned to office, the country was in a total crisis. Politically, major sectors of Chinese society still lived in the shadow of the great terror of Maoist "class struggle" campaigns. Economically, many peasants of even the once most prosperous rural areas had been reduced to beggars; and the urban population suffered from declining income and shortages of virtually all kinds of consumer goods.[1] Psychologically, the whole nation was in a state of depression and despair.

To lead China out of its miserable condition and bring it into the ranks of modern industrial nations, Deng and his colleagues opened China's door to the

[1] Some observers, e.g., Dwight Perkins (1986: 39–40), seem to believe that the post-Mao reforms were undertaken primarily under the pressure of a political crisis, and that the economic situation at that time was not so bad. This judgment is one-sided, as it understands an economic crisis mainly by looking at growth rates reflected in official statistics. But to the insiders of an economic system, the condition of day-to-day material life is a more important indicator in judging the economic situation. To understand how miserable China's economic situation was in the middle and late 1970s, how that situation had produced a strong sense of urgency among the top leaders, and how that sense had contributed to their tolerance for limited economic liberalization, see the vivid narrative by Chen Yizi (1990: 1–44).

outside to admit new technology and capital. In the meantime, they permitted radical changes in a socialist economic system that had proved inefficient. To them, any economic means were acceptable as long as "public ownership" remained dominant. And thus a variety of market mechanisms and entrepreneurially based establishments flowed into the Chinese economy; these included quasi-private farming, "special economic zones" (SEZs), joint ventures and foreign-capital businesses, quasi-private and private enterprises, market pricing, and limited labor and capital markets.

While giving the go ahead to such quasi-capitalistic economic reforms, those in the mainstream of the post-Mao ruling elite refused to carry out parallel reforms in government and to open up the political system. They insisted that the Communist party must monopolize political power and that all reforms should be executed under party committees' organization and leadership. In other words, the party-state bureaucracy must serve as the sole transmitter and interpreter of reform policies, the sole monitor of reform proceedings, and the authoritative judge of reform results.

The Dengist approach to reform was a "dual traffic policy," that is, "anti-Left" in economics and "anti-Right" in politics.[2] "Left" in post-Mao China denotes ideals, methods, and practices typical of Stalinist and Maoist socialism, and "Right" denotes the liberalization tendency deviating from Stalinism and Maoism. Without legally abandoning state dominance over the economy and granting private ownership equal rights, the Dengists wanted to create a dynamic and efficient economic structure free of all the defects associated with the socialist economy. Yet, while promoting economic pluralism, the Dengists refused to undertake political liberalization and wanted to keep the core of the Communist government system intact.

The primary reason the Dengists adopted this contradictory reform policy was their concern for power. Political restructuring was opposed because it would mean sharing power with others. Formally abandoning the commitment to "public ownership" was unacceptable because it would mean giving up the raison d'être for Communist rule. As Marx and Engels (1972: 346) declare in the *Communist Manifesto*, "The distinguishing feature of Communism is . . . the abolition of bourgeois property. . . . The theory of the Communists may be summed up in the single sentence: Abolition of private property." Since that time, communist parties in power across the world have defined this as their ultimate goal and justified their rule by this commitment. If this principle were to be abandoned, the legitimating foundation of communist rule would crumble with it.

---

[2]See Xueliang Ding (1988: 1127–28) for an explanation of that policy.

The Deng regime's effort to keep a balance between change in the economic sphere and continuity of the political structure faced extreme difficulties. The Dengist economic reforms and, in particular, their unintended social consequences offended privileged groups in the party-government and the army. These felt that liberalization of the economy and commercialization and pluralization of Chinese society opened up too much room for "incongruous practices and incompatible elements," which, in turn, undermined the party-state's control of the population and threatened their material and ideal interests. (See Weber 1946: 280 for discussion of "material and ideal interests.") In the eyes of the politically concerned populace, however, the Dengist reforms did too little too slowly to dismantle the self-serving, bureaucratic iron cage in which they had suffered so much and for so long.

The Dengist leadership was thus caught in a two-front confrontation. In defending its right to rule in an age of reform, it had to address two different audiences. In the face of the establishment hard-liners, the Dengist leadership had to justify its legitimacy by invoking the Communist system. In order to access resources controlled by the party-state bureaucracy and the army, the Dengist leadership had to convince these traditional power centers that the current policy was in their best interests. And to the politically conscious social groups, the Deng regime had to justify its legitimacy as a government acting in the interests of its people, in order to secure their conformity and cooperation, for both preventing rebellion and getting socioeconomic tasks done. The regime had to prove to the ruled that their future and the nation's welfare and pride all depended on the current political order.

The reason the Dengist leadership had to fight a two-front war is that during the period covered here, China had turned away "from the emphasis on revolutionary struggle and ideological transformation that characterized the last years of the Maoist era. China's post-Mao leaders, under the slogan of 'Four Modernizations,' . . . stress political stability and economic development rather than ideological struggle and class conflict. Pragmatic adaptation of policy to solve pressing concrete problems has replaced utopian efforts to transform society in the name of egalitarian goals" (Barnett and Clough 1986: 1). To the Communist system under Deng, the objective of regime legitimation was not limited to survival. With the commitment to economic and technological modernization, the Deng regime understood that the better-educated social groups' cooperation was indispensable.

The primary goal of Dengism was to maintain harmony between economic pluralism and Communist dictatorship. This experiment confronted its most serious challenge in the spring of 1989. When a significant part of the urban population went out into the streets to defy Communist rule, the regime, apparently, felt it had little choice but to turn to the army for aid. The nation-wide mass demonstrations and the subsequent military crackdown put an end to a distinctive era dating from the late 1970s.

Description and analysis of the types of difficulties involved in managing a huge communist system in transition are a formidable task that goes beyond any single researcher's capacity. This study has a limited goal and deals with only one aspect of that process. I present here a case study of intraelite conflict and regime delegitimation and destabilization in the post-Mao era. The conflict took place at the national level between the party's ruling elite and what I call the "counterelite," which was made up of politically aware members of the intellectual and professional classes. In examining the processes of regime relegitimation and delegitimation, this study places emphasis on how the two elite groups interacted with each other, not on how they related to other groups such as the local bureaucracy, though this and other segments of Chinese society are touched on in this work from time to time. This study devotes more space to analyzing the counterelite's activities than to the ruling elite's because the former has received insufficient attention in previous studies of regime legitimation and political change under communism. I demonstrate how, in the face of the legitimacy crisis generated jointly by Mao's cultural revolutionary policy and the post-Mao reform program, the Communist regime under Deng attempted to win support from different political and social groups by making various appeals to them. I also explain how, ironically, these appeals created the political space for the counterelite to make counterappeals, which resulted in social consequences contrary to what the ruling elite expected – the deepening of the regime's legitimacy crisis and the acceleration of political instability.

This study covers the period from the late 1970s, when Deng and his allies were just reemerging from Mao's great purge and struggling to launch a reform program to lead China out of chaos and poverty, to the late 1980s, when the Chinese Communist regime faced the most serious crisis since its inception. One of the reasons I confine this study to this time frame has to do with a methodological pitfall in the analysis of legitimacy. Because in communist systems there did not exist a free public sphere where the ruled could express its disapproval of the government, the researcher, some argue, could never be certain of the legitimacy of a communist regime. "At best," says Alfred Meyer (Sinanian, Deak, and Ludz 1972: 66), "we can, perhaps, sense the lack of legitimacy [in] periods when it becomes apparent that legitimacy has broken down." The spring of 1989 was definitely such a period, during which the happenings in China cleared up any doubts, be they on theoretical or empirical ground, about the identification of a legitimacy crisis.

Chapter 1 of this book is devoted to discussion of the analytic framework of this study and of the framework's relevance to the analysis of transitions from communism in the former Soviet bloc. I criticize the mainstream theories of political stability for neglecting intellectual and professional groups' critical activity in late communism, which contributed enormously to the formation of objective and subjective conditions of the revolutions of 1989. I also contend that the standard "state versus civil society" scheme is centered in Western experience and unable to account for the institutional ambiguity and confusion typical of decommunization. I propose instead the concept "institutional parasitism" and argue for its usefulness in analyzing the dynamics of the transitional processes.

Chapter 2 portrays several intellectual and professional groups that made up the Chinese social elite and describes their systematic efforts to build up the institutional basis on which they exerted influence on the country's political process.

The second part of this study is topically organized. Chapter 3 investigates three interrelated social movements in the late 1970s and early 1980s that followed from the official appeal to rationalism – that is, the intellectuals' efforts to dig out the structural roots of terror, poverty, and societal decay in the PRC; their struggle to build institutional barriers against the recurrence of Maoist practices; and educated youth's airing of its despair about the future of communism.

Chapter 4 looks into the political campaign called "Build Socialist Spiritual Civilization" and 5he counterelite's reaction in the early to mid 1980s. In the former, the ruling elite strove to curb the influence of Western political ideas and cultural values on the increasingly nonconformist youth. In its response, the counterelite pressed the regime to abandon its conventional means of social control and accommodate the sociopolitical aftereffects of the open-door policy and of the economic reforms.

Chapter 5 surveys the ruling elite's appeal to patriotism to encourage educated urban youth to identify with the regime, and the counterelite's appeal to patriotism to mobilize popular pressure on the ruling elite to wipe out the institutional arrangements that kept China backward.

Chapter 6 deals with two types of action in the late 1980s reacting to the party's new formula of the "primary stage of socialism," which implicitly admitted that socialism in China had become untenable. To offer alternatives in order to escape from this dead end, one group of intellectuals put forward the "East Asian model" and urged the CCP ruling elite to move toward "economic capitalism plus political dictatorship," which, it argued, was effective in the development of Taiwan, South Korea, and Singapore from the 1950s to the 1970s. In contrast, another group of intellectuals put forward the "Eastern European and Soviet model" and urged the ruling elite to move to "political democratization plus economic restructuring" as the only workable solution to the entrenched problems confronting communist states. This public debate was a prelude to the massive street demonstrations in the spring of 1989.

PART I

1

Theoretical and comparative issues

The major theoretical arguments made in this work can be summarized as follows: First, the mainstream theories of political stability often define what is an elite too narrowly. They usually focus attention on only a small number of national political leaders. In the case of communist studies, for example, the main focus is on the Politburo or the party central committee level, and other levels and types of elites in society are often neglected. I advocate widening the scope of what gets considered as elite in the studies of the transition from communism, to include not only party-state leaders but also a group I call the counterelite, consisting of intellectuals and professionals who were, for the most part, opposed to the communist ruling elite.

The second flaw in the mainstream theories of political stability is that they stress only one aspect of the function of legitimation – to keep a regime surviving. This one-dimensional view justifies the approach in which the researcher pays heed mainly to the process of self-legitimation and solidification among a few power centers. Against this, I advocate a multifunctional view of regime legitimation: The function or purpose of regime legitimation should be understood both negatively – keeping power or securing political survival, and positively – using power or achieving socioeconomic objectives. A multifunctional view of regime legitimation is particularly useful in understanding the predicament of communist systems under reform.

Third, the mainstream theories of political stability tend to treat the organizational strength of the state and its political legitimacy as two processes dynamically independent. I contend that this perspective neglects the fact that any sufficiently developed state machinery is a giant organization. It must employ a large number of individuals to keep the system running. As far as the community of government-office employees is concerned, the top leadership's appeal or political legitimation is an inseparable aspect of building up organizational strength and institutional capacity in the state machinery. Neglecting this, one cannot explain the phenomenal changes in the communist world in the recent past.

Last, I introduce the concept of "institutional parasitism" as an alternate scheme to "civil society versus the state" in explaining the major part of decommunization. By "institutional parasitism" I mean the indeterminacy of the nature and function of individual institutions, and of boundaries between them. In the case of the transition from communism, it refers particularly to the manipulation of official and semiofficial institutions by the critical forces for their own advantage. I argue that, in most countries and for most of the time, this analytic scheme more adequately accounts for the dynamics of decommunization than the "civil society versus the state" concept, which highlights institutional separateness, structural autonomy, the definitive nature of institutions, and the zero-sum relations in sociopolitical life. When applied to decommunization as a scheme of selecting and organizing data, what this dichotomous concept includes and enlightens falls short of what it omits and obscures. And what it omits and obscures is precisely the most characteristic, dynamic, and intriguing parts of the transitional process under question.

Elite: definitional clarification

"Elite" is one of the central concepts employed in this study. According to Pareto (1980: 273–74), an elite is "a class of the people who have the highest indices in their branch of activity." Here the "unit of analysis" is professions – that is, to judge whether an individual is a member of the elite in his society is to observe his status in his own profession. Hence, in Pareto's measurement, a "chess champion is certainly a member of the elite," for he beats everyone in his profession. A lawyer who has made his millions is a member of the elite in comparison to most of his colleagues who can only earn their thousands. The same holds for "a clever rascal who knows how to fool people and still keep clear of the penitentiary" (ibid.). Following this, we have a picture of elite distribution as horizontally structured in accordance with positions in respective professions.

There are two problems with Pareto's model as far as this study is concerned. First, we do not know how one measures elite membership comparatively. For instance, a lawyer who can earn a half million a year might not be qualified as a member of the legal elite, provided that many of his colleagues can earn the same. Can he, however, be regarded as more elite in society at large compared with the cleverest rascals?

Second, we have a simplified polarization. At one pole there is a tiny elite; at the other, the colorless and negligible masses, with nothing in between. In responding to this second problem, later elite theorists, such as Mosca, try to avoid oversimplification. In defining the elite, Mosca not only includes individuals at the very top, but seems to take into consideration "the second stratum" as well. According to Tom Bottomore (1966: 11), there is an element

in Mosca's theory which modifies its original stark outlines. In modern times, the elite is not simply raised high above the rest of society; it is intimately connected with society through a sub-elite, a much larger group. . . . This group does not only supply recruits to the elite (the ruling class in the narrow sense); it is itself a vital element in the government of society, and Mosca observes that "the stability of any political organism depends on the level of morality, intelligence and activity that this second stratum has attained."

With regard to the first problem in Pareto's notion, later elite theorists tend to define the elite by more generalized sociological variables, such as power, authority, achievement, and reward. "Elites are those minorities which are set apart from the rest of society by their pre-eminence in one or more of these various distributions" (Keller 1968: 26). Thus, the unit of analysis in measuring elite status now is not the individual profession but society as a whole. A person can be defined as a member of the elite so far as he is superior to most other social members in terms of power, authority, influence, or wealth, even if he is not at the peak in his own profession.

As elite study is always associated with inquiry into power, political elites have been given special weight in contemporary elite studies. Harold Lasswell (1966: 4–5) believes that "influence" is the attribute of the political elite: "Most simply, the elite are the influential. . . . If influence is equally shared, every participant in the situation belongs to the elite. If sharing is unequal, the most influential are called elite; others are mid-elite and rank-and-file." By assigning influence rather than power as the attribute of the political elite, Lasswell (ibid.: 16) includes in the category of political elite all individuals who have direct or indirect impact upon the decision making in a given political community, regardless of their being members of government or the opposition (as in a democracy), or "political criminals" and "class enemies" (as in dictatorial systems). A notion of political elite taking in both the "ruling elite" and the "counterelite" may cause confusion in certain types of empirical research.

Another point in Lasswell's observation, which identifies a midelite between the very top and the grass roots, is a development of Mosca's "second stratum." This multilayer approach is accepted in recent sociological research. In setting out a scheme for surveying the elite in contemporary British society, Anthony Giddens (Stanworth and Giddens 1974: 13) has resorted to a similar model: "Instead of employing a simple distinction between 'elite' and 'non-elite,' a differentiation is made between 'elite,' what could be termed a 'secondary structure,' and the 'non-elite.'" Even at the elite level per se, a subtle differentiation should be made. The stratification within elite groups has two dimensions (ibid.: 8):

> In determining the relative primacy of elite groups in terms of their possession of power, there are two main factors to be taken into consideration: I shall refer to these as the nature of the *hierarchy* which exists among elite groups, and the *institutional salience* of the forms of social organization or institution which they head. The first relates . . . to . . . the degree of "issue-strength" of the power held by elite groups. A hierarchy exists among elite groups when one such group (e.g. the political elite) holds power of greater issue-strength than others, and is therefore able to exert a greater or lesser degree of control over them. "Institutional salience" refers to the vertical dimension of power: it can be defined as residing in the degree to which a given institution affects the life-chances of the mass of those belonging to it.

Defining the elite in the case of Dengist China

To conclude, the term "elite" is used in this study in the broadest sense: all those who have made themselves stand out from the majority of society in terms of one or more of these variables: power, prestige, authority, influence, and wealth. Of the various elites in post-Mao China, this study focuses on two strategic elite groups (see Keller 1963: 20 for a definition of "strategic elite") that purposefully took part in the political process. I designate these two as the "ruling elite" and the "counterelite," respectively.

My "ruling elite" refers to three of the five subcategories included in Lasswell's concept of political elite (1966: 16): (1) "all individuals who occupy high office during the period"; (2) "all individuals who have occupied high office in previous periods and who regard themselves, and are regarded by others, as continuing to be in harmony with the established order"; and (3) "close family members" of those two. The PRC ruling elite touched by this study is limited to party-state officials holding influential administrative positions in the central or provincial governments.

The Chinese counterelite here refers to roughly the subcategory of counterelite in Lasswell's definition of political elite (ibid.): "all individuals who, though perceived as adherents of a counterideology, are recognized as exercising a significant influence over important decisions." As the focus of this study is on the interplay between one influential social group and the political leadership in post-Mao China, I treat the counterelite and the ruling elite as two independent categories, instead of mixing them in the same category as Lasswell does.[1]

---

[1] In Lasswell's (1966: 16) definition of political elite, there is another subcategory: "all individuals who, though holding no high office, or any office, are perceived as highly influential in important decisions." In the Chinese case under investigation, this classification has no independent value; it overlaps completely with either "retired officials" or "close family members."

The Chinese counterelite was principally composed of intellectuals and professionals. (Thus in this study the terms of "counterelite" and "intellectual elite" are often used interchangeably.) They were cultural, scientific, and professional personnel, with university students as their major source of recruitment. Those covered by this research include: (1) the intellectual and professional elite in the strict sense, that is, individuals who occupied preeminent positions in the national intellectual circles; (2) individuals who, though not preeminent on the national level, were regarded as more influential than most of their colleagues (midelite in Lasswell's sense); and (3) individuals who were not distinguished at all in intellectual and professional circles but nevertheless were, in a society with 25 percent illiteracy, regarded as educationally and socially more elite than the general population.

These intellectuals and professionals were the only status group in post-Mao Chinese society until the late 1980s and early 1990s when a tiny entrepreneurial class emerged. They were respected by the rest of society and had a great influence on the values and attitudes of the general population, but, to borrow from S. F. Nadel (1956) and Geraint Parry (1969: 71–72), they did not command deference and influence "by virtue of [their] coercive power" or any "monopoly of decision-making." They enjoyed such social status because of their educational, cultural, scientific, or professional achievements.[2]

Legitimation crisis and political destabilization

The concept of legitimacy is another major component of the frame of reference for this study. As Samuel Huntington (1991: 46) has noted, this concept is "mushy" but "essential to understanding the problems confronting authoritarian regimes in the late twentieth century." Thus some clarification has to be made before we can apply this concept to the Chinese case.

Felix Oppenheim (1975: 321) points out that the concept of legitimacy has two dimensions, a "descriptive-legal" and a "normative-moral" one. In the former, legitimacy designates legality, lawfulness, and conformity with established procedure. When applied specifically to political processes, it "describes the way in which State activity conforms to the particular rules of the legal system or the general directives which the Constitution lays down" (d'Entreves 1967: 141). This descriptive-legal usage can be traced back to the notion's ancient origin. In classical Latin the word *legitimus* means "lawful, according to law." In medieval texts "*legitimus* is what conforms to ancient custom and to customary

[2]Apparently out of a similar consideration, Moshe Lewin (1988: 148) applies the notion of "social elites" to Soviet intellectuals and professionals who played a critical role in political transition in the USSR.

procedure" (Sternberger 1968: 245). On the eve of the Renaissance a new element, consent, was added to the term's meaning. It emphasizes that rulership should be granted by the consent of the subjects (Schabert 1985: 99). For the founders of modern political theory, especially Locke (1960) and Rousseau (1967), the agreement of the governed is the sole foundation upon which a government can claim its legitimate authority. Here the normative-moral dimension of the concept of legitimacy becomes discernible.

Immediately after the French Revolution, the problem of legitimation became the axis of current political debate. The "legitimists" defended the legitimacy of the Bourbon dynasty, grounded in its royal descent, against the legitimacy of the Napoleonic regime (Ferrero 1972). As Tilo Schabert (1985: 100) has observed, the debate has three major consequences: "First, a formalization of the concept of legitimacy or, in other words, a dissociation of the concept from transcendent truths." Second, "legitimacy becomes the subject of a competition between *principles* of legitimacy that appear to be equally valid." And finally, "a new historic understanding of legitimacy emerges. Legitimacy is from now on being understood as a matter of contingency: legitimacy continually modified by time."

The earlier the usage, the more attention is paid to the outward aspect of legitimacy – legality, lawfulness, procedural formality; the later the usage, the more attention is paid to the inward aspect – the substantial, moral, psychological implications of legitimation (Vidich and Glassman 1979: 76–77; Merquior 1980: 6; Schaar 1981: 20–21). This tendency can be seen clearly in two major figures in modern legitimacy theory, Max Weber and Guglielmo Ferrero. The former's famous statement is that "the basis of every authority, and correspondingly of every kind of willingness to obey, is a *belief*, a belief by virtue of which persons exercising authority are lent prestige" (Weber 1978: 263). The latter stresses that "truly legitimate governments" are those that are "actively or passively, but sincerely, recognized by the people who have to obey them" (Ferrero 1972: 278).

The "inwardness" tendency can be equally seen among leading contemporary political sociologists. Seymour Martin Lipset (1981: 64) maintains that "Legitimacy involves the capacity of the system to engender and maintain the belief that the existing political institutions are the most appropriate ones for the society." A government is accorded legitimacy, says Robert Dahl (1984: 53), "if the people to whom its orders are directed believe that the structure, procedures, acts, decisions, policies, or leaders of government possess the quality of rightness, propriety, or moral goodness – the right, in short, to make binding rules." Jürgen Habermas (1979: 178–79) articulates that:

Legitimacy means that there are good arguments for a political order's claim to be recognized as right and just; a legitimate order deserves recognition. *Legitimacy means a political order's worthiness to be recognized.* This definition highlights the fact that legitimacy is a contestable validity claim; the stability of the order of domination (also) depends on its (at least) de facto recognition. Thus, historically as well as analytically, the concept is used above all in situations in which the legitimacy of an order is disputed, in which, as we say, legitimation problems arise. One side denies, the other asserts legitimacy.

The importance of legitimation described as such is that, as normative integration, it, alone with coercive power and material benefits, constitutes one of the three pillars of a political order (Weber 1978: 212–14; C. Johnson 1970: 192–93).[3] As the mechanism that supplies voluntary, consenting support for government, legitimation grants regimes long-term stability; it helps a government survive its difficult moments such as inefficiency and failure; and it makes it possible for a leadership to carry out bold, imaginative, and unusual measures, which a leadership otherwise could not accomplish. When a rule is respected as legitimate by the members of a political community, they are willing to postpone enjoyment and bear hardship for remote goals. In short, legitimacy allows a political power to run its business more efficiently and effectively with much less cost and coercion (Weber 1978: 31; Ferrero 1972: 134, 144; Lipset 1981: 67–70; Lowenthal 1984: 85).

Interestingly, contemporary mainstream legitimacy theories, which have been developed in the wake of Weber, appear to parallel what has been developed in the Marxist tradition regarding the function of "ruling ideology" in sustaining old political domination (Giddens and Held 1982: 408). Marx argues (Marx and Engels 1972: 136): "The ideas of the ruling class are in every epoch the ruling ideas: i.e., the class which is the ruling *material* force of society, is at the same time its ruling *intellectual* force. The class which has the means of material production at its disposal, has control at the same time over the means

---

[3]Goran Therborn (1980: 171) thinks that the "focus on production and maintenance of legitimacy stems from an unwarranted rationalist assumption that the ruled do not rebel only, or mainly, because they consider the rule of their rulers to be justified. But, economic and political constraints apart, there are a number of other reasons why people do not revolt. They may be broadly ignorant of and disinterested in the form of rule to which they are subjected. They may not be aware of alternative modes of social organization, and, even if they are, they may feel powerless to affect the existing state of affairs." Therborn's comments can be contested on two levels. Theoretically speaking, analysts of legitimacy such as Max Weber do not attribute people's nonrevolt solely, or mainly, to their recognition of the legitimacy of their rulers. Empirically speaking, well-educated segments of communist societies, such as China's counterelite in this study, were not ignorant of, or disinterested in, the form of their government. They might lack information about political alternatives and feel powerless under the leadership of Stalin or Mao, but no longer so afterward (see Havel's [1985: 23–96] famous essay "The Power of the Powerless" and my subsequent discussion on horizontal comparison).

I am indebted to Reader B for calling my attention to Therborn's comments.

of mental production, so that thereby, generally speaking, the ideas of those who lack the means of mental production are subject to it."

Borrowing this idea and building into it his political experience, Antonio Gramsci developed a more sophisticated theory of bourgeois hegemony in the public life of modern Western society. He (1971: 244) remarks that "the State is the entire complex of practical and theoretical activities with which the ruling class not only justifies and maintains its dominance, but manages to win the active consent of those over whom it rules." Inspired by the Gramscian theory, a class of contemporary writers, notably Louis Althusser (1971: 127–88) and Nicos Poulantzas (1974; 1980), has worked out the analytic scheme of "ideological state apparatuses." These writers call attention to the fact that the "State cannot enshrine and reproduce political domination exclusively through repression, force or 'naked' violence, but directly calls upon ideology to legitimize violence and contribute to a consensus of those classes and fractions which are dominated from the point of view of political power" (Poulantzas 1980: 28).

Since legitimation is part of the process of system integration through which a power structure becomes more solidified, a question arises logically: As far as this purpose is concerned, on which organizational level and in whose eyes is legitimation more important? This question in political sociology has been phrased as the dichotomy of elite legitimation versus mass legitimation. Against the earlier treatment of legitimation in which "the focus has generally been on the legitimacy of the *system as a whole* . . . in the eyes of the *population as a whole*" (Teiwes 1984: 7; see also Bialer 1980: 185), later approaches have been increasingly concerned with elite legitimation. They emphasize that whether a leadership, a government, or a policy can be given consent by the elite of a society is more important to the fate of the political authority under question than consent by the masses (see, e.g., Bialer 1980; Rigby and Feher 1982; Lewis 1984; Lowenthal 1984: 104–6; Teiwes 1984). No one has articulated this point more unambiguously than Arthur Stinchcombe (1968: 160–62) does:

A legitimate right or authority is backed by a *nesting of reserve sources of power* set up in such a fashion that the power can always overcome opposition . . . The crucial function of *doctrines of legitimacy* and norms derived from them is to create a readiness in other centers of power to back up the actions of a person with a certain right. Doctrines of legitimacy serve the crucial function of setting up that nesting of powers which usually makes appeals to physical force unnecessary. . . . *A power is legitimate to the degree that, by virtue of the doctrines and norms by which it is justified, the power-holder can call upon sufficient other centers of power, as reserves in case of need, to make his power effective.*

Applying Stinchcombe's proposition to the Soviet case, Seweryn Bialer (1980: 195) further affirms that:

It is the elite dimension of legitimacy that seems to be more crucial from the point of view of the stability of the system and especially its potential for transformation. Most importantly, it is the decline or disintegration of elite legitimacy that either leads to the decline of mass legitimacy or transforms the lack of popular support into an effective popular opposition.

In challenging the previously popular perception of the dependence of political stability on mass support, Theda Skocpol (1979: 31–32) goes so far as saying that the

organizational, realist perspective on the state . . . contrasts with non-Marxist approaches that treat the *legitimacy* of political authorities as an important explanatory concept. If state organizations cope with whatever tasks they already claim smoothly and efficiently, legitimacy – either in the sense of moral approval or in the probably much more usual sense of sheer acceptance of the status quo – will probably be accorded to the state's form and rulers by most groups in society . . . Even after great loss of legitimacy has occurred, a state can remain quite stable – and certainly invulnerable to internal mass-based revolts – especially if its coercive organizations remain coherent and effective.

This approach has long been accepted by many political sociologists and become a mainstream explanatory scheme in the research field of political crisis and revolution (Portes and Kincaid 1985: 51).

Counterarguments against the recent mainstream theories of political stability

Without questioning the fruitfulness of differentiating social strata in discussing legitimation problems, and basically accepting the proposition that elites and masses have asymmetric impact on regime stability, this study makes the following arguments against several blind spots in the previously discussed analytic schemes. These analytic weaknesses render the researcher, when engaged in an investigation of political transition, insensitive to certain subtle yet important processes, and reinforce his insight into one type of phenomena at the cost of depriving him of insight into other key elements that lead to historic changes. The result of such analytic weaknesses, as many have pointed out, is that almost all the Western specialists on communism and revolution failed to grasp the developments that prepared the revolutions of 1989 in the communist world (Brumberg 1990: 3–17; EEPS 1990; Chirot 1991).

First, the recent mainstream theories of political stability often define their elite scope too narrowly. In highlighting the importance of elite legitimation for political stability, these theories usually pay attention to only a few top political leaders and tend to neglect other levels and types of elites, not to mention "specific mobilized groups," which often act as a social catalyst in political change (Tilly 1977: 464). For instance, in two acclaimed studies on legitimation and stability in the Soviet Union and China, Bialer's (1980) scope of the elite covers merely Soviet leaders on the all-union, republic, and provincial levels; Teiwes's (1984) covers no more than the supreme Chinese leader and a small class of personnel immediately below him. An elite scope so narrowly defined, known as the "Kremlinological approach," directs the researcher to notice only the contrast between elite and mass legitimation, not the interaction between the two and not the linkage connecting crises at the top with actions of pivotal social groups below. These missed stories constitute a part of the very dynamics of political destabilization and transition (see Lewin 1988: 103); their inclusion in the researcher's framework enhances theory's ability to explain breakthroughs in political life.

If we take up the narrowly focused Kremlinological approach to look at Dengist China, we cannot appropriately understand how the deepening legitimation crisis eventually led to the general political crisis breaking out in the spring of 1989. In examining the period of 1977–89, if we focus attention on only the upper echelon of the CCP establishment, we will see that, although legitimation difficulties existed within that circle, the leaders could overcome these difficulties, reach agreements, and achieve institutional integration at their level most times and on most important issues. There existed several intellectual groups, however, that did not belong to the top political echelon and had fundamental disagreements with it on major issues. Largely because of this counterelite's consistent efforts, those "dangerous" issues which had been successfully excluded from the official agenda and public debate by the ruling elite were made salient again. Sometimes the issues even reentered the official agenda under the counterelite's pressure.

Moreover, the Communist leaders for many years had succeeded in securing the compliance of ordinary Chinese by, in Steven Lukes's (1974: 21–24) words, "influencing, shaping or determining their very wants," and "controlling their thoughts and desires." Thanks to a high degree to the counterelite's action, these legitimate wants and desires now became partly the consciousness of ordinary Chinese citizens. The process was full of appeals and counterappeals between various levels and types of elMtes, beyond the delimited elite scope that the recent mainstream theories of regime stability have accounted for.

For the reasons stated earlier, my study of regime legitimation relies on a widened elite scheme that goes beyond the conventional Kremlinological scope. It takes into consideration not only China's ruling elite but also its counterelite; not only leading intellectuals but also ordinary and marginal intellectuals (see Chapter 2 for details).

Second, the recent mainstream theories of political stability stress but one dimension of the function of legitimation – to keep a regime surviving. If this were true, then it is sufficient for the researcher to pay heed only to the course of self-legitimation and solidification among a few power centers. But experience tells us that much of the time power-holders keep power not only for the negative purpose of averting popular rebellion but also for the positive purpose of achieving certain socioeconomic objectives. The latter helps the former. In view of this, the one-dimensional approach to legitimation is insufficient and misleading. The limits of its explanatory power are particularly evident when we examine communist systems rather than democracies or authoritarian regimes in general.

What distinguishes communist systems from other systems is that in the latter there exists a relatively higher level of institutionalized mechanisms for private initiative, societal self-organizing and self-functioning, such as private ownership and markets, and autonomous or semiautonomous religious, educational, cultural, and social associations. But in communist systems all these were either nonexistent or they existed at a much lower level. Consequently, the communist party-state had to take over many tasks that were usually taken care of by independent social and economic organizations under noncommunist governments (see Fleron 1969: 153–69; Linz 1975: 230–40; Lindblom 1977; Hayward and Berki 1979: 1–12). Ironically, under the pressure of their own institutional environment, communist ruling elites – except at critical moments when their survival was in danger – cared very much about the masses' understanding of, and support for, official socioeconomic objectives, or, to use Habermas's (1975: 75ff.) term, cared very much about avoiding "motivation crises" in society. Communist leaders were indeed concerned with legitimation within the high stratum, but also invested tremendous energy in appealing to the larger social groups involved in the government's major socioeconomic programs. These groups had to be convinced of the meaningfulness – that is, the moral and practical value – of government programs before they committed to them.

It is particularly telling to contrast the concern for popular legitimation in communist politics with polity–society relations in noncommunist authoritarian systems. In the latter, regimes could get along quite well with a survival-oriented and power circles–centered legitimation policy, insofar as the politically alienated members of the population have their own spheres (mainly the private economy and nonpolitical social life) to work in and in which to pursue their non-political interests. However, in communist systems where the party-state acts as the chief employer and organizer for most socioeconomic activities, if the populace is politically alienated, does not recognize official policies, and withdraws cooperation from the government-set socioeconomic tasks, a general political and social crisis is more likely to occur, as happened in many communist states in the late 1980s.

Thus, the relative weight of various social groups in legitimation depends on the nature of the activity for which the legitimation effort is made. This point was put forward as a caveat in Stinchcombe (1968: 161): "In some kinds of activity, such as learning, which require the active cooperation of the subordinate, the legitimacy of power among subordinates may be very important." Yet Stinchcombe has not fully developed this insight into a multifunctional analytic scheme on legitimation. In other rulership-centered legitimation theories, this point has been almost forgotten.

In short, this study stresses that the function or purpose of regime legitimation should be understood both negatively – keeping power or securing political survival, and positively – using power or achieving socioeconomic objectives.

Finally, this study argues that the "organizational, realist perspective" on political stability as presented by Skocpol is misleading on one point: It treats the "structure and capacities of state organizations" and "political legitimacy" as two processes that seem to be dynamically independent, having no intrinsic connection or interaction. This perspective neglects the fact that any sufficiently developed state machinery is a giant organization and must employ a large number of individuals to keep the system running. The life-chances of most government-office employees are closer to ordinary citizens' than to top political leaders'. These functionaries and office workers are not remote from society but interweave with varying social strata through personal and family relationships. To the huge number of government-office employees, the political leadership's appeals are not abstract, enigmatic statements but messages indicating policy directions that will directly affect their objective and subjective interests. Furthermore, these office employees are human beings and have to be persuaded that what they are told to do makes some sense.[4] Therefore, those appeals, gestures, and messages play a big part in strengthening or eroding the "structure and capacities of state organizations." No government can maintain its institutional integration solely by delivering immediate material and political rewards to its officials and rank and file. All political authorities have at the same time to rely on communications of long-term visions and policy perspectives to keep their subordinates' confidence in and loyalty to the regime. As far as the community of government-office employees is concerned, political legitimation

[4] I am indebted to Reader A for suggesting I stress this aspect.

is an inseparable aspect of building up organizational strength and institutional capacity in the state machinery.

"Vertical comparison," "horizontal comparison," and regime delegitimation

China's experience in the post-Mao epoch has shown that the process of regime delegitimation is a process of constant comparison made by members of the concerned political community. The comparison is conducted along two lines. One is to compare power holders' words and promises with their deeds and deliveries (i.e., "reality check"), and another is to compare the performance of the home government with that of foreign governments. Comparison of the second type is what Chinese term "horizontal comparison" (*hengbi*) in contrast with the officially sanctioned "vertical comparison" (*shubi* – that is, to compare the "old China" with the "New China").[5]

The use of the two lines of comparison, "reality check" and "horizontal comparison," permits the uncovering of the failed prophecy, the exposure of hypocrisy, the weakening of the power of disinformation, distortion, and manipulation, the awakening of a hitherto smothered sense of rights, and the mobilization of the resentful. The Chinese experience has shown that, of the two lines of comparison, horizontal comparison is more effective in producing a sense of "relative deprivation" and eventually the "Tocqueville effect" – accumulation of popular grievances against the old regime and the outbreak of revolutions in times of reform (Tocqueville 1955: 169–79). Without it, only making a reality check may not yield meaningful results under certain conditions. The power holders can water down the magnitude of their failure by promoting intensified "vertical comparison" campaigns, reminding people how miserable pre-Communist Chinese society was and how much progress has been made since then. High-ranking leaders can also blame their subordinates for poor governmental performance and corruption, thereby shifting the focus of popular resentment from the system to incumbents. Only with horizontal comparison can the governed go beyond personalized grievances against incumbents and reach a generalized understanding of the system as a whole. The symptom of a legitimacy crisis is grievances against the system as a whole rather than against individual incumbents (Lehman 1987).

The effect of horizontal comparison has also been demonstrated in Eastern Europe. As graphically portrayed by Timothy Garton Ash, in the "objective

[5]The Maoist method of vertical comparison is *yiku sitian*, meaning "to recall the past bitterness and appreciate the present happiness" (see Solomon 1971: 195–97, 439–41, and Madsen 1984: 135–36). In the official campaigns of anti–bourgeois liberalism in early 1987 and after the spring of 1989, the CCP accused critical intellectuals of replacing vertical comparison with a horizontal one in order to serve their "evil intention" to dishonor Chinese socialism.

reality" of the 1980s, life in East European countries was quite grim; in the "subjective reality" – the mental product of the citizens of these countries – life was even grimmer. This is largely "because the members of the younger generation compare their situation not with their own countries' recent past, but with the situation of their contemporaries in Western Europe" (Ash 1990: 258–59). In constructing the subjective reality, "many young people in Eastern Europe have a rose-tinted picture of the West. But that itself is a reality that their governments have to confront" (ibid.: 260).

Institutional parasitism: a challenge to the civil society versus the state scheme

How would one characterize, within a wider sociological perspective, the Chinese counterelite's criticism and dissent against the party-state establishment in the post-Mao era? Evidently, such opposition signifies the emergence of a new pattern of relations between the party-state and Chinese society. It reminds us of what has occurred in Eastern Europe and the Soviet Union since the late 1950s (cf. Rothberg 1972; Tokes 1979; Rubenstein 1985; Skilling 1989; Taras 1991).

In the practice of social science, the most conspicuous recent attempt at theorizing about nonconformity and opposition in posttotalitarian communist systems deals with the scheme "civil society versus the state." This theorization effort started in the late 1970s, when "the emergence and growth of independent social groups which managed to survive the repressions, especially in Poland and Czechoslovakia, brought to light a complete lack of the sorts of method and theoretical background which would enable scholarly analyses of this problem" (Rau 1987: 574). Thus, one of the central notions of classical political theory – civil society – was introduced to cope with the new phenomenon by students of communism such as Ivan Szelenyi (1979: 187–208), Jacques Rupnik (1979: 60–112), and Andrew Arato (1981). By the late 1980s and early 1990s, when most communist regimes under pressure have abandoned their attempt at total control of society, and certain spheres of human activity have become partially autonomous, to employ the notions of "regeneration of civil society" and "civil society against the state" as a means to conceptualize decommunization became an influential intellectual wave.[6] As an enthusiastic advocate of civil society theory has claimed (Tismaneanu 1990: 181):

[6]The civil society theory was initially applied to the East European and Soviet cases (see, e.g., Keane 1988a; Lewin 1988; Starr 1988; Bialer 1989: 121–48; W. Miller 1989; Nee and Stark 1989: 13–25, 208–32; Skilling 1989; Ash 1990; Brzezinski 1990; Frentzel-Zagorska 1990; Hosking 1990; R. Miller 1992; Seligman 1992; Weigle and Butterfield 1992); many writers have attempted to use it to explain developments in China, though not without considerable hesitation. For a list of recent writings on civil society in China, see Robert Miller (1992: 151–52; Bonnin and Chevrier 1991 should also be included in the list).

The theory . . . is relevant both for its analytic potential – it explains the changes going on in the communist world – and for its predictive power. As a theory it challenges long-held assumptions about the nonreformability of communist totalitarian regimes. It shows that small islands of autonomy can eventually torpedo the continuum of state-controlled heteronomy. It argues that the transition is possible from a totalitarian dictatorship to first an authoritarian and further to a pluralist order.

The use of civil society theory to explain the profound change sweeping through the communist world is very appealing. Communism has been viewed as a perfect example of statism (Jowitt 1971: 82; Westoby 1983: 219; Brzezinski 1990: 3–9). The field of communist studies has long been in the shadow of the totalitarian image. Hence, in the institutional context of communism, any meaningful change cannot but induce its observers to reconceptualize the relations between state and society.

In spite of this, the application of the "civil society versus the state" scheme to nonconformity and opposition in communist systems as a whole is problematical. A brief review of the scheme's history will help to see this.

To most social and political philosophers of the seventeenth and the eighteenth centuries, "civil society" was a concept not in contrast with the "state" but with the "state of nature." The state of nature, more a logical what-if than a historical description, signifies a state in which there exist no law, no public authorities, and no government; everyone can do what his instinct and interest drive him to do. Hence, the state of nature is the state of war, every man against every man. In contrast, civil society indicates a human community in which all members' actions and their relationships are regulated by consensually accepted law. The individual's security, property, freedom, and dignity are protected by the law. Men thereby enjoy a civilized life according to reason and all are able to bring their potentials into full play. Such conditions bode well both for the development of individuals and for the growth of arts and commerce in society in general (see Hobbes 1962: 87–90; Locke 1960: 361–74; Burke 1904: Vol. III, pp. 353ff. and Vol. IV, pp. 175ff.; Ferguson 1980; Kant 1887: 163ff.). Civil society, defined as a civilized political community, pointed to the same thing as "political society" or "commonwealth" did in social and political philosophy of the seventeenth and the eighteenth centuries. Thus, "civil society" then was synonymous with "state" as a normative concept (on "state" as a normative concept, see Sills 1968: Vol. 15, pp. 150–54). Accordingly, it had a strong normative implication too.[7]

---

[7]Among the classic social philosophers, Rousseau (1967, esp. 211–12) holds a very different view on civil society. In Rousseau, "civil society" is transformed from a mainly normative to a chiefly descriptive concept (Carnoy 1984: 19–20), pointing to the social reality in which the philosopher lived. It was a world of greed, inequality, oppression, and evil. In contrast, Rousseau believes, the state of nature was a paradise, free of private ownership and all social evils.

That civil society conceptually became separate from, and in contrast to, the state was first achieved in Hegel (Marx 1972: 72ff.; Pelczynski 1984: 1). In Hegel's view, civil society and the state are two distinct "movements" or aspects of the human community. The former represents a sphere of private affairs and contractual relationships, the battleground of individual interests of each against all, and the realm of necessity. In short, civil society is a network of capitalistic economic and legal institutions. In contrast, the state represents a sphere of public affairs and the realm of freedom; it is the manifestation of the spiritual and the universal. So the state reveals a higher stage in the movement of Reason. While civil society serves as an intermediary point for the individual's self-consciousness, the state serves as the absolute and final (Hegel 1942: sec. 258; Pelczynski 1984: 77–93).

There are two points in Hegel that deserve attention here. First, civil society and the state refer not to two entities, but to two aspects of the same entity – modern Western society. Second, the state is superior to civil society. Methodologically Marx fully inherits the first point. He uses civil society to denote the totality of economic relations in modern capitalist society, and the state to denote the totality of political and legal relations in that society. But the second point in Hegel is completely reversed by Marx; civil society, which he terms "the economic base," rather than the state, which he terms "the superstructure," has the decisive primacy in human life (Marx and Engels 1974: 4).

As Z. A. Pelczynski (1984: 263–64) notes, in Marx's concept of civil society – the core of his historical materialism – the complex contents of Hegel's civil society are reduced to economic relations. Of later Marxists, Gramsci is the leading figure to take civil society as the central concept in his sociopolitical analysis, and simultaneously to try to enrich the contents of civil society once simplified by Marx. To Gramsci (1971: 12), civil society as "the ensemble of organisms commonly called 'private'" is not the economic base as defined by Marx, but a part of the superstructure, an important means and process of domination over working people executed by the ruling class. Yet, the analytic usefulness of Gramsci's concept suffers heavily from his inconsistent explanations of the relations between civil society and state. He sometimes views the two as contrasting (equal to consensus making versus coercion); sometimes he defines civil society as a part of the state; and on still other occasions he identifies civil society with the state (Carnoy 1984: 72).[8]

---

[8] Pelczynski (1988a: 365–66) notes that Gramsci's theory of the state–civil society relation inspired in the late 1970s radical left-wing intellectuals in the West and theorists of the opposition in the East to "conceptualize historical developments [in Eastern Europe] and to map out a programme of . . . the 'de-totalization' of socialism." I wonder how they coped with the inconsistency in Gramsci's theory.

In contemporary social and political theory, civil society is defined as the nonstate, or the limits of state action. The scheme of the state versus civil society is used to refer to the public versus the private, the coercive versus the voluntary, or the compulsory versus the autonomous. The following statements, taken from writers in the classical liberal, Weberian, and neo-Marxist tradition, illustrate its common usages.

Ernest Barker (1951: 2–3):

By "Society" we mean the whole sum of voluntary bodies, or associations, contained in the nation . . . , with all their various purposes and with all their institutions . . . By "the State" we mean a particular and special association, existing for the special purpose of maintaining a compulsory scheme of legal order, acting therefore through laws enforced by prescribed and definite sanctions.

Reinhard Bendix, John Bendix, and Norman Furniss (1987: 33):

In the context of the modern Western world the state has been defined as a country's capacity to act as a corporate whole, based on the monopolization of the legitimate use of force over a territory with clearly defined boundaries. The corresponding civil societies do not constitute corporate wholes in the same way. Rather, they consist of aggregates of families and private associations that "put into effect certain rules of particular interest to them in some special area of social and political life, albeit without seeking direct responsibility in public affairs."

John Keane (1988b: 3):

The relationship between the state and civil society . . . is . . . between the complex network of political institutions (including the military, legal, administrative, productive and cultural organs of the state) and the realm of social (privately owned, market-directed, voluntarily run or friendship-based) activities which are legally recognized and guaranteed by the state. This relationship between the state and civil society must be rethought in a way that affirms the necessity and desirability of drawing stricter limits upon the scope of state action, while expanding the sphere of autonomous social life.

The bifurcated conception of state–society relations genetically bears a deep mark of modern Western experience.[9] Dieter Grimm (1986: 93; see also Black 1984) amply illustrates this development, which began in early modern times in Western Europe:

The new concentration of political power divided the medieval community into two different bodies: a small one consisting of the prince and his staff, characterized by the monopoly of legitimate coercive power, and a large one comprising everybody else being

[9] In his critique of recent social scientific discussions on state–civil society relations, Keane (1988a: 62 and 70; 1988b: 65) remarks that most contemporary writers have a misconception of the distinction. A reading of Keane's (1988a: 1–72; 1988b: 1–68) essays on the subject indicates that, while Keane's review of the classical literature illustrates the existence of "important differences in the geographic distribution, temporal changes and semantic variation of the distinction" (1988a: 62), which have been ignored by many contemporary writers, Keane's own usage of the state–civil society distinction demonstrates no meaningful difference from most of the other approaches that he criticizes. Try to compare, for instance, the works of John B. Thompson (Lefort 1986: 6 and 321) and R. N. Berki (Hayward and Berki 1979: 2) with Keane's (1988a: 21; 1988b: 3).

subject to that power. For the first body, the notion of state, formerly applied in an attributive sense only, came up in this very period. The second one used to be called society. Yet, society no longer signified the community as a whole including all political authorities, but the community without the state. The concentration of all political rights in the hands of the ruler left everybody else behind in the role of a private member. Privateness became the characteristic of society. . . . The legal system reflected the distinction between state and society, private and public sphere. The universal medieval law fell apart into two different sets of rules: the private law regulating the relations within society, and the public law concerning the relations between society and state.

Thus, the defining feature of civil society is institutional autonomy vis-à-vis the state, either in the form of legally protected rights, or in the form of customarily recognized freedom. In a weak sense, a civil society can be said to exist in a de facto form – that is, it keeps operating overtly in spite of the state's prohibition.

Institutional parasitism: an alternate conceptualization

This study contends that the binary conception of civil society versus the state, when bestowed on nonconformity and opposition movements in communist systems, is usually misleading, being applicable only in rare, extreme cases. Based on the Western model of state–society relations in modern (not contemporary, see Gilbert and Howe 1991) times, this dichotomous concept highlights, analytically, the definitive nature of institutions, organizational separateness, structural autonomy, and a zero-sum relationship in sociopolitical processes. When applied to decommunization as a scheme for selecting and organizing data, what this all too neat concept includes and reveals falls short of what it omits and obscures. And what it omits and obscures is precisely the most characteristic, dynamic, and intriguing phenomena in the devolution and disintegration of the mechanism of party-state control in late communism, a process full of uncertainty, ambiguity, opacity, and confusion.

I instead propose the concept "institutional parasitism" as an alternate scheme. Institutional parasitism is distinguished by the following characteristics: (1) the boundary between institutional structures is vague and indeterminate, mainly because one institution grows and is sheltered on or in a different institution from which it draws its partial or total resources; and (2) the nature of individual institutions is amphibious[10] or even indeterminate; that is, a single institution can be used for contradictory or conflicting purposes or functions.

It has been widely observed in the transition from communism that many organizations that were described by outside observers as "independent" or

[10] In *Webster's Third New International Dictionary*, "amphibious" is defined as "belonging to, adapted for, or consisting of both land and water"; or as "having or combining two lives, positions, or qualities."

"autonomous" and working to end communist rule were actually in a symbiotic relationship with party-state structures. They depended, in greater or lesser degrees, on these official structures for legal or political protection and for personnel or material support. What is more fascinating is that the party-state set up institutions for its own use and then these institutions were gradually co-opted by critical forces that used them for counterpurposes, all the while keeping up the front that these were still party-state institutions.[11] Institutional parasitism has manifested itself in all communist countries and in all aspects of decommunization.

In the sphere covered by this study, which East European scholars term as the "public sphere" or the "second polity" or the "parallel polity," evidence shows that, first, some of the Chinese counterelite's critical voice was expressed in the mass media and in meetings owned or organized by party-government organs and official institutions, which were a part of the party-state machinery: Politically they were subject to the direction of party propaganda departments and governmental culture bureaus, organizationally they were administered by personnel appointed by party organization departments and state personnel bureaus, and financially they were supported by the state budget. In the meantime, however, because of the political orientation or personal connections of those working within, these institutions could also be used to support the opposition or paraopposition. This pattern developed at a dramatic level in the Spring 1989 Democracy Movement. Important party-state organs became the mouthpiece of the antigovernment movement, and the state's conventional instruments of political control became organizational frames for mass protest (Walder 1989; Jakobson 1990; Saich 1990: 126–63).

Second, most of the Chinese counterelite's voice was put forward in the "cliquish publications." (See Chapter 2.) These publishing institutions were not directly owned by party-state organs but established and run by the intellectual circles through networks of personal relations. Formally, however, they had to attach themselves to official bodies and their money came mainly from public funds and state enterprises. Only a small portion came from private resources.

Third, the dissent and oppositional activities discussed in this work became possible only through sponsorships, arrangements, and coordination provided by a variety of societies, research groups, institutes, associations, and editorial boards. These organizations were voluntary in the sense that different intellectual circles set them up on their own initiative. Yet, under PRC regulations, a voluntary organization must have a supervisory official institution in order to obtain legal registration; party officials of the supervisory institution must be

---

[11] I am thankful to Rachael Winfree for helping me make this clarification.

politically responsible for all the activities in the affiliated voluntary organization. Although in reality most of the affiliations between voluntary and supervisory institutions were made through personal connections, and though many
party officials in supervisory institutions did not interfere very much in the
activity of voluntary organizations, no voluntary organization could come into
being without an official institution's shelter.

Finally, one must not forget that most members of the Chinese counterelite
were party-state employees. Some of them even belonged to what Geoffrey
Hosking (1990: 45) calls the "establishment nonconformity" class.

Though beyond the scope of this study, material I have collected shows that in
China, among the businesses that were not state-owned, which together were
parallel to the former Soviet bloc's "second economy," very few could be strictly
called "private." Most nonstate businesses had to have state or collective organs
and companies as their "mother institutions" (*guakao danwei*). In addition to
bribes, which were usually given on an irregular basis, those businesses had to
pay a considerable amount in so-called supervisory fees to the mother institution on a regular basis. In exchange, owners of nonstate businesses could use
their mother institutions' "good names" as state or collective organizations to
protect their businesses from harassment from local bureaucrats or hooligans.
When policy changes occurred, "good names" could help reduce financial
losses, because the government periodically tightened restrictions on private
firms. Affiliation with state or collective institutions also helped nonstate enterprises get fuel, raw materials, and transportation. In a word, many nonstate
businesses had state or collective institutions as their supervisors, party-state
officials as their bosses, and official institutions as their profit sharers.[12]

Institutional parasitism was so prevalent in Dengist China that even those
trying to explain post-Mao changes in the light of civil society theory have to give
it considerable weight. For example, David Kelly and He Baogang (1992: 29)
admit that to say companies of the Beijing Stone Group type (a highly publicized computer firm) are "'private' is misleading. Such concerns are better
described as *semiofficial*. Almost all are 'pendant' (*gua*) from some part of the
CCP organizational network." They also note that China's institutional environment in the late 1980s enabled "state entities to act counter to the state" (ibid.:
37). In a similar vein David Strand (1990: 13–15, 18) cites various data to show
the "ambiguity between state and society" in China, in which "elements of the
state . . . have developed an independent social identity. They can attack the

---

[12] Based on interviews with participants in, and researchers of, China's economic reforms: Informants nos. 15, 40, 41, and Chen Yizi (December 1990, Princeton). An American sociologist's
(Wank 1992) fieldwork on the development of nonstate enterprises in Xiamen tells the same
story.

state by creating a Chinese version of the East European strategy of 'social self-defense.'" Strand (ibid.: 12) further comments that because of "the Chinese tradition . . . whereby official, public, and private realms interlock in complex, changing pattern," it is difficult to decide whether the type of factory established in the economic reforms is "in the 'state' or in 'society'?"

Institutional parasitism in the former Soviet bloc

This characteristic relationship between state and society in Dengist China was also present, in varying degrees, in the former Soviet bloc.[13] In the sphere of communications, in pre-1990s Eastern Europe, "the line between the two cultures [of the official and the unofficial] or two forms of communication is not always sharp and distinct, and varies according to the country or the period under consideration" (Skilling 1989: 38). George Schopflin (1979: 142) uses the term "para-opposition" to portray Hungarian intellectuals' counteractivities against the Communist regime from the late 1960s to the late 1970s: "By this, I mean opposition that does not overtly question the ideological bases of the system, but does accept the leeway for a semi-autonomous political role permitted by that system." Even in Poland, a place where Communist rule was under the strongest challenge, in the 1970s and 1980s, the expression of critical voices also fell into the mode of institutional parasitism: "Where the official media are not in total control, or are flexible enough to permit the expression of some nonconformist ideas, there are autonomous elements within the official realm of culture" (Skilling 1989: 38). Opposition-minded Polish intellectuals "created a situation in which intelligent and creative individuals had more and more opportunities for self-realization outside the system" but "mainly inside state institutions" (Frentzel-Zagorska 1990: 766). In the Soviet Union, literary journals and associations in the Gorbachev era became one of the centers for antigovernment protest. Yet, these associations and journals were formally government-owned and sponsored. This phenomenon led an observer (Hosking 1990: 45) to name them paradoxically as "establishment non-conformity." Vaclav Havel (Benda et al. 1988: 233–34) explains vividly why dichotomous categorization has little relevance to the transitions taking place in late communism:

Under a totalitarian system, of course . . . no one is, nor can they be, completely or absolutely independent of the state. Even Czechoslovak or Polish citizens who express themselves most freely are (mostly) employed in state institutions where they are paid a salary by the state, with which they buy food or consumer goods (mostly) in state-owned shops; they make use (mostly) of the state health service; they live (mostly) in state-

---

[13]In discussing institutional parasitism in the former Soviet bloc, I cite evidence mainly from practitioners of the "state versus civil society" theory, in order to demonstrate the discrepancy between the theory they are using and the reality with which they are dealing.

owned flats and they observe the countless laws and regulations issued by the state . . .
Yet it is also true that a measure of independence is available even to the most dependent
citizens . . . In other words, there are not, strictly speaking, two distinct societies or two
types of individual, one dependent and the other independent. Everyone is dependent
and at the same time everyone, in certain areas, expresses himself more or less independently. The difference – and of course it is an extremely important difference – lies in the
. . . proportions of those two "quantities" in relation to each other.

This was very much the state of affairs in the sphere of association making.
Elemer Hankiss (1988: 31), a close observer of sociopolitical transitions in
Eastern Europe and the creator of the concept of "second society," makes the
following comments when relating how the Communist structure of society was
gradually changed in Hungary in the late 1960s to late 1980s:

Community networks and helping systems, working in the border zone between
the formal and the informal sphere, the first and the second society, have . . . become
more active in these years. The most important fact from the point of view of our
argument is the great number of interest intermediating networks operating in this
country. Their parallel working, their interactions and interferences, create a chaotic
situation, a state of opacity and confusion, a society in which an important proportion of
social interactions has submerged in a sphere of latency and informality, escaping the
control of the ruling elite.

Of these organizational networks many "were created from above and supported with public funds" (Hann 1990: 19). For this reason Hankiss (Skilling
1989: 220) later concludes "that the various forms of a 'second society' were not
really separate or independent of the first society, but were really only compo-
nents of the latter, heavily dependent on and influenced by it." Another Hungarian analyst, Mihaly Vajda (ibid.: 232), also believes that "the second society
was not independent from the first or from the totalitarian society, but at best
was an informal relationship inside the first society." In Gorbachev's Soviet
Union, the growth of informal and voluntary associations was phenomenal. By
the end of the 1980s, their estimated number had reached sixty thousand. This
is a chief reason many observers have turned to civil society theory to explain
what had happened in the Soviet Union (see, e.g., W. Miller 1989: 27–35;
Hosking 1990: 63–75). Nevertheless, these observers also notice that most of
those associations were parasitic: They had to attach themselves to official
institutions (Hosking 1990: 64, 67–68). Students of Poland saw a similar pattern
there: Antisystem movements often "found institutional space on the fringes of
official party-state institutions such as youth organizations" (Ekiert 1990: 3). To
characterize this behavioral pattern typical of communist societies such as
Poland and Hungary, Janina Frentzel-Zagorska (1990: 761) has invented the
term "adaptation through opposition," which means "supporting existing state
institutions on the behavioral level; at the same time taking advantage of them

and displacing their goals by trying to achieve private goals at the expense of official ones."

In the economic area, we find the same situation (Seleny 1991). The state-owned (the "first") economy and the nonstate (the "second") economy were interwoven through informal networks of relation between officials and workers in the first economy and employers and employees in the second. "The relationship is symbiotic," remarks a researcher (Judt 1988: 201). "The second economy depends upon the first economy for its survival; it channels resources away from it (often illegally)." As Hankiss (1988: 35) has nicely summarized: "The *second economy* . . . is not nationalized, not centralized, not politicized, not hierarchicized, as the first one is, but, nevertheless, it is not an autonomous alternative economy. It is a complementary economy, grown together with the first one. They encroach upon each other in a more or less inextricable and mutually parasitic way." Hosking (1990: 17) uses exactly the same words to describe the second economy in the Soviet Union. Even in post-Communist Russia, there are many so-called private firms that are actually ambiguous in nature, neither private nor public (*Economist* January 4, 1992, pp. 40–41).

Two explanatory models

In late communism, the evolution of the characteristic pattern of state–society relations as described under the term institutional parasitism is natural. All rulership in human history displays a "suspicious attitude towards association" (Bendix et al. 1987: 12–13; see also Nisbet 1966: 115, 130–31). Communist rulership has carried this attitude to the extreme and created what T. H. Rigby (1992: 15) calls a "mono-organizational" system, whose "most distinctive feature . . . was that the whole life of society was incorporated into a single organizational structure." The party-state has enjoyed the monopolization of institution-making resources, material, personnel, and legal, to such an extent that in prereform communist society "it does not make much sense to speak of a 'state'" (Jowitt 1971: 82; see also Schapiro 1969: 98), for everything belonged to the state. In this context, any structural change in communist countries could not but involve pervasive and significant manipulation and "abuse" of state institutions and facilities by citizens, since almost everyone was the state's employee and could reach certain types of institutional or material resources of the state. As Andrew Nathan (1990: 5–6) has keenly observed in the case of China: "The Chinese Communist Party has always enforced its control of society by placing its members throughout every institution, including those that were nominally independent." The result was, paradoxically, mutual infiltration: Not only did the party-state infiltrate society, but "society was beginning to infiltrate the Party" as well. From the material on the Soviet Union and Eastern Europe cited previously, we know that Nathan's comments are equally applicable to other communist systems.

Thus, against the communist institutional background, liberalization and pluralist developments inevitably brought about and went hand in hand with the phenomenon of institutional parasitism: What formally remained as part of the state system could simultaneously work for functions and purposes contradictory to those of the state; and everywhere there existed institutions that could be said to be both for and against the state. In other words, one can find many amphibious entities that were neither strictly "state" nor "societal." Organizational parasitism, structural indefiniteness, institutional confusion, systemic ambiguity, and double identity were present at all levels of society.

Many of the phenomena that observers of communism have inappropriately characterized as "civil society against the state" are actually societalization of state constituents.[14] In communist countries, there existed extensive networks of social organizations, which bore a strong resemblance to voluntary associations in liberal-democratic society but were actually "preemptive" organizations: They were set up by the communist regime for both "serving the regime's mobilization goals and . . . [in particular] inhibiting the formation of private loyalties" (C. Johnson 1970: 19). They were thus an indispensable part of the communist state system. The term "societalization of state constituents" refers to the partial conversion in which the upper echelon of the communist regime loses control of pseudosocial organizations, and members of society can more or less turn these organizations from agents of governmental manipulation into instruments for the expression of ideals, or mobilization and coordination of interests, against the party-state.[15] Societalization of state constituents is one dimension of institutional parasitism.

The concept of institutional parasitism highlights the indeterminacy of the character and function of individual institutions, and of boundaries between them. It also highlights the interweaving and interpenetration of different forces at play in sociopolitical transitions. As an analytic concept, it is responsive to the dynamics of institutional changes in communist countries and the transitional process per se. On the other hand, the concept of civil society projects a dichotomous, oversimplified image of reality. Even if we take into consideration the ideal-typical nature of the "civil society versus the state" concept, and even if

[14]Lewin (1988: 151) terms these phenomena as "socializing the state." I use "societalization" because "socialization" retains special meanings in political economy and psychology.

[15]Guillermo O'Donnell, Philippe C. Schmitter, and Laurence Whitehead (1986: Vol. 4, p. 49) have observed institutional conversion at a higher level in transitions from authoritarian rule in Southern Europe and Latin America. I have borrowed some phrases from them but avo d transplanting the concept of "the resurrection of civil society" into the communist situation.

we keep in mind Whitehead's and Parsons's caution against the "fallacy of misplaced concreteness" (Parsons 1968: 29), this dichotomous concept based on the modern Western model of state–society relations will prove to have limited power to explain the complex transition from communism.

To sense how civil society theory impairs an appropriate characterization and understanding of the major part of the transition, one might read Lewin's recent book on sociopolitical changes in the Soviet Union that led to the Gorbachev revolution. On the one hand, Lewin (1988: 7), on the basis of his informative and insightful study, contends that "the usual antithesis of 'state' versus 'society' may be inadequate when one wants to explore relations between the two" in the post-Stalin situation. On the other hand, however, Lewin still tries to use the concept of civil society to generalize his empirical findings and thus is caught in a self-contradiction. Read these lines (ibid.: 80; emphasis added):

By "civil society," we refer to the aggregate of networks and institutions that either exist and act independently of the state or are *official organizations* capable of developing their own, spontaneous views on national or local issues and then impressing these views on their members, on small groups and, finally, on the authorities. . . . The concept of civil society operating *in the very fortress of statism – among broad layers of officials, political opinion makers, and the party apparatus –* challenges conventional thinking about the Soviet state. It is a novel idea about a novel situation.

What Lewin describes here resembles closely the Chinese case under investigation.

Here I must make it clear that this study is not intended to advocate a total abandonment of civil society theory in the analysis of transitions from communism. This theory certainly is useful in treating a small number of extreme cases such as the Solidarity movement. But the open confrontation in Poland in the Solidarity era, though significant and dramatic, was not typical of the transitions as a whole. To quote a famous saying, "In Poland it [the collapse of communism] took ten years, in Hungary ten months, in East Germany ten weeks and in Czecho-Slovakia ten days" (Ash 1989: 42).[16] There were substantial differences, in terms of regime–opposition relations, between Poland and other East European countries, between East European countries and the Soviet Union, and between European and Asian communist countries (Brumberg 1990: 9; Kligman 1990: 422; Chirot 1991). In most former and remaining communist coun-

---

[16]Even in Poland itself institutional parasitism was a predominant pattern in the opposition movement before the 1980s. As Pelczynski (1988a: 368–69) says, until the 1980s the critical intellectual groups "owed their existence to the laxity of party control, the relative toleration of the security police apparatus and a degree of judicial independence, not to an infrastructure of genuinely autonomous social organizations. They were beneficiaries of loopholes in the state structure. Hence the application of the civil society concept to Poland before the rise of Solidarity – any meaningful talk of 'the rebirth of civil society' – is in my view highly misleading; indeed, a piece of mystification and wishful thinking."

tries and for most of the time, activities and developments that were not typical of the Solidarity movement constituted the major part of the transition from communism. To apply the "civil society versus the state" framework to such activities and developments causes more distortion than provides accurate description.[17] It is precisely in these places where this framework becomes irrelevant or marginally applicable that the concept of institutional parasitism shows its advantage.[18]

When the radical changes were taking place throughout the communist world in the late 1980s, most observers of communism in the West found the unfolding drama difficult to understand. As one East European scholar (EEPS 1990: 155) has noted: "Why did no one predict the revolutions of 1989? How did we manage to expend a sea of ink and thousands of hours in scholarly discourse only to be totally surprised by what is happening there? How embarrassing to read in a specialized journal, prepared several months ago but received only this year, that the Honnecker regime stands firm, and that nothing will happen in Romania until after the presumably peaceful demise of its dictator!" I think the standard analytic frameworks in the field should take part of the blame. Western observers of communism used to focus on the absence or presence of *formal* civic associations and oppositional organizations in communist countries to predict the likelihood of dramatic changes, unrest, or revolutions. Observers using the state versus civil society model did not see that within or underneath the seemingly monolithic party-state structures, not to mention various kinds of social organizations attached to them, oppositional or paraoppositional activities developed.[19] In many cases, such activities could be sustained precisely because

---

[17] I question the value of the "civil society versus the state" scheme as a generally applicable analytic tool in explaining transitions from communism, but do not question its value as a normative ideal and as a political-strategic concept in the same setting. A notion that has great normative and political appeals to a society does not necessarily have a great explanatory power to that society.

[18] As Alex Inkeles (1971: 419) has well articulated, the role of conceptual schemes is to decide "what is taken into consideration and what is left out, what weight is assigned to one factor as against another, which sets of interrelationships are assumed to exist and which will go largely unnoticed." The criterion of judging the quality of schemes, therefore, is not that which is "right" and which "wrong," but that which is richer and which poorer, which is more sensitive and which less, and which is "more appropriate to one time or place than another."

[19] For instance, in a recent article designed for a summary of the transformation of Soviet-type regimes in accordance to the "civil society versus the state" model, the authors (Weigle and Butterfield 1992: 4) state that "unable to freely choose representatives to the state and thus to influence policy or pursue private interests in a legally protected public sphere, those individuals in society who did not accept the regime's domination of public association and participation either withdrew into the private life of the family or developed alternative, underground networks of association and participation." The authors failed to see that besides these two alternatives, there was a third strategy: to manipulate official and semiofficial structures for antisystem purposes.

of the protection and resources provided by these official and semiofficial structures.[20]

The concepts of the state versus civil society and of institutional parasitism represent two explanatory models. The former suggests that the collapse of communism can be explained only or mainly by the growth of the self-organized opposition that was independent of official institutions and that attacked the party-state system from outside by mobilizing forces from below. The latter suggests that the major reason for the collapse of highly organized communist systems was inside – the internal erosion and disintegration of the sociopolitical organization of communist societies, which were caused deliberately by those working within and which gave opportunities to the development of unofficial structures alongside the official ones.

Here therefore lies the predictive power of institutional parasitism: As a theoretical device it helps the researcher penetrate into the opaque organizational world of communist countries and locate an important source for the dynamics of regime transformation in communist systems. With this insight the researcher is able to foresee political changes despite the quiet and normal surface of a communist system.

[20]To be sure, institutional parasitism also imposes severe limits on dissent and opposition (see Chirot 1991: 132–33).

2

The counterelite and its institutional basis

This chapter discusses the major differences between China's counterelite and ruling elite, explains the counterelite's composition, and describes its efforts to capture existing institutions and form new ones. By presenting a number of cases of the counterelite's ventures, the chapter illustrates the prevalence of institutional parasitism in nonconformity and opposition in China from the late 1970s to the late 1980s.

Before rendering a detailed characterization of the counterelite and its institutional underpinnings, this chapter provides a brief look at the larger population from which the counterelite came, in order to give the reader a sense of the position of the counterelite within Chinese society.

According to China's 10 percent sampling population census of 1982, the most comprehensive data of the kind published so far, "mental workers" with post–high school education totaled about 30 million, 3 percent of China's population of 1 billion. Post–high school education here includes formal schooling, on-the-job training, and vocational and television schooling. Of those 30 million, scientific, technical, medical, and cultural personnel counted about 17 million; educators, 9 million; and administrative and managerial personnel, 4 million (*Shehuixue Yanjiu* No. 5, p. 69; No. 6, pp. 18–19, 1988). In addition, 1.88 million nationwide were enrolled undergraduate and graduate students in 1986, the midpoint of the time covered by this study (*China Statistical Yearbook* 1989: 796). Although these students had not entered the labor force yet, they were regarded by the general public as "intellectuals." Therefore, the category of "intellectuals" has a much broader coverage in the Chinese context than in the West,[1] with professionals or white-collar workers and university students all included.

As a tiny minority in Chinese society, the well educated feel a common

---

[1] In communist systems, in China as well as in the Soviet Union, there were only three basic sociological categories that were used to classify the composition of society: workers, peasants, and intellectuals (see Inkeles and Bauer 1959: 323–24).

identification. This natural identification has been strengthened, however, because the well educated have been subject to suspicion and criticism during most of Communist rule.

Some observers tend to attribute Chinese intellectuals' influence in society to their selectiveness: Of the general population only a few have received tertiary education. There is some truth in this observation but selectiveness alone is not the full explanation. In the Soviet Union of the mid-1980s, people with complete or incomplete higher education accounted for 7.8 percent of the population (22 million out of 280 million, see Lewin 1988: 47), a ratio almost 2.7 times as large as the Chinese one. But Soviet intellectuals, despite being a less selective group, were not less influential in their society. In Poland in the 1980s the university enrollment rate was 5.5 times higher than China's (*The Economist Book of Vital World Statistics* 1990: 208), yet we are told by a keen reporter that "the Western intellectual who visits his colleagues in Poland feels admiration, excitement and, yes, envy. Here is a place where people care, passionately, about ideas. Here is a place where intellectuals matter. Here, in a figure like Adam Michnik [a critical intellectual imprisoned by the Communist regime], is the Intellectual as Hero. Here historians make history" (Ash 1990: 117). This is very much the position Chinese intellectuals enjoyed in their society (Link 1992: 28–29):

The role of [Chinese] intellectuals in state and society is more important than a Westerner might suspect. The behavior of the Communist leadership itself suggests the implicit powe5 of intellectuals. The party's long series of campaigns against intellectuals . . . offers the best evidence of the party's fear of the moral authority, and thus the power, of intellectuals. In March 1989, when thirty-three leading Chinese intellectuals signed a petition asking the party leadership to declare an amnesty for political prisoners, this simple act shook the Chinese polity at its highest levels. Top leaders consulted in haste, the State Council's official spokesman issued a carefully worded rebuke; within days, news of the petition had spread orally throughout Beijing and then to other cities. It was a catalyst in the chain of events that led to the tremendous uprising later that spring. What Western intellectual can imagine organizing thirty-two colleagues to sign a petition that would have such effects?

Intellectuals held special weight in communist societies first of all "because communism itself was primarily created by intellectuals," and because communist rule was justified not by procedure or elections but by ideas and theory (EEPS 1990: 167). Another important reason might be that in communist societies other middle classes were either nonexistent or very weak, so that intellectuals were especially powerful (ibid.: 203).

It is well known that in Chinese history scholars were in an ambivalent relationship with the state: They were the source of recruitment for state officialdom; at the same time they were the center of criticism and protest against the ruler who was guilty of misconduct and misgovernment. In the contemporary Chinese counterelite's enterprise we can find the echo of this critical tradition. But our counterelite is not the simple reproduction of the traditional literati: It has internalized modern democratic values in part because of, ironically, the CCP's propaganda efforts. Before 1949 the CCP claimed itself the representative of the democratic forces against the despotic KMT regime, and promised to bring about genuine democracy and freedom in China. After the takeover the CCP exercised governance always in the name of the people: "the People's Republic," "the people's government," "the people's army," "the people's police," "the people's court." All this is but, in Rigby's (1992: 17) words, "institutionalized hypocrisy, which serves to affirm a value or ideal in the very process of betraying it." But the daily rhetoric of democracy helped to build the ideal of democracy into the consciousness of the citizenry,[2] especially that of the better educated, leading them to conclude that participation in government is their right, a right so sacred that even those who were against it in deeds have to label their institutions as democratic. Thus, while the traditional Chinese literati were committed to the making of a good emperor when voicing criticism, the contemporary counterelite was committed to the making of a good – that is, democratic – government system.

The line of demarcation between the counterelite and the ruling elite

Although this study treats the conflict during 1977–89 over directions of the reform program primarily as contention between the intellectuals and the ruling elite, the line of demarcation between these two should be taken as relative rather than clear-cut. First, the distinction of intellectuals versus political leaders is relative. The boundaries between the two are arbitrary in the sense that they are drawn by the researcher for special analytic purposes. If viewed from their educational background, most Chinese Communist leaders, like most modern revolutionary elites of other nations, were intellectuals (Putnam 1976: 193–95). The standard this study employs to identify intellectuals is one of functional role and not of educational background. Under this standard, the present Chinese Communist leaders are set apart from intellectuals.[3]

---

[2] In the Spring 1989 Movement the citizens of Beijing shouted the slogan "The people's army must not shoot the people!" when facing the troops (see Gwertzman and Kaufman 1991: 62–65).
[3] I believe that there exists no simple relationship between political leaders' class background, such as educational experience, and their political conduct (see Stanworth and Giddens 1974: 102–22, 170–84). If employed in research, class-background reductionism would cancel many politicosociological issues of great interest. Class-background reductionism is particularly dangerous in communist studies. Following it strictly, we would only have in-power communists of intellectual, bourgeois, landlord, worker, or peasant background. In a class reductionist approach, the "communist bureaucracy" as an independent, distinct category would dissolve.

Another fact explains the relativity of this line of demarcation. From the organizational point of view, a good many establishment intellectuals in China were once located near the political power center, even as they fought for the interests of the ruled.[4]

Third, neither the ruling elite nor the counterelite was homogeneous. At both the world outlook and policy preference levels, we can find differences within each group.

Finally, it is rare in politics that a fight is carried on in a clear-cut, bloc versus bloc fashion. Political struggles often cut across group boundaries (Bell 1988: 341–42). This happens particularly in times of great political change (Tilly 1978: 213–14; O'Donnell, Schmitter, and Whitehead 1986: Vol. 3, pp. 50–56). In the empirical part of this study, we can see that from time to time certain factions within the Chinese ruling elite reached out to form temporary, issue-based coalitions with certain groups within the intellectual elite fighting against other factions in the ruling elite. Sometimes elements in the intellectual elite also sought support and protection from one faction in the ruling elite to resist pressures brought to bear by another.

With regard to faction friction within the ruling elite, there has been a widely admitted problem of designation. Observers of both China and the Soviet Union point out that it is inadequate and misleading to use oversimplified labels, such as "Left versus Right," "conservative versus progressive," or "radical versus moderate," to designate opinion and policy differences among communist leaders (Macridis and Brown 1977: 175, 201–2). Methodologically, this polarization model has its roots in a mistakenly assumed consistency. "It assumes that social views can be aligned along a single dimension. . . . If a person is a radical in one realm, he is a radical in all others; and conversely, if he is a conservative in one realm, then he must be conservative in the others as well" (Bell 1978: xi–xii). A polarized picture is especially unfitting to the politics of reform (Huntington 1968: 344–96). As mentioned earlier, the decisive feature of Dengism is the syncretic policy of economic pluralism plus party dictatorship. The adoption of this policy by the dominant faction of the Chinese ruling elite rendered coalition formation within the leadership extremely complex and unstable. Opponents in the economic policy area at the same time could be allies or even comrades-in-arms on the political front. Examples of this sort can be found in many places in the chapters that follow.

Additionally, the factor of personal relationships adds new difficulties to the understanding of group formation within the CCP leadership. That Chinese political figures value personal loyalty and connections enormously makes per-

[4]In any concrete society, there is always some overlap between ruling and social elites (Parry 1969: 74).

sonal relationships a relatively independent dynamic in group formation. If a political leader regards somebody as personally loyal to him, he could keep this person in his close circle or assign important posts to him, even if he knows that the loyalist holds different opinions on policy issues. This dimension of grouping can hardly be explained by schemes of "Left versus Right" or "conservative versus liberal," which are entirely based on political orientation and policy opinion.[5]

Deng Xiaoping's inclusion of Wang Zhen and Deng Liqun in his close circle is a good illustration. Deng Liqun, a senior official in charge of policy studies and ideological affairs, had a stand very different from Deng Xiaoping's on policies such as the open-door policy, the SEZs, urban economic reform, the differentiation of party and government functions, and bureaucratic recruitment. Wang Zhen, a former general and later a vice-president of the state, had been closer to Deng Xiaoping's chief opponents on many policy issues in both the political and economic realms. Yet Deng Xiaoping had given both men influential positions. An important reason is that Wang was the first official to urge the then party chairman Hua Guofeng to rehabilitate Deng Xiaoping at the 1977 "Central Working Conference." Deng Liqun refused to denounce Deng Xiaoping in the "Criticize Deng Xiaoping Campaign" of 1975–76 initiated by Mao. Deng Xiaoping greatly appreciated those loyalties and believed that Wang Zhen and Deng Liqun would never betray him at critical times, that is, during the intraparty power struggle. This personal trust contributed heavily to Deng Xiaoping's favoring of these two men, playing down (but not ignoring) their differences over policy.

Personal relationships as a factor relatively independent of policy stands also plays a part in crossline networking between the intellectual elite and the ruling elite. That some intellectuals obtained a certain degree of political protection from powerful leaders does not necessarily mean that the two sides were fighting for the same cause: They might simply be old colleagues or knew each other through chains of friendship or kinship.

For example, late in 1983 during the Anti–Spiritual Pollution Campaign, Hu Qiaomu, China's ideological tsar, and Deng Liqun were determined to abolish the Institute of Marxism, Leninism, and Mao Zedong Thought led by Yu Guangyuan and Su Shaozhi, an institution termed by many in the party establishment as the "stronghold of bourgeois liberalism." At this critical moment,

[5]For a comprehensive review of the efforts to theorize about patron-client relations in politics, see S. N. Eisenstadt and Louis Roniger (1980). For recent applications of the patronage concept to PRC society, see Andrew Walder (1986) and Jean Oi (1989). Robert Kaufman's (1974) article, though written nearly two decades ago, still contains a good review of some methodological problems involved in extending the dyadic exchange model to macropolitics.

the institute's leadership asked Feng Lanrui, a former deputy director of that institute, to seek help from Bo Yibo, her old boss of the revolutionary movement in the 1930s and 1940s. Bo, known as a hard-liner on many policy issues, was a powerful leader in charge of the party rectification campaign. Because of their long-term personal relationship, however, Feng managed to persuade Bo to issue a directive saving the institute from abolition.

Without ignoring these problems, this study places emphasis on the conflict between the ruling elite and the intellectual elite, rather than on the combat between cross-boundary coalitions. Although there were many differences among the members of the post-Mao ruling elite, and these differences may be of primary importance in other studies, the consensus among the majority of the ruling elite was substantial with respect to regime legitimation and political stabilization, which is the subject of the present inquiry. The ruling elite's consensus defined the setting within which the post-Mao political interaction was carried on. On this point, what Bialer (1980: 195) has said about the pre-1980s Soviet political elite is pertinent to the Chinese case:

The Soviet political elite is, of course, not a homogeneous body; it joins varied interests, diverse outlooks and sympathies. During times of internal crisis and severe stress it tends to divide. Yet one may suggest that a core set of attitudes and beliefs which are strong and persistent permeate the elite stratum as a whole. . . . When considering the context of elite group activity in the Soviet Union, it seems important to suggest that it refers to a relationship among groups who fundamentally accept the system but who compete for advantages within it. These groups exist within consensus relationships of a more general and durable kind than their conflict relationships.

One may list a set of positions that the majority of the post-Mao ruling elite consensually held as a base line. It was permissible to have different interpretations on such positions, but any individual member's attempt to abandon them was defined by the ruling group as a whole as treason.[6]

1. The maintenance of a powerful, authoritarian, and centralized bureaucratic state system; the preservation of the state's authority to interfere in the citizen's social and moral life if considered necessary
2. Emphasis on the CCP's leadership in the state system and on the maintenance of Leninist administration of the party itself, in which decision making must be carried out in a top-down manner and the top leadership must enjoy full autonomy; radical rejection of a multiparty system and a legal system independent of the party bureaucracy's control
3. The desirability of the state's control of key economic resources and its discretion in major economic affairs, and fear of excessive income differentiation in society
4. The urgency of technological-economic development, and insistence on the unconditional subordination of human and civil rights to social stability and economic development

[6]The fate of Hu Yaobang and Zhao Ziyang is a good example. Actually, they did not go so far as abandoning the base line, but only tried to soften some of the positions.

5. The commitment to national independence; the mistrust of foreign political and economic power, and the ambivalence toward China's growing interconnections with the world economy, which benefited China materially but subjected it to the manipulation of foreign powers[7]

In contrast, the basic agreements among the counterelite – again acknowledging that considerable dispute was observable within the group – were as follows:

1. Opposition to the omnipotent state; emphasis on differentiation between state and societal activity, on social autonomy at the grass-roots level, and on government responsiveness to complaints and pressure from the governed
2. Objection to the Leninist one-party dictatorship; a belief in the open, fair competition among various factions in the ruling party, and among various parties in the country
3. Desire for a just legal system independent of the party-state bureaucracy, for the authority of the law above that of the ruling party, and for the authority of due process in political succession
4. Demand for the actualization of civil liberties promised by the PRC Constitution – for example, the rights of free information, free expression, free press, and the freedom of assembly, association, worship, and migration
5. Opposition to the CCP's command of the army; demand for a depoliticized, professional national defense force, which must be precluded from involvement in domestic politics
6. Revulsion against political, legal, economic, and social privileges enjoyed by officials and their families, and against nepotism, cronyism, and patrimonialism in politics; insistence on severe punishment of bureaucrats who use public office to promote their own interests, and on equal opportunities, fair competition, and a merit system in selecting recruits for all official posts
7. A belief in the efficiency of a market economy, in which the state bureaucracy's intervention should be minimized and the public and private sector be appropriately empowered

These two different sets of positions, to be sure, were not the starting point of the post-Mao political drama; rather, they developed during the course of the interplay. In Part II of this study we will observe how the two sides parted company step by step and became antagonistic.

This study focuses on the tension between the intellectual and the ruling elites also because the post-Mao experience has shown that, despite certain patron–client relations developed between individual members from the two sides, the patron in the ruling elite would sell out, or at least ignore, his clients' interests when his clients went too far, provoking strain in the Communist leadership. At this point the ruling elite would conclude that something must be

[7]Jurgen Domes (Michael et al. 1990: 184) labels the post-Mao ruling elite's shared position on major policy issues as "enlightened Stalinism." For "the Stalinist or Bolshevik policy elements provided the basis, and the elements of enlightenment were supplementary." Domes's description fits well the ruling elite's common attitude toward political issues, but not its stances on economic policies. In the economic field, the practice of the Dengists – the dominant faction of the leadership – has deviated from Stalinism so far that the preceding description appears inappropriate.

done in order to keep the situation in control and to display the ruling elite's "unity" to the general public. Examples considered in this study include Deng Xiaoping's treatment of the Democracy Wall activists in 1978–79, who supported Deng's return to power but then were attacked by the Communist leadership, including Deng, for demanding "too much democracy." Another example is Hu Yaobang's desertion of Hu Jiwei, Wang Ruoshui, Li Honglin, and Ruan Ming in the mid-1980s, when he was under pressure from his colleagues to punish these intellectuals. Still another is Zhao Ziyang's deal with the top hard-liners over the fate of Liu Binyan, Su Shaozhi, Zhang Xianyang, and others in 1987, when the hard-liners insisted on disciplining those "bourgeois liberals" in exchange for a compromise on economic policies. This standard practice shows clearly how the political leaders identified their interests versus the intellectuals'.

From the late 1970s to late 1980s, there was a consistent and remarkable growth in the collective self-consciousness of Chinese intellectuals as a politically awakened, independent social stratum with a unique role and responsibility. There was a corresponding rise in political activism among them. Immediately after Mao's death, China's critical intellectuals, like the earlier dissidents in Eastern Europe (Skilling 1989: 182), were basically socialist in their orientation, hoping to make changes within the framework of the existing order. With their reform objectives being repudiated by the Communist leadership again and again, with themselves being frequently victimized by the reformist leaders in inner-party struggles, and with their expanding knowledge of political change in the Soviet block and Taiwan, Chinese intellectuals increasingly saw themselves not as a supplementary force attached to certain factions in the Communist leadership but as a counterelite – an independent sociopolitical force engaged in discourse, competition, and confrontation with the party establishment.[8] In the late 1970s, this movement toward a counterelite role was observable only among a few educated youth, such as Wei Jingsheng and Ren Wanding. In the mid-1980s, among elite intellectuals, only Fang Lizhi, a physicist, dared to pronounce:

To a large extent, whether China can advance to a modern and democratic society will depend on how the present generation of Chinese intellectuals can remold themselves. . . . Chinese intellectuals must stand erect, must not submit themselves to higher authorities and await for their instructions in everything, still less to entrust their future to favors bestowed by certain officials. Once Chinese intellectuals become independent, they will show their strength immediately . . . The present generation of Chinese intel-

---

[8] For consistency in terminology I use the term "counterelite" to designate the object of my study throughout this work. But the reader should keep in mind that the intellectual and professional groups under study were less counter to the regime in the late 1970s than in the late 1980s.

lectuals begins to show an independence-consciousness and entertains a strong aspiration to become masters of their own fate. (Rosen's translation, 1990: 88)

In the late 1980s, Chinese intellectuals made public pronouncements about what their role in government should be. In the "First National Conference on Modernization Theories," held in early 1988, most participants reached a consensus, which strongly recommended an "elite democracy" model, in which two elite groups, the political and the intellectual, share power. The recommenders believed that only through an "elite democracy" phase could China move to the higher stage of "popular democracy" (*Guangming Daily* March 24, 1988). In the "First National Symposium on Problems Concerning Intellectuals" in the summer of 1988, many contributors remarked that in the past, political participation by Chinese intellectuals too often resulted in persecution when the ruler became disenchanted with their proposals, as in the Anti-Rightist Campaign of 1957.

If intellectuals have no independent personality, their participation is meaningless. Independent personality means a self-consciousness of the duty and character of one's class or stratum. . . . After the 1949 Liberation, Chinese intellectuals put faith in the ruling party led by Mao Zedong as the sole body capable of revitalizing the nation. Regrettably, the Chinese intelligentsia abandoned its independent and critical spirit as it adopted a faith in and worship of the party and its leader. The 1957 disaster crushed the intelligentsia's spine. Since then it could no longer represent the conscience of society. . . . We thus must call for the preservation of the intelligentsia's sense of independence. (*Guangming Daily* September 8, 1988; *World Economic Herald* September 12, 1988)

In their journey from the role of a good-minded "repairer" of the existing system to that of a determined antagonist of it, Chinese intellectuals' experience was not unique. In communist countries, too often within-system reformers were forced to become overt opponents, as in the Soviet Union during the 1970s and early 1980s (Brumberg 1990: 32) and in Hungary before the late 1980s (Ash 1990: 293; Frentzel-Zagorska 1990: 765). The nondemocratic nature of communist systems expressed itself precisely in their denying of legitimate opposition within the political system.

Four categories of the counterelite

The objects of this study are those members of the well-educated social strata who were deeply involved in politics and dared to voice criticism and dissent against the Communist regime. Members of this counterelite can be roughly grouped into four categories: radical marginal intellectuals, critical cultural intellectuals, politically active technical intellectuals, and independent-minded official intellectuals. Although in many of the events that constituted the post-

Mao political drama members of different categories acted together and their work became inseparable, each category possessed unique characteristics.

1. Radical marginal intellectuals

Most members of this category were born around 1949 when the PRC was founded. They participated in the Cultural Revolution as Red Guards, farmed in the countryside as the "sent-down youth," and afterward returned to cities to work in factories, service sectors, research and educational institutions, or government offices. Some also served in the army.

The vicissitudes that marked the MIs' lives crystallized in them special qualities: extensive knowledge about the many faces of social reality and direct experience of different social strata; close contact with almost every walk of life; knowledge of and sensitivity to the thoughts and expectations of low classes such as the peasantry, poor urban-dwellers, and rank-and-file soldiers; a strong sense of responsibility for the destiny of the Chinese nation and the welfare of the people; a commitment to action; a deep concern with political affairs and susceptibility to political winds; a sophisticated and realistic approach to political issues; familiarity with schemes and tactics in Chinese politics; critical, skeptical thinking; and an immunity to official propaganda.

In this study, these people are called "marginal intellectuals" because of the level of formal educational or vocational position they attained. The majority received conventional educations but reached only senior high school. By self-teaching, or attending evening schools and television colleges, or on-the-job training, many of them achieved the equivalent of college or even graduate degrees. Strictly speaking, they were not all white-collar professionals but ranged between the mental and manual laborers.

The radical MIs are not well represented in this study. Their relatively low status in the Chinese intellectual strata made it difficult for them to enter the center stage. Realizing this difficulty, some MIs worked hard to move up in the intellectual hierarchy, mainly by attending good schools or passing certificate examinations. Thus, some names that appear first in the category of MIs later appear in other categories, such as Min Qi and Lü Jiamin, who were merely office workers when involved in the Democracy Movement of 1978–79 but became well-known critical intellectuals in the late 1980s.

Yet the MIs' status as outsiders allowed them to appear to be a cohesive group – perhaps more so than they actually were. Most participants in the Democracy Movement of 1978–79 and the "Responses to Pan Xiao's Letter" in 1980–81 were MIs (see Chapter 3). Some also appeared in the debate over China's "global membership" in 1988 (Chapter 5). In other events examined here, the MIs' role was visible only in the background. Such individuals as Wei Jingsheng, Ren Wanding, Xu Wenli, Li Shenping, Li Jiahua, and Chen Erjin, who all were activists of the Democracy Movement, and Huang Xiaojiu, one of the authors of "Pan Xiao"'s letter, are well-known examples, but for the most part the MIs received little publicity and as individuals are little known.

2. Critical cultural intellectuals

Research fellows in social-scientific research institutes, university teachers and students in humanities, social sciences, and legal studies programs, and the editorial staff of scholarly journals and publishing houses constituted the second category, the CIs. During the post-Mao era, these people combined the roles of the political and the professional intellectuals. On the one hand, they were required to devote their specialties to official goals and were involved in discussions over policy formation and implementation; on the other hand, they fought for professionalism and tried to dissociate their work from party-state guidance. Under Communist rule, however, to make the cultural and social science enterprises independent of politics, practitioners involved in these enterprises have to be first engaged in politics. Post-Mao CIs purposefully played a role in political battles, hoping their contribution would make a difference in the choice of directions for reform and development.

The Dengist regime, compared with the Maoist one, adopted a more rational policy toward intellectual life, similar to the Soviet bloc after Stalin (cf. C. Johnson 1970: 113; Lewin 1988: 85–100). After the natural sciences, economics as a tool for economic development was the first branch of the social sciences to win some degree of autonomy from party interference. Second was empirical social research, the area that indicated the effects of policies on society. "Bourgeois disciplines" once abolished, such as sociology and political science, were restored,[9] and "imperialist pseudosciences" once denounced, such as business administration and decision science, were instituted. In the humanities, in fields less related to the party's core doctrines, such as pre–twentieth century Chinese history, logic, and linguistics, party officials no longer kept their eyes on what was said or written.

The less a field touched on sensitive political issues, the more its practitioners had opportunities to communicate with Western colleagues. In areas of great practical value, such as business management and international law, lecturers were allowed to use parts of Western textbooks for teaching purposes. In jour-

---

[9]After the Spring 1989 Movement, Hu Qiaomu regretted having permitted the restoration of sociology, for, said Hu, this discipline had propagated tremendous "bourgeois ideas" on campuses and sociology students had been particularly active in demonstrations (Informant no. 1). (For a discussion of the informants used in this study, see the Appendix.)

nals, the number of officially assigned articles declaring support for the current party line declined, as more and more publications were willing to adjust to internationally recognized analytic concepts and research techniques. On the basis of the "Rules for Awarding Academic Degrees" and "Criteria for Assigning Academic Ranks" established in the early 1980s, attaining degrees in school and promotion in academia were determined less by candidates' party cards and political attitudes and more by their professional publications, ability to use foreign languages, recognition by colleagues, and international renown.

Such progress, however, was contingent on relaxation of party supervision of the cultural and social sciences, not on independence from party hands. The party-state leadership continued to view most branches of social and cultural science as political, in the sense that their problematics directly or indirectly referred to the theory and practice of the existing order. Even fields related to the "four modernizations" effort, such as economics, business management, and decision science, were not free from party interference, because they were linked to the sensitive problems of property rights and the decision-making process in the party-state hierarchy.

From the institutional point of view, most critical CIs studied here were employed by organizations under jurisdiction of the Party Central Propaganda Department (PCPD), which supervised the Chinese Academy of Social Sciences (CASS) and provincial social science institutes; the Ministries of Education, of Culture, and of Radio, Film, and Television, with all the organizational bodies under them; news agencies and newspapers; the State Bureau of Religious Affairs; the Communist Youth League (CYL); the All-China Students' Federation, and other organizations.[10] The PCPD had a say in the appointment of leading officials, the making of middle- and long-term development projects, and the handling of serious dissident activities in these institutions. To illustrate the impact of its supervision on the professionalization of activity in these institutions, I cite the case of the Ministry of Education.[11]

In the summer of 1984, a group of establishment intellectuals proposed to Premier Zhao Ziyang that the State Council take the Ministry of Education's business under its direct control. They argued that the modernization program depended on modernizing science and technology in China, and that modernizing science and technology was in turn dependent on modernization of the educational system. Education, they argued, should be treated not as part of the

---

[10]Originally, the PCPD also supervised the Chinese Academy of Sciences (CAS), the State Science and Technology Commission, the Ministry of Public Health, the State Physical Culture and Sports Commission, the All-China Federation of Trade Unions, and the All-China Women's Federation. During the Dengist era, supervision was limited to ideological affairs in these institutions.

[11]The following is based on Informants nos. 2 and 25.

"political and ideological front" but as an essential part of the productive forces and the economy, meaning that it be politically neutral.

Before 1984, however, the educational system under supervision of the PCPD had kept narrow-minded officials like He Dongchang in leading posts and imposed outdated ideological schemes on educational programs, textbooks, and entrance examinations. It erected excessively elaborate procedures for programs to permit Chinese students to study abroad; emphasized students' political reliability in job assignments and directed the activities of the CCP and CYL cells in schools; and controlled publications and communications within the entire educational system. Through these means, the establishment intellectuals argued, the PCPD had created great obstacles to modernizing teaching and research programs and the useful adoption of Western practices in Chinese schools; to training "open-minded, creative, and competent personnel"; and to introducing university professors and students to the "frontiers of socialist economic and political reforms." In fact, what was taught in classrooms conflicted with the course of reform in China, so that the educational system was largely "counter to economic reform."

To Premier Zhao, these arguments appeared both true and attractive, but he failed to take control of the Ministry of Education. Instead, he told the establishment intellectuals that because the PCPD had been in charge of educational affairs since the founding of the PRC, it was hard to make changes regardless of his preference. This incident illustrates that to the party bureaucracy, for the most part, educational affairs, not to mention social research and communications, were political.

Amos Perlmutter (1981: 13) remarks that an essential feature of the Leninist system is institutionalization of "parallel structures": "each state and societal structure and geographical unit is directly controlled by a functionally equivalent unit in the party." In China, in addition to parallel structures, the party's "penetration, domination, and control of society and of the state" (ibid.) was further ensured by functionally diffuse party organizations, such as the PCPD and the Organization Department, whose duty was to oversee a wide range of state and societal institutions that had loose relationships to each other.

A cohort of critical CIs analogous to, but more sophisticated than, the radical MIs were the former Red Guards and "sent-down youth." Able to enter undergraduate and graduate programs during the late 1970s and early 1980s and then provided positions in teaching, research, and publishing, this generation of CIs combined colorful social and political experience with educational and cultural capital. They had been politically active and skillful, and among the well educated they were the most pluralist and creative. In particular, they were capable of grasping undercurrents in Chinese society and translating them into provocative topics in political discourse.[12]

The critical CIs, compared with the radical MIs, are better represented in this study. Many widely known individuals will appear throughout the political drama to be examined here.

3. Politically active technical intellectuals

This category includes intellectuals and professionals in natural science, applied sciences, and engineering and university students in those fields. The Deng regime, owing to the need for technological and economic development, had a policy of favoring TIs over CIs. During the Anti–Spiritual Pollution Campaign of 1983–84, while CIs suffered from "criticism and self-criticism" imposed by the party-state for allegedly having spread antisocialist ideas, TIs were comforted by the statement of Politburo member Fang Yi that "with the approval of the State Council [the Central Government], the State Science and Technology Commission announces that the combat against spiritual pollution will not be carried on in the fields of natural sciences and technology. . . . The purpose of this policy is to further develop a social atmosphere in which knowledge is respected, and to encourage the scientific-technological personnel to be free from fear and engage in research and innovation" (*People's Daily* January 6, 1984). Early in 1987, when the official campaign against the so-called leading bourgeois liberals Fang Lizhi, Liu Binyan, and Wang Ruowang was at its peak, top party-state leaders invited nineteen scientists and engineers, named as "model intellectuals," for discussion and formal dinner at the CCP's headquarters, hoping to convince their colleagues that the regime would not turn its back on them (*People's Daily* January 13, 1987).

More important, the Deng regime's policy of distinguishing between intellectuals was demonstrated by its practice of favoring TIs in bureaucratic recruitment (see Lee 1991 for detail), a tendency parallel to post-Stalin development in the Soviet bloc (cf. Ludz 1972: 10–11). As shown in Table 1 in post-Mao China, of 2,185 senior civilian and military officials, 1,340 had post–high school education: the education of 44.6 percent of these officials was technical, 22.8 percent in the humanities. If engineers trained in military academies (mixed in column IV) and personnel trained in business management programs (mixed in column VI) are taken into account, technocrats clearly predominated in senior officialdom of post-Mao China.

---

[12]For a characterization of this generation, see Li Zehou and Vera Schwarcz (1983–84) and Zhang Yongjie and Cheng Yuanzhong (1988: 94–110).

Table 1. *Educational backgrounds of PRC senior officials (1977–88)*

	I[a]: Total senior officials	II[b]: With post–high school education	III: With technical education	IV[c]: With special training	V[d]: With humanities education	VI[e]: With economics education
Number	2,185	1,340	597	312	306	125
% of I	100.0	61.0	27.3	14.3	14.0	5.7
% of II	N/A	100.0	44.6	23.3	22.8	9.3

[a]For detailed discussion of ranks included here, see Editorial Board of *Who's Who in China* (1989: XI–XIII).
[b]The biographical dictionary omits educational backgrounds of the remaining 845 individuals. In this dictionary, only those who had reached the level of post–high school education are indicated for educational backgrounds.
[c]Includes those who attended military academies, higher party schools, and higher cadres schools (in China or the Soviet bloc) and schools with unidentified specialties. In this group, educational quality varies widely.
[d]Includes those in the humanities, legal studies, and the social sciences.
[e]Includes those in economics and business management.
Source: Editorial Board of *Who's Who in China* (1989). This dictionary is the most comprehensive of its kind published so far in the PRC by an authoritative body. Its range extends beyond the data Hong Yung Lee used (1991: 256).

Although China under Deng witnessed a tendency toward technocracy, TIs did not see themselves as a category that was socially or politically different from other intellectuals,[13] because, under the Chinese Communist system, those in the government "were not allowed to represent any particular social group or class [but acted] as agents of the state" (Lee 1991: 395). As soon as professionals with a technical education became full-time officials, their political and material interests were determined by their administrative position. They no longer shared work or living conditions with TIs but instead identified with party-state functionaries. Hence, no institutional mechanism linked changes in the status of the very few ex-TIs selected to become administrators to changes in the lives of ordinary TIs. Therefore, ordinary TIs identified their interests with those of CIs rather than with those of party technocrats.

For instance, in November 1987, the State Science and Technology Commission conducted a survey (the sample size was 34,000) among 10.03 million technical professionals. Only 16 percent of the respondents said their administrators listened to them on professional matters with respect. In contrast, 25 percent said their administrators suppressed different opinions and mistreated

[13]George Konrad and Ivan Szelenyi (1979: 207–19) once predicted a division, because of technocratic development, between TIs and other intellectuals in state-socialism.

those who voiced criticism. In addition, 50.3 percent believed their administrators appointed people not on the basis of merit but of conformity with the bosses. When asked whether their specialty had been used in the present assignment, 14.6 percent said yes, 30 percent said partially, 10 percent said most of their skills had been wasted; 31 percent said they had tried unsuccessfully to change jobs. Commenting on the existing personnel system and the residence register system – both central to the state's sociopolitical control mechanism – most respondents expressed dissatisfaction; 37.4 percent even said the residence register system should be abolished (*People's Daily* May 25, 1988).

According to another survey (with a sample size of 40,000) released in August 1988, among the country's 5.21 million middle-aged (36–55) technical personnel, 61.6 percent had health problems caused by overwork, malnutrition, or depression. The average income of middle-aged professionals was only 95 percent of that of blue-collar workers in the same age group. The survey concluded that middle-aged professionals with such a low income suffered greatly both physically and psychologically. The successive premature deaths in the mid-1980s of some of the best Chinese scientists and engineers were merely a small indication of the terrible situation middle-aged professionals faced (*Science and Technology Daily* August 22, 1988). A comparison of the lives of TIs and CIs shows no great difference.

In post-Mao China, as in the Soviet Union, because the Communist regime claimed socialism was scientific and defined scientific and technological advancement as a national priority, science and technology became something ideological. Anything put forward under the banner of science appeared to possess universal truth in the eyes of the leaders as well as the general public. Science and technology became safe careers. A small number of intellectuals here labeled politically active TIs deliberately used their identity as scientists to play political roles (Buckley 1991; Williams 1990).[14] In the name of science they raised key social and political issues too sensitive to touch otherwise. A few journals and newspapers with titles linked to science or technology, such as, *Science and Technology Daily* and *Reports on the Dialectics of Nature*, printed articles that most political and social-scientific publications did not dare to print.

---

[14] In post-Mao China, the following individuals symbolize intellectuals of this type: Fang Lizhi (astrophysicist, former vice-president of the Chinese University of Science and Technology); Wen Yuankai (chemist, former vice-chairman of Anhui Provincial Commission on Education); Xu Liangying (expert on history of sciences, former editor in chief of *Science Gazette*); Chen Ziming (graduate student in biology at the CAS when he was involved in protest movements in the early 1980s); Wang Juntao (physics student at Beijing University and then researcher at the Beijing Institute of Nuclear Energy while a democracy activist in the early 1980s); Jin Guantao (research fellow at the Institute of Science-Technology Policy and Management Science of the CAS); and Wan Runnan (researcher at the Institute of Computer Science of the CAS when he erected the "Stone Institute for Research on Social Development" under the Stone Company).

Because critical opinions were couched in, or justified by, scientific reasoning, the articles carried significant weight.

The strategy of using one's scientific status to play the role of political dissident has also been observed in the Soviet Union, the best-known examples being Zhores Medvedev and Andrei Sakharov (Rothberg 1972: Parts I and IV). The most famous scientist-turned-dissident in the PRC, Fang Lizhi, has been named "China's Sakharov," well symbolizing parallel developments in these two countries.

4. Independent-minded official intellectuals

These were both officials or ex-officials and intellectuals. They were party members and persons of authority: heads of cultural and social research institutes; senior editors or reporters for official newspapers and radio and television stations; heads or senior staff members of publishing houses and journals; responsible individuals in educational institutions; senior research fellows in party organizations; instructors in party schools and cadres schools (both served as training centers for officials); and consultants in think tanks.

Although many OIs studied here were party ideologists during their career, party ideologists, unlike these OIs, had no independent points of reference for theoretical and practical activity and displayed unconditional conformity to the current party line. In contrast, the independent-minded OIs retained their own normative standards and professional ethics and were orientated to the people's interests rather than the party's. Deposed from influential positions because of that orientation, they were led further in the direction of independence and opposition.

These OIs were professionals well trained in certain fields. They were recognized by colleagues for achievements in academia and some were even leading authorities in their fields. They were regarded by ordinary intellectuals as professional leaders, rather than political ones like the party ideologists. Their respectable intellectual backgrounds were an important factor in appointments as heads of communicative, cultural, and academic institutions and advisors to decision-making bodies, and occupation of these positions strengthened their authority in intellectual circles. These OIs were highly influential and visible throughout the Dengist era, and for this reason are highlighted in this study too.[15]

[15] It is easy to name individuals typical of this group: Hu Jiwei (former director and editor in chief of the *People's Daily* and former chairman of Beijing Journalists Association); Wang Ruoshui (former deputy editor in chief of the *People's Daily*); Su Shaozhi (former director of the Institute of Marxism, Leninism and Mao Zedong Thought, CASS); Li Honglin (former deputy director of

Institutional resources of the radical marginal intellectuals

The regime under Mao is known for control of public information and communications, with a sternness and sophistication unparalleled even among communist systems.[16] How the post-Mao counterelite competed with the ruling elite in the public sphere and what the counterelite used as a basis for authority against the ruling elite's political power[17] are important issues. With each of the categories of the counterelite discussed here, different institutional and material resources were available. The group most easily explained, the radical MIs, provides a starting point.[18]

The combination of relatively low status in the intellectual strata and a direct manner of political expression excluded most radical MIs from established political platforms. They had to pick from whatever means were available, and some ventured to create their own institutional bases.

Until April 1980, when the party decided to rescind Article 45 of the Constitution granting citizens the rights to public debate and the use of wall posters, both basic techniques for mass mobilization endorsed by Mao, the MIs relied heavily on these primitive means of expression. A wall poster of five pages (each about 80 by 100 centimeters) cost about one Chinese yuan, or three-quarters of a young worker's daily wage, a significant financial burden for the average Chinese. During 1966–69, the peak of the Cultural Revolution, the materials for creating wall posters were available from official institutions, but afterward, to address issues of one's particular concern, materials had to be purchased on one's own.

the Theory Bureau of the PCPD and former president of Fujian Provincial Academy of Social Sciences); Ruan Ming (former deputy division director at the Central Party School); Guo Luoji (former professor at Beijing University and chief of staff to the university president); Sun Changjiang (former professor at the Central Party School and deputy editor in chief of the *Science and Technology Daily*); Qin Benli (former party secretary of the Institute of World Economy of the Shanghai Academy of Social Sciences and editor in chief of the *World Economic Herald*); Yu Haocheng (former director of the Masses Publishing House and editor in chief of the *Legal Consulting*); Yan Jiaqi (former director of the Institute of Political Science, CASS); Xue Dezhen (deputy editor in chief of the People's Publishing House); Ma Peiwen (director of the Theory Department of the *Guangming Daily*); Yu Guangyuan (former vice-president of the CASS); Ge Yang (former editor in chief of the *New Observer*); Dai Qing (senior reporter and columnist for the *Guangming Daily*); Zhang Zhonghou (senior editor of the *China Legal System Press*); Wu Jiaxiang (former research fellow in the General Office of the CCP Central Committee); and Yuan Zhiming (lecturer at the Cadres School of the CYL's Central Committee).

[16] Both traditional Chinese political culture and statecraft contributed to the quality of the control (see Urban 1986: 316–47 and Harding 1987: 24–29).

[17] See Robert Nisbet (1966: 108–12) for elaboration of the difference between power and authority.

[18] The following is based on interviews with Informants nos. 3 and 4 and Hu Ping (Boston, spring 1987). See also Xu Xing (Widor 1981–84: Vol. 1, pp. 31, 33–45); Chen Ruoxi (*China Times* [Taipei] April 26 and 27, 1981); and Rong Xing (*Contending* [Hong Kong] No. 5, pp. 28–32, 1979).

By late 1980, when the Communist regime prohibited unofficial publications, China had had a variety of unofficial magazines similar to the Russian *samizdat*, founded mainly by the MIs. Except for one issue of *Beijing Spring*, which was printed by the Beijing Foreign Languages Press's printing factory, all unofficial magazines were printed on stencil paper, using stencil pens, steel boards, and manual printers. Equipment of this kind cost about 250 Chinese yuan, plus variable expenses for paper and ink for each issue. To balance the costs, activists publishing unofficial magazines necessarily resorted to such means as collecting money from among their own circles, selling magazines on the street (charging, for example, 25 cents to Chinese citizens and 1 yuan to foreigners), and borrowing equipment or material from official institutions, mainly ones at which they were employed, with fabricated "legitimate" reasons.

During 1978–79, publishers of most unofficial magazines appealed to the police for registration as legal publications. Some publishers from establishment families asked their relatives in high places to help them become legal. A few OIs also lobbied for them. But by directives from top party-state leaders such as Deng Xiaoping and Peng Zhen, all such petitions were turned down by local police (see Party Literature Research Center 1982: 702–4). To make the rejection appear lawful, the "Publication Regulations" issued in 1952 were cited, according to which a nongovernment publication must have two legally registered private firms as guarantors in order to apply for legal status. In the late 1970s no such private firms existed in the PRC, and thus the petitions were necessarily rejected.

Dedicated democracy activists also engaged in building small organizations around their magazines, with the editors as the core and contributors, informants, and committed readers as supporting members.[19] Like unofficial magazines, these embryonic organizations were also outlawed. Although many such organizations based in the same locality often met to discuss and exchange ideas and experiences, coordinated actions were rare. Crossregion contacts were even rarer. But contact and coordination did occur in exceptional circumstances. In 1978 when many editors of "Enlightenment Society" left their base in the city of Guiyang to go to Beijing, democracy activists in both these localities began to have contact. When Wei Jingsheng, Lu Lin, and Yang Guang (editors of the *Quest*, Beijing), Chen Lu and Ren Wanding (members of "Human Rights League," Beijing), and many members of the Guiyang-based "Thaw Society" and "Enlightenment Society," and the Shanghai-based "Democracy Association," "Democracy Discussion Society," and "Human Rights Committee" were arrested between March and April 1979 in an official campaign, these organiza-

---

[19]The party-state leadership was very disturbed by these efforts to create independent organizations at local and national levels (Deng 1984: 182).

tions coordinated their efforts to demand the release of those arrested and to protect others in danger.

Troubled by the relative isolation of unofficial magazines, in January 1980 the editors of the *Spray*, the *People's Road*, and *Life*, all based in Guangzhou, appealed to other unofficial magazines for nationwide unity. Their proposal received immediate responses from roughly twenty magazines in Shanghai, Kaifeng, Changsha, Changchun, Ningbo, Wuhan, Anyang, Qingdao, Guiyang, Wenzhou, and Shaoguan. By the summer, delegates from thirty-three unofficial magazines met to found the "All-China Folk Magazines Association." The magazines decided to take turns publishing a new journal named *Duty*. One issue was put out in July by the *People's Road*. Because of pressure from the party-state leadership, the association and its members were soon banned by local police.

For nonconformists under communist rule the most difficult thing was not the creation of unofficial organizations, which could be done locally in times of reform or political crisis, but the national coordination among or coalescence of unofficial organizations. This would raise the political challenge to monopoly communist parties to a critical level. In the second half of the 1980s, the Soviet Union experienced an explosion of informal groups, but for several years these groups, like islands, "exist[ed] primarily in big cities" (Brovkin 1990: 238). Intracity contact and national coordination became possible only at the end of the decade when the Communist party itself was being dismantled.

The Chinese Communist regime's abolition of rights to public debate and wall posters and the ban on unofficial magazines and organizations took almost every means away from the MIs. As will be discussed, after 1980 some of them sought other opportunities.

Institutional resources of the independent-minded official intellectuals

The radical MIs and the independent-minded OIs sharply differed in resources: the former were poor, the latter rich.

First and foremost, the resourcefulness of the OIs can be explained by their role as heads of work units (*danwei*). As has been observed, in the Communist Chinese social structure the unit was a self-sustaining, relatively closed, micro-social system with substantial political, personnel, financial, and social power. The head of the unit had considerable discretion over the opportunities of the members (Kleinman 1986; Walder 1986; Shue 1988). With the decentralization of administration and economic management induced by the Dengist reforms, the "grey area" of legal–illegal, right–wrong, and regular–irregular, which was largely dependent on the judgment of the unit head, expanded. For the purpose of this study, the importance of the independent-minded OI as a unit head lies in that, under his leadership, the unit could be partially converted from an instrument of the party-state into an agent for the struggle against the ruling elite. The case of the People's Publishing House in Beijing can serve as an illustration.[20]

The Publishing House came under direct supervision of the PCPD. Its official function was publication of works by Marx, Lenin, and Mao, as well as current top party leaders and of party documents and material important for political instruction throughout the party networks. The Publishing House edited two major journals, *New China Monthly (Xinhua Yuebao)* and *New China Digest (Xinhua Wenzhai)*. The former was designed to collect major party and government documents, news reports, and official records released in the past month; the latter to collect notable or controversial works in the social sciences, legal studies, science and educational policy studies, the humanities, literary criticism, investigative reports, short and medium stories, and poetry published in the country during the past month. Admired as a pocket library for its wide range of selections and circulation (around 180,000 in the mid-1980s), *New China Digest* has had a tremendous impact on intellectual life in all of China.

Because its deputy editor in chief, Xue Dezhen, was an enthusiastic champion of humanism in the early 1980s, the Publishing House was one of the leaders in the debate on humanism and alienation in socialism. It edited and published major nonconformist works, such as *Man Is Marxism's Point of Departure* (1981; 20,000 copies for the first printing), *A Philosophical Inquiry into Theories of Man* (1982; 33,000 copies), *A Defense of Humanism* (by Wang Ruoshui; 1986; 30,000 copies), and *An Anthology of Discussions on Human Nature and Humanism* (1983; 20,000 copies).

Strategically, the publishers made full use of *New China Digest*. In the political climate of the time, it was very difficult to publish prohumanism works in major Chinese journals. Most editors were aware that senior party officials detested these themes, and they did not want to offend them. Advocates of such themes, lacking choices of where to publish, could only look to minor journals in remote provinces. Most major journals with huge circulations printed articles criticizing humanism and the concept of alienation.

To counteract this situation, the senior editor of *New China Digest*, backed by Xue Dezhen of the Publishing House, gave favorable weight to prohumanism articles when making selections. Reprinted in *New China Digest*, these articles immediately received national attention and became "hot topics" among the

[20]The following is based on personal observation and Informants nos. 5 and 6.

better educated. In the provinces, reprinting of an article by a local writer in *New China Digest* was interpreted as quasi-political approval, because the journal was under the People's Publishing House, the highest-ranked publisher in the country, with a direct relationship to the "above." When questioned by the PCPD about favoring prohumanism writings, the editors of *New China Digest* excused themselves by saying, "We didn't write these articles. Our job is but to digest what has been printed somewhere else. What is reprinted in our journal does not necessarily reflect our opinions." Similar stories could be heard even at the *People's Daily*. With an open-minded and courageous man as head of a unit, more leeway was possible for employees to use the institution's title, money, and facilities for purposes counter to those of the party-state.

Having an independent-minded OI as a unit head also meant that, under his leadership, the unit attracted opposition-inclined elements and functioned sometimes as a quasi-voluntary association. As mentioned earlier, in the PRC the unit had the final say about the allocation of resources key to the urban resident's work and daily life. One's political fortune, promotion, wage, housing, individual and family health insurance, child care, and opportunities for job change depended principally on the unit. If one was an intellectual, this list could include opportunities for studying abroad, on-the-job training, and even publication. It was a commonplace that a gifted person with an independent mind could waste himself, year after year, should his boss refuse to give him what his work needed. He could be subject to his boss's undisguised mistreatment for years, applying for transfer but unable to leave the unit if the boss forbade him to go. On the other hand, if a unit head was of a more independent mind-set, the microclimate of the unit could differ remarkably from the macroclimate of the surrounding society.

When the macropolitical climate was mild, open-minded individuals in the unit could be pioneers in controversial ventures, but when it was harsh, the unit head could greatly reduce the pressure on the unit from above and even save troublemakers from political discrimination and persecution. Drawn by the microclimate, individuals with the same disposition worked to move into units headed by open-minded leaders. Gradually, such units became rallying points for nonconformists, and, as a group, they could exert a power they could not separately. The function of units as rallying points is particularly important in a society where there is no right to association. The case of the Institute of Marxism, Leninism, and Mao Zedong Thought is a good example.[21]

In the spring of 1979, Hu Qiaomu (Politburo member and president of the CASS), Deng Liqun (director of the Research Center of the party's Central

---

[21] The following is based on personal observation.

Secretariat and vice-president of the CASS), and Yu Guangyuan (advisor to the PCPD and vice-president of the CASS) came to Hu Yaobang (secretary-general of the Central Secretariat and head of the PCPD) to suggest there should be an institute within the CASS in charge of research projects on Marxism, Leninism, Mao's theory, and socialism. Hu Yaobang approved their suggestion. In June 1979, Yu invited Su Shaozhi, a senior editor of the *People's Daily,* to take part in organizing the institute. Su responded that he would like to join but wanted a consensus among the organizers. Because Marxism, Leninism, and Mao's theory had been exclusively defined as the "party-state's guiding ideology," Su wanted the establishment of the institute to make those theories the object of social-scientific inquiry. Restoration of the true faces of these -isms would be emphasized, with an awareness of competing currents in contemporary Marxism and socialism and on revision of Marxist concepts.

Yu agreed with Su on these points, and the institute was formed in August 1979. Originally, Hu Qiaomu was to be its director, but he found he was too busy to take the job; instead, he let Yu head the institute, and Yu asked Su to be deputy director in charge of administration. (When Yu retired in 1982, Su took over the directorship.) Yu, Su, and Wang Huide, another deputy director of the institute and deputy head of the PCPD, initiated the Chinese Society for Studies on Works by Marx, Engels, Lenin, and Stalin as a network to support the institute.

Yu's and Su's purpose was to make the institute a stronghold of *sixiang jiefang pai* (literally, "the intellectually liberated," meaning the liberal minded). Thus, the prerequisite for admission was a strong commitment to intellectual pluralism and political tolerance. Recruiting efforts included: (1) soliciting long-known intellectuals from university faculties, publishing houses, and party-state organs in Beijing; (2) asking old friends to recommend professionally outstanding men and women; (3) targeting outspoken scholars at seminars and meetings organized by the Chinese Society for Studies on Works by Marx, Engels, Lenin, and Stalin; and (4) searching for graduate students of distinction at universities in and outside Beijing, when senior members of the institute went out to give lectures.

Under the conventional PRC personnel system, the composition of a unit was decided by the party organization department and the state personnel bureau on the higher level. This system ensured an arrangement that can be called "principled particularism" (a term borrowed from Walder 1986: 123ff.). Formally, the higher level of party-state organs could claim that the unit was in the hands of "genuine Communists" who always followed the party line. Privately, the leaders of the higher party-state organs could make sure that they had their personal loyalists in the unit. Such "genuine Communists" or loyalists would keep their patrons informed of what was going on within the unit and, in times of official campaigns, act as "hatchet men."[22]

The implication of the recruitment procedure adopted by the Institute of Marxism is that this type of "genuine Communist" or loyalist was precluded from entering and thereby the higher level of party-state apparatus lost informants and potential "hatchet men" within the unit. Under these circumstances, the unit could keep much of its operation from being checked by those above and enjoy more freedom of action. Many of the professional associations and official and semiofficial institutions that formed during the 1980s had a recruitment policy similar to that of the Institute of Marxism. This explains why these organizations had a semivoluntary nature and could be manipulated for acts contradictory to the ruling elite's will.

Through such channels, the Institute of Marxism recruited a company of intellectuals who contributed notably to the post-Mao political and intellectual development.[23]

In addition, the leadership of the institute designed a special graduate program to enlist fresh forces. During the late 1970s, a lot of young people – former Red Guards and "sent-down youths" – made themselves stand out in the movement to "emancipate the mind." As mentioned, the majority of these young people were MIs, without formal higher education or backgrounds in social science, even without jobs. To offer opportunities to these young people, the admissions policy of the institute's graduate program, unlike most others, did not require an applicant to have a bachelor's degree and an official institution's recommendation. On the other hand, it did require applicants to take an oral examination in addition to the standard written one. Its intent was that while the standard examination might measure an applicant's knowledge of certain fields and of official doctrine, the specially designed oral examination could test whether he was independent-minded and committed to political and social reforms. Helped by its admissions policy, the institute took in and then sent out a number of outstanding students.[24]

[22]Chinese call them *da xiaobaogaode* (makers of small reports) and *zhengren zhuanjia* (experts of persecution).

[23]These intellectuals, in addition to Yu and Su themselves, include Liao Gailong (known for his design of a reform program for the Chinese political system – see a major speech by him in Burns and Rosen 1986: 87–101), Feng Lanrui (coauthor of the theory of primitive stages of socialism), Zhang Xianyang (activist of the "Forum on the Principles for the Party's Theoretical Work" in 1979, expelled from the party in 1987 and condemned after June 1989), Peng Kehong (enthusiastic supporter of the Spring 1989 Democracy Movement when he was made executive deputy director of the institute, arrested after June 1989), Lin Chun and Li Yinhe (known for work on socialist democracy and legality), and Li Shengping (activist in the Democracy Movements of 1978–79 and of spring 1989, arrested after June 1989).

[24]These included Cao Siyuan (chief drafter of the PRC's first Bankruptcy Law, director of the Stone Institute for Research on Social Development, arrested after June 1989); Zhou Duo

To be sure, the institute could not get everyone it wanted. For instance, in the spring of 1984, it opened the door to Wang Ruoshui, recently deposed as deputy editor in chief of the *People's Daily*. Wang deeply wanted to work in the institute, but the party's Central Secretariat and the PCPD closed the door, explaining that the authorities did not want all the criticized intellectuals to band together.

Because its membership included a high concentration of nonconformists, the institute became a target in major political storms of the Dengist era. In 1983, Deng Liqun described it as the "anti-Marxism base camp." During the 1983–84 Anti–Spiritual Pollution Campaign and the 1987 Anti–Bourgeois Liberalization Campaign, the party's Central Secretariat and the PCPD planned to disband the institute. It survived these major crises,[25] but with many changes in personnel and research projects. After spring 1989, the central authorities once again proposed to disband the institute.

The resourcefulness of the independent-minded OIs can be explained also by their special relationship to party-state leaders. This relationship was not simply a working relationship, but one that was highly personalized. In this study, the special relationship will be shown to have two main uses. First, the relationship could be used by the OI to protect his own or his comrade's position in times of crisis.[26] For instance, Sun Changjiang was one of the five persecuted by the

(project director of the Stone Company, a key figure in the Spring 1989 Movement, arrested after June 1989); Lu Jiamin (former editor of the unofficial *Beijing Spring*, associate professor at the Cadres School of the Federation of Trade Unions, a key figure in the Spring 1989 Movement, arrested after June 1989); Wang Yizhou (associate professor of the Institute of Marxism, a spokesman for political reforms, persecuted after June 1989); and Cao Wuqi (section director of the Stone Company, activist of the Spring 1989 Movement, in exile after June 1989).

[25] As touched on before, the institute was saved once by Bo Yibo, whose directive was: "The institute has problems. But the current party rectification campaign is designed to resolve ideological rather than organizational problems. Ideological problems in the institute must be answered. The organizational issue of its existence shall not be decided for the time being" (Informant no. 7).

   After Hu Yaobang's dismissal, the party's Central Secretariat, under its new secretary-general, Zhao Ziyang, met in Beidaihe in mid July 1987. On July 22, the Secretariat resoluted to dismiss Su Shaozhi as party secretary and director of the institute, and to disband the institute itself. (Persecuted at this time with Su were Wang Ruoshui, Zhang Xianyang, Wu Zuguang, and Sun Changjiang.) Hu Qiaomu directed the institute to integrate its personnel into that of the Central Party School. The Party School leadership was very familiar with the institute's members and did not want to take all the "troublemakers" among them into the school. They wanted only some, not all, of the personnel. Those CASS leaders inwardly sympathetic with the institute responded to the Party School leadership, "You take either all or none. Selection is out of the question." The two sides were not interested in working out a solution. The integration thus met an impasse. Yu Guangyuan reported the situation to Zhao Ziyang, who said: "Put off integration." At the Politburo Standing Committee meeting in May 1988, the CASS president, Hu Sheng, was called on to report. Zhao asked him: "What do you think about the integration?" Hu said: "I think there should be an institute on Marxism within the CASS." Zhao did not say no to Hu's comments. The institute thereby survived again (Informant no. 2).

[26] The following is based on Informant no. 8

party's Central Secretariat at the Beidaihe meeting in July 1987. Even though the central authorities had decided to persecute Sun, Lin Zhixing, head of the *Science and Technology Daily* and former secretary of Marshal Nie Rongzhen, managed with Nie's help to defend him. Nie wrote to Chen Yun, the second most powerful party leader, suggesting that the Central Secretariat's decision should be revised. This was done. With Sun still deputy editor in chief of the *Science and Technology Daily*, the newspaper was important to later political developments in China, especially during the Spring 1989 Movement. The newspaper was the first among the Chinese media to defy the Politburo's order to objectively report the student protests in Tiananmen Square of April 18, thus contributing immensely to the general rebellion of the media against censorship (Jakobson 1990; Saich 1990: 145–63).

This special relationship between the OIs and party-state leaders could also serve in institution building. Institutions established in this manner enjoyed more autonomy than conventional units, as the *World Economic Herald* best demonstrated.[27]

The *Herald*'s founder, Qin Benli, was a journalist working for the underground Communist party in Shanghai before 1949. After the Communist takeover he was director of the International News Department of the *People's Daily* in Beijing, then transferred to Shanghai as party secretary of *Wenhui Bao*, a leading newspaper on cultural and educational affairs. During the Anti-Rightist Campaign of 1957 Qin was condemned, deposed, and sent down to an "internal reference material" editorial department of the Shanghai Party Committee as a regular staff member. After Mao's death, Qin was rehabilitated and appointed party secretary of the Institute of World Economics in the Shanghai Academy of Social Sciences. He planned to found a newspaper that would be as independent as possible from control by the party apparatus. To realize his ambition, Qin mobilized many long-established connections. He persuaded such figures as Wang Daohan (mayor of Shanghai), Huan Xiang (vice-president of the CASS and director of the Center of International Studies under the State Council), Xu Dexing (vice-president of the CASS), and Qian Junrui (chairman of the Chinese Society for Studies on the World Economy) to be advisors to or members of the editorial committee of the newspaper. Qin asked these powerful people for help in getting old fellow journalists, such as Li Hongli, Lu Ping,

---

[27]The following is based on Informant no. 9 and Qin Benli's talks in New York in February 1989. See also Shen Yiao: "*Qin Benli Qiren Qishi*" (*Ming Pao Monthly* [Hong Kong] No. 6, pp. 116–19, 1991). On some of the newspaper's activities, see Cheng Li and Lynn T. White III (1991), but their statement that the *Herald* "became the main journal of China's technocratic movement" (ibid.: 344) distorts the newspaper's role. To attempt to interpret Chinese politics in the Dengist era exclusively within the framework of technocracy, as the two authors have suggested, is to place the subject on the procrustean bed.

and Hu Sai, back to work for his newspaper. Most of them had been persecuted during the Maoist political campaigns and kicked out of the media industry; some had been transferred to other provinces. Without help from the powerful, it would not have been possible to get them back to Shanghai and into the media.

On June 21, 1980, the *Herald,* a weekly, began circulating. Formally owned by the Chinese Society for Studies on the World Economy and the Shanghai Institute of World Economics, the newspaper was the first created since 1949 that was not directly controlled by the party-state organ but by a nonpolitical professional association. At first, money for the newspaper came from the government budget allocated to the Chinese Society and the Shanghai Institute. But in case of budget shortages, Qin and his colleagues had to borrow money, paper, and printing equipment from *Wenhui Bao;* sometimes they even had to purchase office supplies on their own. Later the weekly relied on income from subscriptions and commercial advertisements. Since 1982, the newspaper had been independent financially and editorially. It no longer received any state money but was itself responsible for all its expenses, including its staff salaries. Its editorials and main articles no longer needed to be examined and approved by the Shanghai Party Propaganda Department before going to press, and it soon became independent in personnel administration too. Thus, in recruiting reporters and editors, the senior staff could go to campuses to select new staff rather than accept those assigned by the state personnel bureau. This was a crucial step to ensure the solidarity of the staff in times of political crises and the voluntary nature of the newspaper as an organization.

The *Herald* established bureaus in major cities across the country and sent correspondents to North America, Western Europe, and Japan. It was the first mainland newspaper to attempt news exchange services with a major Taiwanese newspaper, the *United Daily News.* At the outset, the *Herald* limited its coverage to domestic and international economic news, a special priority under the Deng regime, but beginning in 1982 it gradually extended coverage to sensitive issues like political reform, ideological openness, intellectual freedom, educational reform, reform of personnel administration, and foreign policy. By 1982 its subscriptions had reached 80,000, and by early 1989, nearly 300,000. It became the most outspoken and influential newspaper in China and the barometer of PRC politics in the 1980s.

Finally, the resourcefulness of the independent-minded OIs was reflected in their possession of "personal connections capital," that is, a wide range of long-term *guanxi* networks owing to their status and fame.

The great sufferings caused by wave after wave of "class struggle" during the Maoist era led to a shift in human relationships in the 1970s and 1980s from "comradeship" to "friendship," exactly the opposite of the 1950s' trend "from friendship to comradeship" (see T. Gold 1985 and Vogel 1965 for contrast). Residents in the PRC tended more and more to appreciate and rely on mutual help, personal loyalty, and particularism in private and political life, which ran counter to the revolutionary norms and discipline sanctioned by the official value system. The networks of personal connections developed by independent-minded OIs with equals or even inferiors were less critical than special relationships with party-state leaders but were nevertheless stabler, because they were based on shared interests and political preferences. Such networks could survive the drops in one's political fortunes.

Not only the Chinese relied on *guanxi* or informal relationships to mobilize resources for dissent and opposition. In fact, the practice is common in communist countries where the state has monopolized all formal organizational structures. As students of the Soviet Union have noted (Remington 1990: 178):

A striking feature of communist societies (which distinguishes them from more open, market-oriented societies) has been the importance of primary ties, such as family and friendship, in shaping social opinion and behavior. Certainly in the Soviet Union, there is a good deal of evidence on the crucial role of such bonds in oppositional and unofficial behavior. A number of studies demonstrate the continuing centrality of face-to-face means of gathering information and forming opinions, despite the penetration of society by modern print and electronic communication. . . . In the words of Vladimir Shlapen-tokh, friendship and other primary bonds are valued in Soviet society primarily because they are milieux within which trust is established outside and sometimes against the state.

In the case of the Chinese nonconformity and opposition, networks of personal connections served two major purposes. First, they offered the OI opportunities to call on others' resources; for instance, if his friends were in trouble in their home units and his own unit did not have openness, the OI could arrange with the heads of other units for better places for his friends. If certain writings were either too inconvenient or sensitive to print in his own journal, the OI could recommend them to other journals and get them published. If he was deprived of an institutional base by the party-state, the OI could still be heard by society frequently through the public space provided by his friends. This help was particularly important, because the ruling elite's last ditch effort was to silence dissent and thereby have the independent-minded, outspoken OIs killed by being forgotten.

Networks of personal connections provided the independent-minded OIs leeway for semifree association. For example, in the urban economic reforms of the mid-1980s, the giant Capital Steel and Iron Company pioneered bold managerial experiments in reform and made a great deal of money as well as a name for itself as a "new model enterprise."[28] The head of the company, Zhou Guan-wu, was ambitious, wanting to be a public figure on the national scene. Zhou turned to a group of OIs for advice on how to make the most of the huge profits gained from reform. They told him that sponsoring the cultural enterprise would be a good choice. It could win him a reputation as an entrepreneur concerned with public interests and as an official of great vision. Zhou was pleased with this idea and agreed to sponsor an institute for legal and social research. Late in 1987 three men were recommended by the circle of OIs to organize and run the institute: Yu Haocheng, deposed in 1984 from the direc-torship of the Masses Publishing House for advocating an independent juridical system; Zhang Zhonghou, who was unhappy about his position in the *China Legal System Press;* and Zhang Xianyang, recently deposed by the party's Central Secretariat as division head in the Institute of Marxism. Once in charge of the Capital Institute for Research on Legal Systems and Social Development, the three worked to attract intellectuals of their own type. Although the institute existed only for a short time, it contributed notably to debates in the late 1980s on China's "global membership crisis," on "new authoritarian versus liberal democratic choice," and on the rule of law versus the rule of man in socialism.

In another example,[29] in September 1988 Wang Yuanhua, a senior advisor to the Shanghai Academy of Social Sciences, and the deposed Wang Ruoshui, Yu Haocheng, and Ruan Ming and the criticized humanistic philosopher Gao Ertai met in Shanghai to prepare to found a monthly named the *New Enlightenment.* This journal was designed as a *tongren kanwu,* literally translated as "a col-leagues' journal" although it actually means "a cliquish journal." In the PRC, the difference between a conventional and a cliquish publication was that the for-mer was normally established and run by a formal organization, political or professional, and it must be open, at least legally, to all its membership, such as *Social Sciences in China* of the CASS, *Fudan Journal* of Fudan University, and *China's Youth* of the CYL. In contrast, a cliquish journal was initiated and run by a voluntary group, who would describe their journal not as private, but rather for those who shared their disposition, and if the editor always turned down one's manuscripts, one had nowhere to complain. A *tongren* journal, therefore, was quite exclusive; its editors and regular contributors formed a quasi-voluntary association. Although *tongren* journals had a long history in China before 1949, their reemergence in the PRC was a phenomenon of the second half of the 1980s. Journals such as the *Youth's Forum* in Wuhan, *Toward the Future* in Sichuan and the *Thinker* in Shanghai belonged to this category.

---

[28] The following is based on Informants nos. 10 and 17.
[29] The following is based on Informants nos. 8 and 11.

When Wang Yuanhua and his circle wanted to apply for registration of the planned monthly, they faced a big problem: Under PRC regulations, a new periodical must apply to a party propaganda department and a public security bureau for registration. Wang and his circle had no hope of registering their journal: They had been viewed as too outspoken by both institutions. After deliberation, they chose a "not illegal" alternative – to change the category of the planned *New Enlightenment* from "periodical publication" to "book series." Under state rules, the procedure to legalize a new book series was to apply for a book number (*shuhao*) from the publishing house that was to print the series, rather than apply to a party propaganda department and a local public security bureau for registration.

Having devised this new strategy, Wang Yuanhua began to look around for a potential publishing house willing to take risks. He turned to the Hunan Education Publishing House for help: He had known its director for a long time, and more important, the chief of the Hunan Publication Administrative Bureau, supervisor of the Publishing House, was a friend of his when Wang was in office. Matters were settled smoothly. The publishing house agreed to offer a book number and money. Beginning in October 1988, the *New Enlightenment* came out in print once a month, but without the mark "monthly." In this way, it opened up a space for many who had been deprived of means of expression. Its contributors included well-known figures.[30] Owing to the number of outspoken intellectuals gathered around it, the *New Enlightenment* was denounced as the Chinese "Petofi Club" by senior leaders Peng Zhen, Wang Zhen, Hu Qiaomu, and Deng Liqun in early 1989.[31]

Institutional resources of the critical cultural intellectuals and the politically active technical intellectuals

These categories, usually separated, are here treated together in relation to their resources, because, although TIs generally held independent views on social and political issues, only a small portion of them made systematic efforts to take part in political action. This minority in most cases either relied on resources at the disposal of the critical CIs or joined them in an attempt to build

[30] Such as Hu Jiwei, Su Shaozhi, Li Honglin, Ruan Ming, Zhang Xianyang, Sun Changjiang, Tong Dalin (former vice-chairman of the State Commission for Restructuring the Economy), Yan Jiaqi, Bao Zunxin (an outspoken historian at the CASS), Jin Guantao, Liu Xiaobo (an iconoclastic literary critic at Beijing Normal University), and Wang Xiaoqiang (deputy director of the IRESR).

[31] The Petofi Clubs were the intellectual discussion groups that contributed to the Hungarian rebellion of 1956. On January 29, 1989, the *New Enlightenment*'s editorial board held a party to celebrate its birth. The event shocked the authorities. See *New York Times* January 30, 1899 for details.

quasi-autonomous institutions. In this section these two groups are termed general intellectuals.

The general intellectuals had naturally made the best use of resources controlled by the independent-minded OIs. Many institutions, by the joint maneuver of the OIs and the general intellectuals, had acquired a *tongren* nature. Although still "public" in name, they were almost closed to people of disparate political preferences. This tendency had gone so far by the late 1980s that during the 1987 Anti–Bourgeois Liberalization Campaign and the post–spring 1989 "revolutionary criticism," hard-liners in the party and the army repeatedly complained, "While bourgeois liberals have aired their views everywhere, genuine Marxists have been deprived of chances to speak" (*People's Daily* January 29, 1987; *Red Flag* No. 3, pp. 2 and 24, 1987; *Qiushi* No. 15, pp. 15 and 20, 1989).

The general intellectuals did not confine their efforts to the capture of existing institutions, they also invested great energy in creating new ones, mainly book series (*congshu*)[32] and cliquish (*tongren*) magazines (both functioned as publishing facilities and quasi-voluntary associations), and professional associations at the margin of state control. Institution building of this kind usually involved the following efforts, which illustrate vividly institutional parasitism.

First and foremost, the initiator needed to find a *guakao danwei*, which means "an official unit on which a nonofficial unit depends" and which can be roughly translated as "a supervisory official institution." Under state regulations, the head of such a supervisory institution was to be politically responsible for all activities of the affiliated voluntary institution; if the latter made political troubles, not only were its members punished, but the head of the supervisory institution was punished as well. Understandably, few heads of official institutions were willing to form a relation with voluntary institutions. To find someone willing to accept that relation, the initiator of the voluntary institution needed to call on networks of personal connections as well as to go through innumerable procedures.

Second, core members of the voluntary institution needed to find material resources, such as money, offices, and equipment, to support themselves, usually by combining illegitimately used resources of their official home units (see further for details); by exchanging "cultural capital," such as influence and reputation, for financial support from enterprises; by engaging in profitable businesses; and by collecting funds from official institutions with attractive joint venture–like projects.

---

[32]"Book series" here do not mean the masked periodical publications like the *New Enlightenment*, discussed earlier, but a group of books thematically connected.

Third, many voluntary institutions solicited ranking officeholders or OIs and leading scientists to be their honorary leaders and advisors, for the appearance of legitimacy.

Finally, the initiator of the voluntary institution had to find suitable personnel to staff it. In China, even the most dedicated individuals were reluctant to quit their jobs in official or semiofficial bodies to work full-time for unofficial ones. For nobody could be sure how long an unofficial organization would survive. Working for an unofficial body provided the opportunity to fulfill one's long-time ambitions, but keeping a name on the list of state employment provided socioeconomic security that could include regular wages, personal and family health insurance, subsidized housing, and retirement benefits. Therefore, most personnel of unofficial organizations were state employees, who, in the words of a popular Chinese saying, "pick up pay envelopes from the state and work for somebody else." Only a few voluntary institutions could afford to hire full-time employees.

The following examples are selected to indicate institution making of this kind in post-Mao China:

1. *Book series* (congshu). In the second half of the 1980s, China witnessed an epidemic of book series. Scores of intellectual circles across the country set up their own series projects. Books thus published were targeted to a wide audience with senior high school or college education rather than to merely the professional strata. There were several advantages to publishing book series. One was to enhance the editors' social influence. By claiming to introduce "novel ideas," "new branches of social and cultural science," and "modern classic works" in an attractive, thematic format, backed by an advisory committee composed of important figures, the editors could quickly win a reputation for being a "new school" or the "leaders in shaping China's intellectual climate."

Another reason was to form a solid clan. By gathering an editorial committee for a series project that would last for years, a group with compatible concerns and goals could legally meet on a regular basis. With time, the committee could evolve into an organizational framework for activities beyond its original definition.

A final reason for this publishing venture was to make money. Profits gained from series – usually tens of thousands of copies of each title were printed – could be appropriated for programs that would have a hard time getting support from the state budget.

Well-known book series projects included *Toward the Future (Zouxiang Weilai)* published by the Sichuan People's Publishing House; *Facing Modernization, Facing the World, and Facing the Future (Mianxiang Xiandaihua, Mianxiang Shijie, Mianxiang Weilai)* by the People's Publishing House at Beijing; *Cultures: China and the World (Wenhua: Zhongguo yu Shijie)* by Beijing Sanlian Press; *Development Series (Kaifa Congshu)* by a group of young Beijing economists; *The Eastern Scholarship (Dongfang Xueshuo Congshu)* by Shanghai's and Beijing's young sociologists and historians; and a number of cultural studies series. (See Chapter 5 for a list.)

Among these book series projects, *Toward the Future* was the first founded and the most influential;[33] it became the model for those that followed. It was the idea of Bao Zunxin and Jin Guantao, who proposed it in the fall of 1982. They initiated the project with several objectives. The first was to create a channel for new Western social scientific theories, methods, and branches of research, such as cybernetics, systems theory, game theory, econometrics, comparative sociology, quantitative methods in social research, developmental studies, and sociobiology. These fields had been unavailable to well-educated Chinese for decades, and many needed the information.

Bao's and Jin's second objective was to inform the general public about the remarkable changes in the economies and social structures of the industrial nations since World War II. China's modernization program could not succeed, they believed, without this knowledge.

Their third objective was to promote empirical research on practical issues of great concern to Chinese – population, family problems, juvenile delinquency, cultural conflicts, labor mobility, unemployment, and industrial inefficiency.

A remote but overarching objective was to bring together young and middle-aged intellectuals with distinguished professional stature or extensive connections in an association that would be of great benefit in a time of reform and change. With this fresh force, Bao and Jin expected, they could exert great influence on better-educated urbanites and possibly even some top leaders.

Bao's and Jin's blueprint was very positively received among their friends. To set up the book series, however, they needed to find three things: a supervisory official institution, a publishing house, and financial support. Although they reached out to several official institutions, none wanted to do business with them. With help of friendships, they eventually made an arrangement with Tang Ruoxin, a young official in charge of research planning in the Institute of Juvenile Studies of the CASS, who argued Zhang Liqun, the institute's director, into accepting the editorial committee of the book series as an affiliated body, with Bao as editor in chief and Jin and Tang deputy editors in chief.

Like the official institutions, most publishers turned down the project; the subjects proposed sounded heretical. At last, the editors won over the Sichuan

---

[33]The following is based on Informants nos. 12, 13, 14, and 15, and my own records as a member of the editorial committee.

People's Publishing House at Chengdu. The head of the house was convinced that the series would prove very popular and might win the publishing house not only big profits but also a national reputation. The publishing house even agreed to provide financial support for the editorial committee's regular meetings.

To help this highly controversial business endure political trends, those who initiated the book series looked to every side for protection. The editorial committee included both noted professionals from established institutions, such as the Institute for Research on the Economic System Reform (IRESR) and the China Rural Development Research Center under the State Council, the PCPD, the CAS, the CASS, prestigious universities, leading publishing houses, and family members of high-ranking officials, including Deng Liqun's son Deng Yingtao and vice-premier Yao Yilin's son-in-law Wang Qishan. In addition, the series invited senior people to become advisers, including Du Runsheng (director of the Rural Policy Research Center under the party's Central Committee), Yan Jici (vice-chairman of the National People's Congress's Standing Committee and executive chairman of the Presidium of the CAS), Qian Sanqiang (vice-president of the CAS), Chen Hanbo (head of the Publication Administrative Bureau under the State Council), Zhong Peizhang (head of the News Bureau under the PCPD), and Chen Yizi (director of the IRESR).

From late 1983 through 1988, the series published seventy-four titles in print runs of 38,000 to 85,000 copies each, and these publications had a tremendous impact. Having gathered big profits, in the spring of 1986 the editorial committee founded a *tongren* journal *Toward the Future*. The book series group was influential in the intellectual and political discourse of the 1980s. After June 1989, when many members were persecuted[34] and the whole project – as well as its supporter, the Sichuan Publishing House – was attacked, the series ceased.

2. Tongren *magazines.* Those devoted to organizing *tongren* magazines were mainly intellectuals under forty years of age. Aside from their political activism, their lack of seniority within the intellectual strata provided a major reason for their devotion. Conventional magazines reserved much less room for them than for senior authors, and these young intellectuals felt need for institutional space under their own control. Their adventure in opening up such space began in the

---

[34] Among its editors and advisors, the arrested, deposed, condemned, and exiled were Bao Zunxin, Wang Yan, He Weiling, Xie Xuanqun, Wang Xiaolu, Yan Jiaqi, Chen Yizi, Du Runsheng, Zhang Gang, Jin Guantao, Wang Xiaoqiang, Zhu Jiaming, and Liu Qingfeng. Their misfortunes were, of course, not caused by the book series alone.

late 1970s, when many university students were working to institute campus magazines.[35]

These magazines were different from the general unofficial magazines discussed earlier in several ways. Unlike them, they were not publications of political dissent. Whereas the general unofficial magazines were completely run by private individuals, the campus publications often obtained both approval and financial support from university administrations. The general unofficial magazines directly touched on political taboos, but the campus ones avoided frontal attack. Some of the better-known campus magazines were *Luojiashan*, put out by Wuhan University students; *Jinjiang*, by Sichuan University students; the *University Student*, by Fudan University students; *Red Beans*, by Zhongshan University students at Guangzhou; *Nankaiyuan*, by Nankai University students at Tianjin; and *We*, by Hangzhou Normal College students. In response to a proposal by the editors of *Luojiashan*, from July 25 to August 10, 1979, eighteen delegates from thirteen campus magazines located in Beijing, Tianjin, Jilin, Guangtong, Zhejiang, Shanxi, Jiangsu, and Guizhou held a meeting in Beijing, where they voted to set up a nationwide university students' magazine, *This Generation*, which was prepared quarterly and whose publication was rotated among members of the group. Its first issue was put out in November 1979 by Wuhan University students. This proved also to be its last issue, because it contained sensitive material that exposed official corruption. Although permission to found it had been obtained from several university administrations, *This Generation* was banned by order of the top party leadership.

Not until the mid-1980s could young intellectuals renew their attempt to have their own legal magazines. From that time on, the number of *tongren* magazines run by relatively junior people multiplied. One of the earliest of these was the *Youth's Forum*, based in Wuhan.[36]

Wuhan's young intellectuals had sought the chance to make their own base for a long time and they found it in the fall of 1984, when Hu Deping, son of then party chief Hu Yaobang and himself a bureaucrat in the United Front Work Department under the party's Central Committee, was sent to Wuhan as a liaison officer for the powerful Central Leadership Group for Party Rectification. Several young men of Wuhan, led by Li Jinhua (a research fellow at the Hubei Provincial Academy of Social Sciences), came for help to Hu Deping,

---

[35] The following is based on conversations with campus press activists in several universities in Shanghai in the late 1970s and early 1980s. See also Chen Ruoxi (*China Times* April 26 and 27, 1981) and *Contending* No. 3, pp. 7–8, 1980.

[36] The following is based on Informant no. 16, who was on the magazine's editorial board, and Hu Ping (December 1990, Princeton), a regular contributor.

who, like his father, was known for open-mindedness. After listening to their proposal for founding a magazine – to mobilize young intellectuals' creativity and expertise to work for reforms, with special attention to problems of great concern to the educated youth – Hu expressed his "understanding and support." With Hu's endorsement, Li Jinhua and his friends applied to the Provincial Party Propaganda Department for registration. Although the head of the department disliked the idea of a youth's magazine, he did not want to make an enemy of the party chief's son. The department therefore issued a document approving the new magazine and indicated that "the idea has been approved first by comrade Hu Deping," implying that the fault, if any, was not the department's.

Knowing that the prospective magazine had received approval from people in high places, the Hubei Provincial Academy of Social Sciences immediately agreed to become its supervisory institution. Funding for the magazine came partly from the academy, partly from donations from universities, the CYL branch in Hubei, Donghu Intelligence Development Cooperation, and Hubei Second Motor Company. The editorial board was composed of young research fellows from the Provincial Academy and junior professors and graduate students from universities at Wuhan, such as Li Jinhua, Xu Sumin, Huang Kejian, and Cai Chongguo. The first issue of the *Youth's Forum* (a bimonthly) came out in November 1984, with a contribution by Hu Deping – "Speaking Out for Freedom." The article was less radical than its title but nevertheless provided a sign of the themes that could be publicly discussed.

New China Digest immediately reprinted Hu's article, causing a nationwide shock. Four months later the *Forum* initiated the "National Conference of Young Theorists," at Guangzhou, and called for nationwide support for the magazine, in the form of either manuscripts or money. Young people's articles on sensitive issues that could hardly appear in other journals flooded into the *Forum*. The magazine brought out writing that analyzed the political and social origins of the 1957 Anti-Rightists Campaign and the Cultural Revolution, that called for formulating a press code and a publication law to substantiate the citizen's right to free speech, and that proposed democratization in the polity and denationalization in the economy. The *Forum's* articles were often reprinted or reported in *New China Digest, People's Daily, World Economic Herald,* and *Chinese Youth News,* thus exerting a national influence. To shelter their magazine, the editors of the *Forum* managed to have high-ranking officials or established scholars contribute a few "guiding" or "encouraging words" for each issue. The magazine survived until February 1987, one month after Hu Yaobang's dismissal.

3. Professional associations. Professional associations in the PRC were origi-

nally part of the mechanism of party-state control, few in quantity and huge in scale, and had high-ranking party bureaucrats as chief officers. In the early 1980s a new type of professional association appeared that included societies, discussion groups, workshops, clubs, and research institutes. These associations were more diverse and local. They were started usually by professionals themselves, rather than by party-state organizations, and their chief officers were usually professionals elected by members, not party-state bureaucrats appointed by the higher authorities. In most instances, they organized their own regular activities with funds mainly from academic institutions and economic organizations, rather than directly from the government budget.

The growth of semiautonomous professional associations was a cause of concern to the party apparatus. During the Anti–Spiritual Pollution Campaign of 1983–84, the PCPD and the Ministries of Education and of Culture ordered a nationwide check on professional associations and attempted to disband those displaying a tendency to sponsor "antisocialist speeches and acts."[37] Yet the premature end of the campaign rendered this directive inoperative. Professional associations bloomed again afterward, but in reduced size, which allowed activities to be organized more independently, promptly, and economically. The organizational efficiency of these professional associations proved critical to their impact on the larger society as the Chinese political drama came to a climax in the late 1980s.

The financial resources of the associations varied, as already shown in general terms. Two of the necessary resources need to be discussed in detail here: the illegitimate use of money from the home units of core members and material support intellectuals received from "cultural capital" exchange. As regard to the former, many units in the PRC had established "small treasuries" (*xiao jinku*)[38] no later than the 1960s, which the Cultural Revolution suppressed in most places, but which afterward came back in a much bigger way. A "small treasury" was a unit's semisecret account, but was secret from the higher authorities and outsiders, not from its core members. The money was, in most cases, illegally transferred from units' business gains or official budget – for example, annual profits of a furniture factory, part of the tuition and fees a college gained from its evening school, or part of research funds an institute received from the government. Serving as a unit's "small treasury," the money was used mainly for its

---

[37] I personally heard this directive.
[38] I came to know the "small treasury" practice during the late 1960s, when a great number of officials confessed such wrongdoing and were punished in the Socialist Education Campaign. In 1970, when I was an assistant accountant in a village, the senior accountant admitted that some rural cadres still kept the practice, but on a smaller scale. In the mid-1970s, I discovered the practice again in the factory where I worked for more than five years.

employees' extra welfare (e.g., ten kilograms of pork and two bottles of wine for each employee on a holiday free of charge) and its leaders' networking activity (e.g., gifts to and entertainment for guests). Because units usually kept two kinds of accounts, one for higher authorities and outsiders and one for its core members, checking on this practice was difficult: The unit's members would not damage their interests, and the higher authorities and outsiders could not get hard evidence.

Since the mid-1980s[39] "small treasuries" have increased significantly because of the decentralization of administration, which gave the grass roots more freedom in financial affairs, and because of the commercialization of society, which engaged most institutions in urban China, whether cultural, educational, administrative or military, in commercial activities. Such activities brought these institutions new sources of income that were uncontrollable by the government. When a unit's core members entered into voluntary professional associations, they regularly used the "small treasury" to support such activity.

Practices of this sort seem to be shared by many societies undergoing political liberalization, wherein corruption feeds embryonic opposition. For instance, during the second half of the 1980s when Taiwan began political pluralization, those businesses financing the opposition often kept four kinds of accounts, the "true internal account" (*zhenneizhang* – every transaction was on record; it was for the owner's use only), the "false internal account" (*jianeizhang* – most transactions were on record; it was for the hired manager's use only), the "credit application account" (*daikuanzhang* – used for applying for a bank credit), and the "tax account" (*baoshuizhang* – used for reporting taxes to the government). The businessmen kept the money that was donated to the opposition out of record in the latter three accounts, in order to avoid retaliation from the government.[40]

Material support from the "cultural capital" exchange was a by-product of China's mixed economy, partially coordinated by the governmental bureaucracy and partially by underdeveloped market mechanisms. In such an environment, managers of Chinese enterprises who wanted to increase market sales often needed help from intellectuals and professionals. They saw that a favorable report on a company in the media had more effect on the customers' response than numerous advertisements. Chinese customers tended to view advertisements as braggadocio but media reports as praise by a third party. To the politically ambitious, positive reports on their enterprises in the media or theoretical generalizations about their reform experience by researchers, which

[39]The following is based on my notes and Informants nos. 17, 18, and 19.
[40]Based on my interviews in Taiwan in December 1989.

could be sent to the higher authorities for reference, meant more customers and better chances for promotion. Managers were hence willing to contribute financial aid to professional associations in exchange for a good word from the professionals. Many of the collective doings of the intellectuals covered in this study were made possible in this way.

The most successful of the professional associations established voluntarily during the 1980s may have been the Beijing Institute for Research on Social and Scientific-Technological Development.[41] In one sense it was atypical: It managed to have greater autonomy than most of its counterparts. But in another sense it was truly exemplary: The strategies of its organizers to found and preserve the organization were so comprehensive that others could rarely invent new ones.

The chief organizers of the institute were Chen Ziming and Wang Juntao, both with backgrounds in science but a deep interest in politics. For their ambition, Wang quit his job at the prestigious Beijing Institute of Nuclear Energy in 1983; Chen left graduate study at the elite Chinese University of Science and Technology in 1984 and applied to a graduate program at the Institute of Philosophy of the CASS. But their involvement in the democracy movement of the late 1970s meant Chen and Wang had been blacklisted by the police and were thus excluded from membership in key think-tanks, in which they both had a great interest. Their only option was to found a research institution of their own.

In late 1984 and early 1985, Chen and Li Shengping (an office worker at the *Baike zhishi* magazine in Beijing) established the North Books and Magazines Distribution Agency to bring the ex-democracy activists together as well as make money for future ventures. (The agency's supervisory official institution was a Beijing factory where Chen's wife worked as the CYL branch chief.) Later in 1985, when the nation was rapidly opening correspondence and television schools, Chen and his friends, with the money from the agency's business, founded the Administration and Management Correspondence School and the Beijing Correspondence College of Trade and Finance, both with an enrollment of tens of thousands. They paid about 15 percent of the school's huge income to the supervisory institution, the Beijing Western District Education Bureau, as "supervision fees" and kept the rest for their secret plan. Under official regulations all gains from the education industry had to be reinvested in it again, but Chen and his colleagues planned to use part of the profits as funds to start a research institute, and to do so they regularly falsified their accounts.

---

[41] The following is based on Informants no. 10, who was on the Institute's executive board, and no. 17. One of the institute's organizers published two articles, under two pseudonyms, on its history; see Li Yuan and Shao Jun (*China Spring* [New York] No. 1, pp. 7–9 and 10–13, 1990).

In August 1986, Chen Ziming and his friends founded the unofficial Chinese Institute of Political and Administrative Sciences, whose membership included Li Shengping, Min Qi (office worker at the *Social Sciences in China* journal under the CASS), Guo Xia (graduate student at the Central Party School), Yang Baikui, Chen Zhaogang, Wang Zhigang (all researchers at the Institute of Political Science of the CASS), Qian Jianjun (reporter for the *Economic Daily*), Li Ming (lecturer at the Cadres School under the Ministry of Civil Affairs), Zhang Lun, Fei Yuan (Beijing University's graduate students), Hou Xiaotian (graduate student at the Beijing Economics Institute), and Jiang Hong (graduate student at the Chinese People's University). This institute existed only a short time. At a conference it sponsored in late 1986 on "Discussions of Military Modernization," many of the presentations exceeded official political limits. Yang Shangkun, Deng Xiaoping's chief assistant in military affairs, harshly criticized the institute, and as a result it was dissolved.

Shortly afterward, in August 1987, Chen Ziming and his comrades made a comeback when all members of the dissolved institute, plus Wang Juntao, Chen Ziming's wife Wang Zhihong, Xie Xiaoqing, Zheng Li, and Bi Yimin, formed a new body, the Beijing Institute for Research on Social and Scientific-Technological Development. The biggest difficulty in forming the new institute was, not surprisingly, obtaining a supervisory institution. Chen Ziming and Wang Juntao were so well known as troublemakers that most people in office refused any formal relation with them. After long, exhausting work Chen, assisted by an old friend of his father in the Beijing Municipal Association for Sciences and Technology, established an affiliation with that association, which had its advantages and disadvantages. The association did not keep an eye on the doings at the institute, so Chen, Wang, and their colleagues almost had a free hand in running their own business. But the association was municipal, not national, so that as its subordinate the institute was limited to activities within the Beijing area. To carry projects in other provinces, Chen and his colleagues had to cooperate with national institutions such as the *Workers' Daily* and institutes within the CASS.

To secure the institute's political safety, Chen stayed behind the scenes, exercising leadership while letting Fei Yuan be director. In the meantime, Chen and his colleagues invited several important figures and put these "safe" names on the institute's list: Li Zhengwen (former deputy minister of education and secretary-general of the Chinese Union of Societies for Economic Studies) as honorary director; Xie Tao (vice-president of the Chinese People's University) as advisor; He Jiadong (deputy editor in chief of the Workers' Publishing House), Ding Wang (deputy editor in chief of the *Economic Daily*), Xu Lianquan (director of the Institute of Psychology under the CAS), and Yuan Fang (chairman of the Sociology Department at Beijing University) as special research fellows.

The institute had forty-nine full-time and about thirty part-time employees. Of these, a dozen were senior research fellows, Chen Ziming's and Wang Juntao's comrades in the Democracy Movement of the late 1970s, who, as former MIs, had become semiestablished.

The institute was entirely self-supporting, with an annual budget at its highest of 350,000 Chinese yuan. Part of this money came from gains from the two correspondence schools, part was business profits from the North Books and Magazines Distribution Agency and its printing workshop. The institute rented as office space two stories of a building, about sixty rooms, from a suburban automobile repair factory.

In March 1988, the Chinese Union of Societies for Economic Studies decided to close its *Economic Weekly* due to budget constraints. Chen Ziming immediately offered an attractive price, 300,000 yuan, to the union in order to take over the editorship of the *Weekly*. Chen wanted to run the weekly because the institute had no publication of its own and because establishing a newspaper was extremely difficult, requiring approval from the party propaganda department and the police. Having made this deal, Chen's institute could run the *Weekly*, even if it could not own the publication legally. Out of concerns for political safety, Chen and his colleagues asked the union's officer to be the *Weekly*'s director and He Jiadong to be editor in chief. The de facto editor was Wang Juntao, and under him, the *Weekly* became one of the most courageous Chinese newspapers, second only to *World Economic Herald*. Its subscriptions jumped from several thousands to around 30,000, and its influence on the general public increased.

From its birth until the spring of 1989, the Institute sponsored several controversial projects, including a nationwide "Survey Research on Chinese Citizens' Political Minds," a questionnaire on the opinions of 1,172 delegates to the National People's Congress about restructuring the congress, and a survey of university students' attitudes and life-styles. The institute also co-organized in early 1988 the "First National Conference on Modernization Theories," a meeting on intellectuals' problems that took place that summer, and early in 1989 several public debates on the new alternatives – authoritarian versus liberal – to China's socialism. When the Spring 1989 Movement started, the institute's members offered, besides money, much advice to students, urging them to peaceful action and prudent strategy, and to take into consideration the demands of the working classes. After June 1989, the government dissolved the institute and arrested several members; Chen Ziming and Wang Juntao were sentenced to thirteen years in prison.

The social context of ehe emergence of the counterelite in post-Mao China

To borrow Anthony Giddens's (Stanworth and Giddens 1974: 8) notion of elite differentiation in terms of "issue-strength" and "institutional salience," a hierarchy might be sketched to indicate the relative weight of the PRC ruling elite and the counterelite in the political contention of the Dengist era (Figure 1).

As many have pointed out, the revolutions of 1989 in Eastern Europe and the Soviet Union were led primarily by intellectuals: writers, journalists, poets, dramatists, musicians, philosophers, historians, scientists, university professors and students (Ash 1989; EEPS 1990; Chirot 1991: 18, 22). These educated specialists had been "heavily brutalized" under Stalinism. Thanks to the industrialization and professionalization of Soviet society after Stalin, they "have had time to recreate themselves or to recover" (Lewin 1988: 147). Being an elite of prestige and influence in society, they "are widely considered to be voices of the 'nation'" and "frequently become political counter-elites" in times of political transition (Remington 1990: 179).

The Chinese case under question resembles closely the Soviet and East European experiences. Although for many centuries scholars in Chinese society enjoyed a celebrated status, they were reduced to the bottom of the social hierarchy during the Cultural Revolution of 1966–76. In the PRC, intellectuals and professionals went from being the "stinking ninth" (i.e., one of the nine social categories that were officially discriminated against) of the Maoist era to being the counterelite of the Dengist era, capable of capturing existing institutions and creating quasi-autonomous associations to voice criticism and dissent against communism. These developments were undoubtedly the outcome of profound changes in the state system, in Chinese society, and in the relations between the two during the era of reform.

First and foremost was the change in the definition of goals of the state and of the means to achieve them. For the party-state under Mao, especially during his last years, the principal goal was construction of a society of absolute equality. As part of the program to achieve this goal, China's educational system ceased being a chief mechanism for determining opportunities for social mobility, and intellectuals were denounced and forced to go to the countryside and factories to learn from the uneducated. In these circumstances, the possession of "educational and cultural capital" was not the key but a barrier to membership among the elite. In Maoist China, the only possible elite was the political elite, whose members were recruited according to class background and political reliability.

For the party-state under Deng, however, the principal goal was to modernize China's economy. Having witnessed the failure of the Maoist method, which

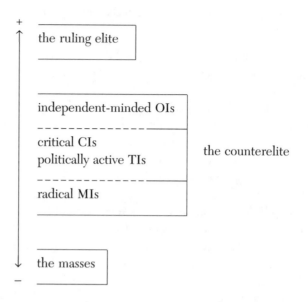

Figure 1. Relative weight of the PRC elite groups in comparison with the masses

was to enhance productivity by class struggle and mass mobilization, the Deng regime reinstated experts to former positions to carry out professional activities, with the hope of updating China's education, technology, and economy (see Goldman, Cheek, and Hamrin 1987; Simon and Goldman 1989; Lee 1991). The well-educated strata once again were situated superior to workers and peasants, if not in pay, at least in prestige, status, and influence. Thus, the Maoist principle was reversed. A familiar social hierarchy returned, one analogous to the social structure in most noncommunist and communist industrial countries. As Barrington Moore (1951: 406) observes of the Soviet experience, it is hard to throw away "the inherent requirements of constructing a modern industrial society," among them "the need for a functional division of labor and for inequality of rewards. All of these requirements add up to the necessity of a system of organized socal inequality." Under the pressure of industrialization, ruling communist parties had to cast aside extreme egalitarianism, and in this situation Chinese intellectuals rose as an elite stratum in the post-Mao era.

The second important change contributing to the emergence of intellectuals and professionals as a counterelite was the CCP's loss of moral authority and political legitimacy. The CCP had claimed to be "the sole and the best" representative of the people's interests, and for quite a long time most intellectuals, like other major sectors of Chinese society, had accepted that claim. This trust made the intellectuals voluntarily relegate their own functions of thinking, questioning, and voicing their views to the party.[42] Disillusioned by the party during the 1970s and 1980s, the intellectuals began to think for themselves and for society. They believed they were responsible to the Chinese people for taking back the rights they had been deprived of by the party-state (see Link 1992: 249–90). Conscious of themselves as a counterelite, they developed an antiestablishment program.

Yet another change that helped bring about the counterelite's institution-building ventures was the weakening of the political center's control of the party-state machinery. This change was brought about by the joint effect of Mao's Cultural Revolution and, more important, Deng's reform program (Harding 1987; Lee 1991). While the Cultural Revolution heavily damaged the morale of party-state officials, created bitter factional fighting at all levels of leadership, and significantly diminished the effectiveness of the party-state bureaucracy, Deng's reform program opened the door to a large number of former victims of Maoist purges who could now reenter office, some of whom had learned from the past and were less willing to follow the party line in new waves of political persecution during the Dengist era.

The Dengist reforms introduced a generation of better-educated people into officialdom, many of them more tolerant than the older generation of Communists. Several administrative reforms, such as the decentralization of decision-making and the functional differentiation between party and government, loosened coordination among levels and sections of the government and eroded discipline in the party-state organization. Because the center had difficulty getting the periphery to toe the line, and superiors had difficulty getting subordinates to obey orders, it became possible for the counterelite to societalize the state constituents and to develop quasi-autonomous structures within rifts of the party-state organization, from which they could carry out nonconformity and oppositional acts. The development of the set of phenomena characterized as institutional parasitism would have been out of the question if the party-state apparatus had been well disciplined.

The final major factor that made possible Chinese intellectuals' nonconformity and opposition was the Dengist economic reforms and their social results (on these results, see Davis and Vogel 1990). These reforms included decentralization of economic management, partial marketization and privatization of the economy, and greater commodification of goods and services. As a result of these reforms, the role of money in society and local financial autonomy were increased; personnel mobility was enhanced; and the power of the reader mar-

---

[42]This phrase is taken from Liu Binyan, who repeated this point when speaking at the Harvard-Yenching Institute in 1988.

ket expanded. The counterelite thus had more leeway to collect material support from a variety of sources, to shift from one institutional setting to another, and to hire necessary personnel to staff their unofficial organizations. With a growing market of readers, the publishing industry had to be more responsive to demand, and members of the counterelite found a place in which they could sell their products (see Bonnin and Chevrier 1991: 577). All this added up to a remarkable widening of areas uncontrollable by the party-state apparatus.

PART II

3

The movement to "emancipate the mind" and the counterelite's response

The preceding chapter deals with the question of how it was possible for the counterelite of post-Mao China to voice its criticism of the Communist regime. The rest of this work will answer the question of what criticism the counterelite expressed during the late 1970s to late 1980s. Having surveyed the institutional basis of opposition and paraopposition in post-Mao China, we can now turn to the major events that symbolized the conflict between the ruling elite and the counterelite. My analysis begins with the ruling elite's appeal to rationalism and the counterelite's response, which formed much of the background against which the political drama of Dengist China developed.

Background: obstacles to Deng's advance and to his four objectives

Late in 1974, when China's premier Zhou Enlai was hospitalized for an incurable cancer, Deng Xiaoping, an early victim of the Cultural Revolution, was appointed by party Chairman Mao Zedong as vice-premier for day-to-day administration of state affairs. After taking over this key post, Deng began to push bureaucrats to make systematic adjustments to correct the disastrous consequences of the Cultural Revolution. This move disappointed and enraged Mao, who regarded the Cultural Revolution as his last political masterwork. The aging chairman put his remaining energy into a "Criticize Deng Campaign" and early in 1976 replaced Deng with Hua Guofeng, a Politburo member in charge of the police.

Mao died on September 9, 1976. Four weeks later, his wife, Jiang Qing, and three close assistants, Zhang Chunqiao, Yao Wenyuan, and Wang Hongwen – since then labeled the "Gang of Four" – were arrested by Hua, with the help of several veteran leaders. In about ten months, Deng formally returned to office, assuming his previous positions as vice-chairman of the party, deputy premier of the government, and chief of general staff of the army (Domes 1985: 123–47).

The first major campaign in which the newly rehabilitated Deng and his allies put great efforts was "the great debate on the criterion of truth," which will be treated at length in this chapter. Why was the reformist leadership so interested in this controversy? Michael Schoenhals (1991) has documented Deng's stake with regard to the once purged leader's claim to office. But was this the only reason? Apparently not. When Deng threw himself into the debate in the early summer of 1978, he had already resumed all his previous positions and held them for almost a year. In other observations (see, e.g., Womack 1979; Schram 1984; Pye 1986), the reformist leaders' motivation is described as policy-oriented. These observers argue that Deng and his allies orchestrated the truth criterion debate in order to create a political climate in which they could implement pragmatic policies to deal with pressing economic and social problems facing the country. These observations are correct but too general; one wants to know what specific policy proposals the reformers had in mind at that time.

Various sources suggest that the newly returned Deng and his allies particularly sought four major accomplishments at that point: securing their personal positions in the leadership, the replacement of incumbent Maoists by previously purged veteran officials, the upgrading of intellectuals' social status and restoration of professionalism, and the uprooting of the theoretical foundations of the cultural revolutionary radicalism.

The first task was annulment of the Politburo's April 7, 1976, resolution on the "April 5 Incident." In late March and early April 1976, millions of Chinese people had spontaneously gone to Tiananmen Square to express mourning for the late premier Zhou, as well as grievances against continuation of the cultural-revolutionary policies endorsed by Mao and his radical assistants and sympathy for Deng, who was then under heavy official criticism. The mourning and protest at the square climaxed on April 5, the traditional Chinese Memorial Day. With Mao's approval, the authorities mobilized tens of thousands of militia, police, and military forces to crack down on the protestors that night. This bloody incident offered a timely pretext for Jiang Qing and her associates to push Deng out of power in the succession struggle. He was accused of backing the activities at the square (just as Deng and the octogenarian Communists accused Zhao Ziyang thirteen years later). The Politburo, under Mao's directive, made a resolution on April 7, condemning the activities at the square as "counterrevolutionary." Accordingly, Deng was stripped of all titles, and Hua was appointed the party's first vice-chairman and premier.

Emotionally as well as strategically, Deng could not help reversing the earlier official decision on the "April 5 Incident." In doing so, he intended not only to clear his own political history but also move further in an offensive against those who benefited from the incident.

The beneficiaries understood the situation well. In December 1976, while the fight at the top level over Deng's rehabilitation was unfolding, the *People's Daily* under Hu Jiwei investigated the Gang of Four's plot to manufacture a "counterrevolutionary, violent revolt" at Tiananmen Square to serve their purpose in the power struggle. When the editors of the *People's Daily* asked to publish the investigative report, Wang Dongxing, the party's vice-chairman and Hua's ally, rejected their request, saying the judgment on the incident was made by Mao and to reverse it would be damaging to the Great Banner, that is, the late chairman (*People's Daily* History Editorial Group 1988: 199–205; Yu Guangyuan and Hu Jiwei 1989: 258). At the "Central Working Conference" in March 1977, where the leaders finally reached a compromise on Deng's rehabilitation, Hua made a statement: "The 'Criticize Deng Campaign' was initiated by Chairman Mao; it was necessary" (Party Literature Research Center 1985: 477). Hua agreed to let Deng return to office soon, with the condition that Deng accept the earlier official judgment on the "April 5 Incident" (Hao Mengbi and Duan Haoren 1984: 670–71).

Deng's second objective was to bring back high-ranking officials deposed in the Maoist political campaigns. Most of them were purged during the Cultural Revolution when charged with "practicing Liu Shaoqi's and Deng Xiaoping's revisionist policies." Deng wanted his old colleagues eventually to replace the beneficiaries of the Cultural Revolution then in office. Naturally, this move met with fierce resistance.[1] On April 3, 1978, Hu Yaobang, new head of the party's Central Organization Department, announced when taking over the position: "All unfounded judgments on cadres must be reversed, no matter when, in what circumstances, at what organizational level, and by whose directive had these judgments been made." As Hu's speech was sent to press, these words were crossed out by Li Xing, deputy director of the General Office of the party's Central Committee, an act fully supported by Wang Dongxing, who declared: "Many of the judgments were made by Chairman Mao himself. How could the Organization Department's head possibly have the right to change what was decided by the Chairman?" (*People's Daily* History Editorial Group 1988: 223; Yu Guangyuan and Hu Jiwei 1989: 262–63).

Deng's third objective was to repudiate the "Two Appraisals of the Educational System." The "two appraisals" referred to a major document entitled "Summary of the National Conference on Education" resulting from a 1971 meeting led by Zhang Chunqiao, Yao Wenyuan, and Chi Qun, Jiang Qing's representative for educational affairs. According to this document, during the seventeen

---

[1] For a vivid description of the opposition to Deng's proposal, voiced by Guo Yufeng, then head of the party's Central Organization Department, see Yu Guangyuan and Hu Jiwei (1989: 262), and Ruan Ming (1991: 23–24).

years (1949–66) prior to the Cultural Revolution the bourgeoisie exercised dictatorship over the proletariat in China's educational sphere; the world outlook of the majority of Chinese intellectuals had been bourgeois, and it remained so. These two notorious appraisals justified the systematic persecution of the well educated beginning in 1966 and the abolition of the old schooling system, which emphasized academic performance.[2] To revoke the "two appraisals" was a prerequisite of upgrading intellectuals' social status and restoring professionalism.

Deng, who had a technological-economic modernization program in mind, was terribly worried by both the demoralization of professionals and the antiintellectualism in schools (1984: 82). He proposed reinstatement of the pre–Cultural Revolution educational system, with national entrance examinations instead of the Maoist admission policy based on class background and political reliability, as well as elite schools for the gifted, graduate programs, and international students-exchange programs. He urged cutting down on political studies imposed on professionals in order to give them time for research. He even suggested that experts should replace party functionaries and run research institutes themselves (Deng 1984: 53–54, 61–72).

Deng's bold ideas resulted in nothing, however. Liu Xiyao, the education minister, who had participated in drafting the 1971 "Summary," neither wanted nor dared to do what Deng proposed. Instead, Liu admitted he "was scared" (Dai Qing 1988: 9) and did not want to make further mistakes by following Deng's advice (Deng 1984: 82). Liu's fear was not groundless. In 1975 his predecessor, Zhou Rongxing, had attempted under Deng's direction to put the educational system on a reformist track, and when Deng was purged the following year Zhou also got into trouble. Zhou was accused of restoring "revisionist educational policies" and died from a heart attack after the torture of a "struggle session" (Informant no. 26). The 1971 "Summary" carried Mao's signature, and any attempt to override it invited enormous risk. Liu therefore did his utmost to prevent matters under his jurisdiction from running counter to the "Summary." His efforts directly caused the failure of the national conference on college admission policy in the summer of 1977, which had been intended to carry out the Dengist reforms (*People's Daily* History Editorial Group 1988: 217–19).

Finally, Deng wanted once and for all to discard the theoretical foundations of cultural-revolutionary radicalism. Deng's assistants selected two targets for this battle. One was a joint editorial of the *People's Daily, Red Flag,* and the *Liberation Army Press* entitled "Advance Along the Road Opened Up by the [Russian] October Socialist Revolution" (*Peking Review* No. 46, pp. 9–16,

[2]On the damage the Maoist policy did to the Chinese educational system, see Jonathan Unger (1982).

1967). Published in November 1967, the editorial was prepared by Kang Sheng, Chen Boda, and Yao Wenyuan, Mao's chief ideological assistants. (All three were officially condemned by 1977.) Its theme was: After communist parties take power, revolutions should go on without interruption. The new target of the revolutions is revisionists within the party, or "capitalist roaders" as Mao termed them; they are the most dangerous enemy of the working class, for they control the state power.

Another target was a pair of articles by Yao Wenyuan and Zhang Chunqiao published in early 1975, "On the Social Basis of the Lin Biao Anti-Party Clique" (*Peking Review* No. 10, pp. 5–10, 1975) and "On Exercising All-Round Dictatorship over the Bourgeoisie" (*Peking Review* No. 14, pp. 5–11, 1975). Grounded in Mao's speeches of late 1974, these articles specified the social basis of revisionism and in-party "capitalist roaders": the "bourgeois rights" in socialist society, for example, the operation of farms, factories and workshops, and stores that are not owned by the state; pay according to performance; the existence of money and exchange in economic life; wage differentials; and material incentives. To prevent revisionism and in-party "capitalist roaders" from rising, radical programs are needed to uproot such "bourgeois rights" in socialism.

Deng and his comrades were understandably uneasy with these theories, which had been devised primarily to bring down officeholders like Deng and Liu Shaoqi. Worse still, Deng's opponents continued to hold these theories over him like the sword of Damocles. In July 1978, a year after Deng's rehabilitation, Xiong Fu, head of *Red Flag* and a spokesman for Hua Guofeng's camp, dared to declare in public that "We must follow Chairman Hua and be prepared to employ the cultural-revolutionary methods again in the fight against potential unrepentant capitalist roaders like Liu Shaoqi, Lin Biao, and the Gang of Four" (Yu Guangyuan and Hu Jiwei 1989: 34). "An unrepentant capitalist roader" was the catchword reserved for Deng during the 1976 "Criticize Deng Campaign."

In the meantime, Deng saw that his opponents were using Maoist doctrine to block his policy proposals. In a major report to the Central Working Conference in March 1977, Hua adopted all the central points in Yao's and Zhang's anti–bourgeois rights articles, which, of course, ran completely against what the Dengists preferred – market mechanisms, bonuses, managerial authority, and the like. From the spring of 1977 on, Chinese economists discussed pragmatic economic measures for a whole year but offered no recommendation to the government. The economists feared persecution as "counterrevolutionaries" for contradicting the late Mao's anti–bourgeois rights teachings.[3] Since early 1977,

---

[3] Based on Yu Guangyuan's speech at the "Seminar on the Relations between Theory and Practice," Beijing, July 5, 1978.

members of the *People's Daily* had worked on projects attacking Yao's and Zhang's articles, but Wang Dongxing told them: "Chairman Mao read the articles. You cannot criticize them directly" (Yu Guangyuan and Hu Jiwei 1989: 266).

In May, reporters of the *People's Daily* discovered that a key concept in the 1967 joint editorial, "all-round dictatorship," denoting the cultural-revolutionary policies, had been written into the manuscript not by Mao but by Chen Boda. When this discovery was reported in the newspaper's internal newsletter, Wu Lengxi, a senior official in charge of editing Mao's work, angrily telephoned the newspaper's leaders: "We have the final version of the manuscript. Although Chen Boda added the term 'all-round dictatorship' to the text, Chairman Mao agreed and said: 'A good addition.'"[4] Wu's warning prevented the newspaper from releasing the discovery to the public, which could have encouraged further moves to reproach the joint editorial.

It was clear to Deng and his allies that their conflicts with the beneficiaries of the Cultural Revolution over power and policy all led to one question: How to deal with Mao's legacies? To Deng and his allies, most of the legacies were an obstacle to their move toward reorganization of leadership and redefinition of policy goals. To the beneficiaries, however, Mao's legacies were a shield, protecting the interest structure built up during the Maoist epoch. The necessity of these Maoist legacies to them was best reflected in a formula produced by Hua, Wang Dongxing, and Li Xing in early 1977, known as "two whatevers":

When Chairman Mao was alive, we united and fought under his banner. Chairman Mao now has passed away, but we should hold and defend his great banner better than before. . . . Whatever policies Chairman Mao formulated we shall all resolutely defend; whatever instructions Chairman Mao gave we shall all steadfastly abide by! (*People's Daily* February 7, 1977. For how this statement was made, see Hao Mengbi and Duan Haoran 1984: 670; and Dai Qing 1988: 7)[5]

The question posed by Mao's legacies reflected a profound problem that the post-Mao ruling elite confronted: the source of legitimacy. To the question of whether the late Great Helmsman should remain the sole source legitimizing power and policy in the PRC, exactly as he was alive, the beneficiaries of the Cultural Revolution answered yes. They wanted to keep China as it had been shaped since the mid-1960s by what Howard Becker and Robert Bellah (Finkle and Gable 1966: 188–89) call a "prescriptive" system.

It "is characterized by the comprehensiveness and specificity of its value commitments and by its consequent lack of flexibility. Motivation is frozen, so to speak, through commitment to a vast range of relatively specific norms governing almost every situation

---

[4]Hu Jiwei's speech at the Central Party School, September 13, 1979.
[5]In Part II of this book there are many quotations taken from Chinese sources. Unless other translators are indicated, the translations are mine.

in life. Most of these specific norms, usually including those governing social institutions, are thoroughly integrated with a religious system which invokes ultimate sanctions for every infraction." Small changes in the society "tend to have ultimate religious implications."

In this mode, any policy shift that Deng and his allies were to make predicated a declaration of position on Maoism, and any reevaluation of the legacies of Mao in turn touched on the emblem of the Chinese Communist system. Clearly, until the reformers obtained independent legitimacy for their political line through redefining their relation to the Maoist creed, they would not be able to take a single meaningful step forward.

The appeal to rationalism

From October 1977 to May 1978, under the direction of Hu Yaobang (de facto head of the Central Party School) and Luo Ruiqing (secretary-general of the Central Military Commission and a leading victim of the Cultural Revolution), a team of OIs[6] worked on two major statements, "Practice Is the Sole Criterion in Testing Truth" and "A Fundamental Principle of Marxism" (see Schoenhals 1991 for details). The first one appeared on May 11, 1978, in the *Guangming Daily* and one day later was reprinted in the *People's Daily* and the *Liberation Army Press*. The second one appeared in the *Liberation Army Press* on June 24. The national campaign of "great debate on the criterion of truth" was thus started. The statements were based on four main arguments.

First, the ultimate criterion for testing truth is practice, rather than theories such as Marxism and Maoist doctrine.

Second, the superiority of practice to theory is a fundamental Marxist principle endorsed by Mao himself, and thus to respect practice is to hold high Mao's banner.

Third, all theories are subject to revision. "Once a theory has been proved wrong or unsuitable to practice, it must be modified immediately" (*Guangming Daily* May 11, 1978).

Last, there should be no "forbidden zone" in political studies. "'Forbidden zones' . . . are fettering people's minds. We must have the courage to touch these 'forbidden zones' and tell right from wrong" (*Guangming Daily* May 11, 1978).

Once this rationalistic movement got started, Deng's camp endorsed it in all possible ways. In addressing the "All-Army Conference on Political Work" on

---

[6]Among them were Yang Xiguang (editor in chief of the *Guangming Daily*), Hu Fuming (philosophy lecturer at Nanjing University, later deputy director of the Jiangsu Provincial Party Propaganda Department), Wu Jiang (section head at the Central Party School), Ma Peiwen, and Wang Zhaohua (senior editors of the *Guangming Daily*).

June 2, 1978, Deng himself launched a fierce attack on dogmatists in high places (1984: 128). Politburo member Fang Yi called on natural scientists, such as Fang Lizhi, to justify practice as the sole criterion of truth from the point of view of the sciences. Deng Liqun and Zhou Yang organized a large meeting in Beijing and took more than 160 participants from party schools, universities, research institutes, publishing houses, the army, and government offices all around the country in an attempt to "set fire at every corner." Beginning in August 1978, provincial leaders and Great Military Area commanders were asked one by one to declare their positions on the "criterion of truth" (Dai Qing 1988: 27–32, 42–43).

Assisted by the popular campaign to "emancipate the mind," Deng and his allies had achieved, by late 1978, most of their objectives: Leading beneficiaries of the Cultural Revolution such as Hua Guofeng and Wang Dongxing were stripped of substantial power; Deng became de facto head of the party-state; the "April 7, 1976, Politburo Resolution" was reversed and the "April 5 Incident" redefined as a "popular revolutionary movement"; many of the primary victims of the Maoist purges were restored as heroes or high-ranking officials; a company of Deng's allies, for example, Hu Yaobang and Wang Zhen, entered the central leadership; on the official policy agenda, economic development replaced class struggle as a priority; peasants were allowed larger private plots and even permitted to dismantle their collective farms (Li Yongchun, Shi Yuangin, and Guo Xiuzhi 1987: 39–43).[7] At the central leadership meetings late in 1978, which symbolized the beginning of the "Deng Xiaoping era," Deng and his allies showed their great appreciation to the campaign to "emancipate the mind": "The debate is of far-reaching historic significance. . . . To a political party, a state or a nation, if everything has to be done according to books and if the thinking becomes ossified, progress would be impossible, vitality would be over, the party and the state would perish" (*Peking Review* No. 52, p. 15, 1978).

The consequences

Although the rationalistic movement to "emancipate the mind" was carried out in the Marxist rhetoric,[8] purposefully encouraging a limited flexibility in politi-

---

[7]There have been numerous publications in English on the power struggle among the PRC ruling elite during this period, many, understandably, containing speculation. See Harry Harding (1987: 312–14) for a list.

[8]The appeal to the "higher truth" (e.g., "true socialism" or "genuine Marxism") and the call for "returning to the original" are the basic tactics of reformers who act in a canon-bound political system. In Eastern Europe in the 1960s and 1970s and in the Soviet Union of the 1980s, such tactics were used again and again by those who advocated remolding the Stalinist structure, including, of course, Gorbachev (Gorbachev 1988: 81–82; Brovkin 1990; 238–39; EEPS 1990: 165).

cal life, the symbolic message it sent was revolutionary in the immediate post-Mao milieu. It granted the living individual license to judge right and wrong in the social world around him. Until then in the PRC the tiny ruling elite had had the exclusive privilege of making such judgments. The movement also shifted the reference point for judging: Previously it had been the teachings of the supreme leader and the party, but now it was the life experience, or "practice," of average men and women. Combining these two elements, the movement had the effect, largely beyond the initiators' intention, of teaching the individual Chinese, "Don't believe any theory, -ism, statement, or promise that you are told to believe. Don't belittle yourself. Trust only what you have seen. Rely on your own brain only." Encouraged by this rationalistic spirit, many people began to think over matters they had never before dared to ponder. Some began to express what they had dared to contemplate but not to express. A few who had dared to speak out in the past but had been suppressed instantly now became the engine of antisystem collective action. In this intellectual and political climate, three currents emerge in public life during the late 1970s and early 1980s, reverberating each other.

The first was the independent-minded OIs' drive to uproot systematically Stalinist and Maoist practice in Chinese politics. Their efforts concentrated on the "Forum on the Party's Theoretical Work" (*Dang de lilun gongzuo wuxu hui*) held in Beijing from January 18 to April 3, 1979.[9] The forum developed from a dispute. After the *Guangming Daily* published the article on practice by the "special commentator" on May 11, 1978, all the leading mass media were quickly involved in the discussion, their tone favoring the "practice first" side. Only *Red Flag*, the theoretical journal of the party's Central Committee, was an exception. Directly controlled by Wang Dongxing and Xiong Fu, it refused to publish work on the debate. In August, under growing pressure from both leading Dengists at the top and independent-minded OIs below, Xiong drafted a statement; in it, however, he emphatically intoned that "for the time being, special regard should be given to preserving and defending the fundamentals of Marxism-Leninism and Mao Zedong Thought" (quoted from Dai Qing 1988: 32–33). In late September, Xiong's draft was sent for comments to the Institute of Philosophy of the CASS, where its tone invited sharp criticism. The editors of

[9]The 1978 debate on the criterion of truth and the 1979 forum on theory were two major, closely interconnected events in post-Mao political development. While the first has consistently received attention among China scholars, the second has been little known to the outside. A recent paper by Merle Goldman (1991) reveals for the first time some interesting details about the 1979 forum but also contains many factual errors. What is missing in her paper are important details about the connections between the two events in question, the internal processes themselves, and their consequences. The discussion here is intended to fill in that information as well as provide contextual analysis that is indispensable for understanding the significance and consequences of the two events.

Red Flag submitted this draft with the comments to the Politburo's Standing Committee. Ye Jianying, the party's vice-chairman, suggested that the party's Central Committee organize a forum to air all sides, in order to reach a consensus on the issue of the truth criterion (Dai Qing 1988: 32–36).

Hu Yaobang, then head of the PCPD, was put in charge of organizing the forum, which was divided into two phases. The first phase was sponsored by the PCPD and the CASS and invited about one hundred participants from institutions in Beijing and one delegate from each province. The second was sponsored by the party's Central Committee and invited nearly five hundred people, including those who had attended the first session and more delegates from provincial party propaganda departments and research institutes all over the country (Hao Mengbi and Duan Haoran 1984: 693). Simultaneously each province was asked by Hu Yaobang to organize similar meetings, thereby achieving "the effect of mutually echoing and learning" (Party Literature Research Center 1982: 50–51).

Participants in the first phase of the forum included party leaders and the OIs that this study focuses on.[10] At the start of the forum a common understanding was reached among the majority: In order to search for a new road to make China rich, strong, and prosperous, no zones should be "forbidden"; nothing would be immune to reexamination and reevaluation. The dark age of the Gang of Four was over; we all were mistreated then and we should not now do the same thing to ourselves (Informant no. 4; Yu Guangyuan and Hu Jiwei 1989: 32).

Several critical views were voiced at the forum:[11]

[10] In addition to those Goldman (1991: 231) lists in her paper, participants in the first session also included Li Chang, party secretary of the Chinese People's Association for Foreign Friendship and a close friend of Hu Yaobang's when they worked together in the CYL; Wang Huide; Li Zhenwen, head of the Political Theory Education Division in the Education Ministry; Wu Lengxi and Xiong Fu; Shao Huaze, senior editor of the *Liberation Army Press;* Lu Zhichao, deputy head of the Theory Bureau in the PCPD and Deng Liqun's assistant; Jiang Liu, division head of the Central Party School; Sun Yefang, a leading economist in the CASS; Qin Chuan, He Kuang, and Wang Zisong, all senior editors of the *People's Daily;* Ma Peiwen; Xing Fensi, deputy director of the Institute of Philosophy in the CASS, who was active in promulgating the "practice first" principle but shifted his position to the hard-line during the 1983 Anti–Spiritual Pollution Campaign, and was promoted to vice-presidency of the Central Party School afterward; Ru Xing, deputy director of the same Institute of Philosophy; Hu Fuming; Wang Guixiu, Hu Yaobang's assistant at the Central Party School; and Li Xiulin, philosophy professor at the Chinese People's University. For a more detailed list, see Ruan Ming (1991: 105–19).

[11] The question of who did voice what at the forum is important. As the meeting was an "internal" one and most of the materials were not allowed to be distributed publicly, we are unable to reconstruct the proceedings on the basis of original presentations. Goldman (1991: 232) uses the method of approximation to solve the problem: looking at the participants' publications during and around the forum. But this method must be cross-checked by other sources of information.

My representation of the forum below resulted from several sources: (1) interviews with the participants, although here one must trust their often unclear memories; (2) recollections about the forum, such as those by Yu Haocheng, Ma Peiwen, and Guo Luoji (Yu Guangyuan and Hu

1. Raising questions about Mao's motives in launching the Cultural Revolution, Wang Ruoshui was a leading voice. By the time of the forum, the wholesale affirmation of the Cultural Revolution, held by such leaders as Hua Guofeng, had been rejected by the majority of the ruling elite. The new party line was: Mao "initiated this great revolution primarily because the Soviet Union had turned revisionist and in order to oppose revisionism and prevent its occurrence in China" (*Peking Review* No. 52, p. 15, 1978; with my editing). This view implies that the Cultural Revolution was a bad thing done by a great man for virtuous reasons (Deng 1984: 160–61). Wang Ruoshui, however, argued[12] that Mao had made the Cultural Revolution out of an evil desire – to purge his "revisionist" colleagues from the party-state leadership, on the promise that whoever was "unconditionally and absolutely loyal to his person" was a Marxist, and to be otherwise was to be a revisionist (Wang 1989: 236). According to this view, Mao's theory of class struggle, which was the justification of all his political campaigns, was only an excuse to mistreat those who disagreed with him (ibid.: 222).

Worse than Mao's ends were his means, the method of "luring the snake out of his hole" – first inspiring one to pour out true opinions and complaints, and then taking these as evidence of crimes (ibid.: 220). Mao used this technique in

Jiwei 1989: 20–22, 32–70, 290–91), although these recollections, because the forum has been a highly sensitive topic, usually omitted names and most details; (3) the hard-liners' criticism of the liberal participants, heard of from time to time in the intellectual and political circles; and (4) publications by the participants during and around the forum in both the internal and open press.

In using these publications one must be aware of two pitfalls to which Goldman (1991: 232) fails to call to the reader's attention. First, in the PRC people express themselves more directly and informatively in oral presentations than they do in formal writings, for published articles are *baizhi heizi* (black characters on white paper). If one gets in trouble someday, these can be used as the records of one's "crime." For example, at the "central working conference" of November–December 1978, Fang Yi, a Politburo member and vice-premier, condemned Mao as "the most tyrannical emperor in China's history," but his statement was deleted when the internal newsletter was printed (communication in spring 1983 with a functionary working in central party organs).

.   Another pitfall about the participants' publications is that they were "generalists" in the broadest sense and ready to comment on any subject so far as the political climate permitted them to do so. Without sufficient clues, one simply cannot be sure which publication contains the key points the author presented at the forum.

The following discussion is based on my cross-checking of the previously mentioned sources of information but is by no means free of mistakes. It is subject to further verification as more data become available.

[12]Wang's speech at the forum was widely disseminated in intellectual circles in Beijing and Shanghai at that time but never published in the PRC. The Hong Kong-based *Ming Pao Monthly* published most of the speech – with errors – in No. 2, 1980 (English translation: *China Report* No. 66, March 1980, FBIS). Early in 1989, a collection of Wang's writings was printed in Hong Kong, which contains a corrected, complete version of the speech. I use the later version, with several lines taken from the FBIS translation.

the 1957 Anti-Rightist Campaign and the 1959 anti–Peng Dehuai campaign, as well as, of course, in the Cultural Revolution (ibid.: 219, 221, 225).

On the basis of these observations, Wang at the forum challenged the current official assessment of Mao's motives for the Cultural Revolution: "If Chairman Mao launched it purely to oppose and prevent revisionism, and to consolidate the proletariat dictatorship and construct socialism, without unclean personal purposes, he should have discerned the vastly destructive effects the Cultural Revolution had caused." Mao failed to do so, mainly because he "placed his personal prestige above the interests of the people" (ibid.: 235).

2. Of those suggestions that the power of the state should be weakened, Yu Guangyuan was a leading voice.[13] He pointed out that during the Cultural Revolution, the prevalent theory was that "the class struggle in socialist society tends to intensify." Corresponding to that theory, the party line insisted on "strengthening the dictatorship of the proletariat over a long period of time." This viewpoint, although typically Stalinist, contradicted both Marx's and Lenin's theories of state, according to which the state should weaken, not strengthen, after communists take political power.

The dictatorship of the proletariat as a special form of the state, Yu argued, had two stages. The first was the "party dictatorship." A "dictatorship by minority," instead of a "rule of majority," immediately after the revolution was not desirable but was a necessary compromise, owing to the low level of political consciousness and of education at this stage among workers and other laboring masses. With enhancement of their political consciousness and education, the dictatorship of the proletariat should move into its second stage, in which the rule of the party gives way to the rule of the whole working class through its various popular organizations, for example, the trade unions and the people's congress.

Yu's criticism concentrated on the core of the Stalinist system – the definition of the party dictatorship as the desirable power structure that must be sustained throughout the entire socialist period. Citing Soviet and Chinese lessons, Yu underlined that the party dictatorship is extremely prone to neglect the working people's will and interests, the total bureaucratization of the party, and the conversion of state officials from "servants of the people" to "rulers of the people." Through these obscure, philosophical terms, Yu put forward a simple postulation: The Communist Leviathan must be crippled; power must be

---

[13]Yu's speech has not been published in the original in the PRC, but his basic argument on this matter was expressed in an article that came out on the eve of the forum (*Baikezhishi* No. 1, pp. 24–30, 1979).

distributed more widely among a variety of representative bodies; the decision-making process must be opened to people outside the party.

3. Of those demanding open discussion and public debate of political issues, Guo Luoji was one of the leaders.[14] His presentation attacked an official stand often cited as a symbol of the liberalism and kindness of the post-Mao regime: The Gang of Four equated academic and political issues, and as a result millions of intellectuals were mistreated. To avoid such mistakes and encourage scholarly competition, the post-Mao regime was determined to draw a clear line between the political and the academic and never allow officials to treat scholarly dissent as the same as political dissent.

Guo offered the counterargument that political and academic issues are often inseparable, and that opinions in such disciplines as political science or legal studies can be both scholarly and political. In socialist countries, even philosophy and economics function as theoretical foundations of the political. To ground academic freedom in the separation of scholarship and politics, in Guo's view, is problematic. He defended genuine freedom of expression:

Why should political issues be excluded from open discussion? Is discussion permissible only in areas remote from politics? . . . Political, academic, and other issues all should be subject to open discussion. So, even if somebody blurs the dividing line, he would not get into trouble. It is wrong to promote scholarly competition by drawing the line. . . . The right way is to substantiate sufficient, genuine freedom of speech. . . . [Compared with other issues] Political issues require more discussions, which all people should take part in. Generally speaking, academic issues could be discussed only by experts and scholars, but political issues must be discussed by all the people because they are important to all the people's interests.

Whether an anti-Communist should be granted the right to free speech was then hotly debated, and Guo ingeniously spoke for universalism: "How to handle the situation in which some individuals [use the right to free speech to] publish counterrevolutionary views? That's easy. You can publish revolutionary views to debate and criticize them. We should not indulge in counterrevolutionary statements. But we should not arrest the speaker either. . . . The past has shown that legally punishing individuals for their thoughts and words easily led to . . . suppressing independent-minded people, people of great vision, and far-seeing." In the PRC many people with great intelligence lost their lives, to the nation's calamity and shame. China should not have prisoners of conscience. Guo concluded: "If it is a democratic polity, people will be permitted to talk about it; if people are not permitted to do so, it must be a despotic polity."

[14] A digest of Guo's speech was printed in the *People's Daily*, November 14, 1979, under the title "*Zhengzhi wenti shi keyi taolunde.*" The following quotations are taken from it.

4. The nature of the PRC society was assessed, mainly by Su Shaozhi and Feng Lanrui,[15] who saw the PRC as not yet having entered but still remaining in the process of moving toward socialism.

Before the Liberation, China was a semicolonial, semifeudal country. Small-scale production was predominant. The level of the productive forces, of socialization of production, and of education all were very low. In this society, the transition toward socialism would be much longer [than expected]. In our country, the transitional period has not ended. China has not entered the first stage of communism (i.e., a socialist society) as Marx and Lenin conceived.

According to this view, to impose strictly socialist socioeconomic policies on Chinese society, as the Maoist leadership had done since the mid-1950s, was both unjustifiable and premature. China must instead systematically adopt policies that fit its social conditions. In other words, the government must allow nonsocialist institutions and methods to operate in the PRC for a long time.

5. In the critique of the socialist bureaucracy, one leading voice was Zhang Xianyang,[16] whose main point was: Lin Biao and the Gang of Four had treated the majority of party-state officials as capitalist roaders and persecuted them. That was wrong. Yet, the rejection of the theory and practice of Lin Biao and the Gang of Four should not lead to denial of the problem of bureaucracy in socialist states. The combination of a 2,000-year-old tradition of despotism and inheritance of Stalinist institutions in China had produced a bureaucracy mainly concerned with itself. In this system, once a person became an official, he stayed in officialdom forever, subject only to promotion, not demotion, and to appointment from the top, not election from the bottom. The bureaucratic system was a pyramid; as one moved higher, more and more power was concentrated in the hands of a few men until at the top, in only one man's hands. This structure acted against the growth of democracy within the party and in public life. As China struggled for modernization, the pyramid system became an obstacle, suppressing grass-roots vitality, initiative, and innovations.

Many other important views were also presented at the 1979 forum.[17] Yan Jiaqi proposed abolishment of life tenure in leading posts, arguing that replacement of this entrenched system by elections could institutionalize the transition of power and effectively reduce political instability. Liao Gailong suggested that the People's Congress should become the de facto sovereign power; currently,

[15] The theoretical part of Su's and Feng's presentation was printed in *Economic Research* No. 3, pp. 3–7, 1979, under the title "*Wuchanjieji qude zhenquan hou de shehuifazhan jieduan wenti.*"

[16] Part of Zhang's speech was printed in an internal publication, *Newsletter of Research on Marxism and Leninism*, early in 1980. The *Newsletter* was not allowed out of China. The following discussion is based on my reading notes and conversations with Informant no. 20 late in 1983.

[17] The following recapitulation is based on Yu Guangyuan and Hu Jiwei (1989: 21, 32–70); Tao Kai, Zhang Yide, and Dai Qing (1989: 146); and Wu Jiang's memory (*New Observer* No. 1, p. 30, 1989).

its only function was to vote for what had already been decided. "We often attack bourgeois democracy," Liao cynically remarked, "saying it is nothing but a form. Yet we don't even have the form." Yu Haocheng called for a judiciary that would judge cases according to law, not party committee directive. Li Honglin opposed the official norm requiring people be loyal to their leaders, and said it should be the other way around. Li Shu observed that one of the biggest mistakes the CCP had made since 1949 was the judgment that capitalism was the chief danger to China's socialist system. Actually, as the experience since then had showed, the influence of feudalism (read: despotism) was the chief enemy. The CCP had gone so far as to rely on feudal forces for revolutionary dynamism in the fight against capitalism, as was clear in Mao's resort in his last years to the Legalist School.

The overwhelming majority at the forum was critical. Few participants stood up, like Xiong Fu, for Maoist theory and practice, and these few failed to counterbalance the majority (Tao Kai, Zhang Yide, and Dai Qing 1989: 173). The top leadership, kept apprised of criticism in the forum by Hu Qiaomu, Deng Liqun, and the like, was divided about what was going on. The differences were less between supporters of Hua Guofeng and Deng Xiaoping (Hua's allies had lost considerable influence by that time) but among Deng's allies, as can be observed in the addresses of Hu Yaobang at the opening of the forum and Deng at its closing. At the opening on January 18, Hu had called on the participants:

We should exchange views on whether any ideological and theoretical obstacles remain to block our road and must be broken up for further progress. Any remaining forbidden zones? Any mental shackles? . . . As theoretical workers, you must have courage and vision, daring to proceed from the actual conditions to raise and deal with new questions; maintaining a scientific attitude and holding firmly to truth in serving the people's interests; and opposing the abominable behavior of selling one's principle for personal interests. (Party Literature Research Center 1982: 57, 60–61)

Deeply worried by the proceedings, Deng (1984: 180–81), whose views differed sharply from Hu's, on March 30 for the first time put forward the "four cardinal principles":

In order to achieve the four modernizations we must keep to the socialist road, uphold the dictatorship of the proletariat, uphold the leadership of the Communist party, and uphold Marxism-Leninism and Mao Zedong Thought. The Central Committee considers that we must now repeatedly emphasize the necessity of upholding these four cardinal principles, because certain people (even if only a handful) are attempting to undermine them. In no way can such attempts be tolerated. No party member and, needless to say, no party ideological or theoretical worker, must ever waver in the slightest on this basic stand.

Deng and many other leaders, somewhat understandably, were angered in particular by three of the themes addressed at the forum (Informants nos. 2, 8, and 20). The first of these was Wang Ruoshui's critique of Mao's moral quality (see Deng 1984: 180, 284, 347). Wang's reasoning easily led to the conclusion that Mao, the personification of the ruling party, actually was an immoral man, and such a moral judgment is harmful to a leader in the tradition of Chinese political culture, which admits a man's right to rule wholly on his moral quality (Fairbank 1983: 55–60, 419). Wang's critique provided a paradigm for understanding CCP politics: The leaders' theories and statements were only a mask to cover their heartless, evil pursuits. This generalization was indeed damaging to the rulers, as Deng (1984: 287) realized: "Comrade Mao Zedong was not an isolated individual, he was the leader of our party. . . . Discrediting Comrade Mao Zedong . . . means discrediting our party and state."

The second theme that angered most CCP leaders was embodied in Guo Luoji's proposition that people should not be punished for what they think and speak. In 1979, protests were rising and gaining momentum in the streets of many Chinese cities, and coping with the dissident movements was a matter of urgency. In light of these protests, Guo's proposition was seen as an attempt to legalize political opposition (Party Literature Research Center 1982: 683, 688; Deng 1984: 181–82).).

The third theme was the push for the withering away of the state. Yu Guangyuan's proposal to diminish the "party dictatorship" was obviously a thrust against those who had ruled society in the name of the "vanguard of the proletariat."[18] Deng Xiaoping called Yu's proposal "muddy."

The forum on theory led many of Deng's allies at the top to conclude that the same OIs, who had been immensely helpful to them against the beneficiaries of the Cultural Revolution, were now no longer dependable. Deng Liqun later described the forum as "the first of five major struggles between right and wrong in the party" after the fall of the Gang of Four (Tao Kai et al. 1989: 136), implying a new "two-line conflict" (*luxian douzheng*). In 1987 Wang Zhen recalled that starting at the forum "a few theorists in the party parted company with the party" (*People's Daily* February 17, 1987). The forum was even condemned, as early as 1979, as "a black meeting," "a troublemaking conference," "a gathering of rebelling intellectuals" (Yu Guangyuan and Hu Jiwei 1989: 53). Yu Guangyuan, who, with Hu Qiaomu and Deng Liqun, had been Deng Xiaoping's chief assistant in ideological affairs, lost favor largely as the result of his presentation at the forum. In 1982–83, Wang Ruoshui was charged with "manufacturing Chairman Mao's black material" by the party's Central Commission for Discipline Inspection. Deng Xiaoping, informed of Hu Yaobang's admiration for Guo Luoji's ideas, exiled Guo from Beijing to Nanjing, to prevent Hu's

---

[18]The conflict between theorists like Yu and the CCP ruling elite had its precedent in Russia (see Inkeles and Geiger 1961: 113–26).

contamination by Guo's "liberal influence" (Informant no. 21). Activists in the forum were afterward labeled *wuxuhui fenzi* (elements of the forum), with the connotation that they were members of a political opposition, and treated as "dangerous persons" by the party's central organs of propaganda and organization.

Another current to emerge in public life during the late 1970s and early 1980s, encouraged by the campaign to "emancipate the mind," was the Democracy Movement, led chiefly by radical MIs. This short-lived but notable movement has been examined in several reports in English (Seymour 1980; Tong 1980, 1981; Goodman 1981; Nathan 1985) and will not be covered in detail here. The two aspects of the movement discussed here are its extent and its political and intellectual affinity with the tide led by the independent-minded OIs.

Because the movement was known in foreign reports as "Beijing Spring" and the "Democracy Wall Movement," it has been perceived as being based only in Beijing. But the material collected by observers in Taiwan and Hong Kong, although by no means complete, shows that the movement had spread to many other areas, as shown in Table 2.

It has been generally observed that intellectually the radical MIs and the independent-minded OIs echoed each other but organizationally the latter stayed away from the former. This observation is not so accurate. There were a good number of attempts to form political linkage between the two sides.[19] Among elite intellectuals, there were many people supportive of the movement. For instance, Bai Hua, author of the screenplay *Unrequited Love,* openly expressed his endorsement of the Democracy Wall. Yan Jiaqi and Huang Yongyu, a noted painter, submitted their manuscripts to unofficial presses for publishing. Yu Guangyuan invited a group of radical MIs for roundtable discussion. Xie Changkui, a fellow at the Research Center of the CYL Central Committee, made a very positive survey report about unofficial presses. The journal of *China's Youth* invited editors of several unofficial presses, including Lu Lin, who worked with Wei Jingsheng for the *Quest,* to attend discussion meetings. Some OIs assisted radical MIs in their struggle for legal status, and helped them obtain material support and sensitive data. We see that during the 1979 forum, reports about the OIs' activity appeared promptly in an unofficial magazine.[20] The majority at the 1979 forum was sympathetic to the protests in Beijing that

---

[19]The following is based on Informants nos. 3 and 4 and Hu Ping (*China Spring* No. 12, pp. 10–11, 1988). See also Deng (1984: 238–39) and Party Literature Research Center (1982: 706).

[20]See *Fruits of the Autumn* (*Qiushi*) No. 1, 1979, in Institute for the Study of Chinese Communist Problems (1980–85: Vol. 9: 181–83).

Table 2. *Geographic distribution of unofficial magazines (1978–80)*

Province	City	Unofficial magazines
Beijing	Beijing	34
Guangdong	Guangzhou	9
	Shaoguan	2
Zhejiang	Hangzhou	6
	Ningbo	2
	Wenzhou	2
Shanghai	Shanghai	8
	Chongming	1
Guizhou	Guiyang	7
Hunan	Changsha	6
Henan	Kaifeng	2
	Anyang	4
Sichuan	Chongqing	4
	Wanxian	1
	Chengdu	1
Tianjin	Tianjin	5
Hubei	Wuhan	5
Shandong	Qingdao	3
	Linqing	1
Jilin	Changchun	3
Shanxi	Taiyuan	2
Heilongjiang	Haerbin	1
Liaoning	Jinzhou	1
Shaanxi	Xian	1
Hebei	Baoding	1
Total		116

Sources: Institute for the Study of Chinese Communist Problems (1980–85); Widor (1985–84); Luo Bin (1981); *China Spring* (No. 4, p. 9, 1990).

occurred during this period – the "Fu Yuehua event," the "Democracy Wall," and peasants' demonstrations for more food.[21]

Contact between the two sides was helped by the fact that some of the radical MIs were children or relatives of party officials and elite intellectuals, like Wang Juntao and Wei Jingsheng, allowing exchange of opinions and information to be carried on informally.

Born in the late 1940s and early 1950s, the majority of the radical MIs bore a heavy Marxist intellectual stamp,[22] acquired in long and serious independent

---

[21] Communication with Informant no. 4. On these events, see Andrew Nathan (1985).

[22] Although many members of the Chinese counterelite, OIs as well as MIs, were Marxist in intellectual orientation at early stages of their critical activity, this fact does not diminish the historical significance and political implications of their activity, because the direction their efforts consequently led to is the dismantling of fundamental features of the Leninist structure.

study. Only a few radical MIs were inclined toward non-Marxist concepts in their analyses or appeals – for example, Wei Jingsheng's application of Lockean and Montesquieuean theories of the separation of powers (Widor 1981 – 84: Vol. 1, p. 163), and Ren Wanding's use of the human rights concept (ibid.: Vol. 2, pp. 421–24). Politically and apparently out of strategic consideration, most radical MIs did not wage a frontal attack on the primacy of the Communist party and the socialist system but showed sincere support for Deng's reforms.

Several themes prevalent in unofficial publications indicated that certain sociopolitical concerns were widely shared by both the MIs and the independent-minded OIs.[23]

1. Both criticized the political structure of the PRC, a critique that was generally conducted along two lines. The majority contrasted what the regime promised with what it delivered, but did so without repudiating the Marxian socialist fundamentals, concluding that the ruling elite had betrayed Marxist ideals of universal suffrage and popular governance embodied in the Paris Commune of 1871.[24] The minority contrasted what Chinese socialism delivered with what Western capitalism offered, concluding that the Communist system was nothing but organized brutality clothed by beautiful words.[25]

2. Mao's doctrine was condemned and he was held personally responsible for the horrible crimes committed by Lin Biao and the Gang of Four and for the socioeconomic backwardness of the country; de-Maoization was put forth as a precondition for modernization.[26]

3. For the propagation of democratic reforms, most people saw the Yugoslavia model of "workers' self-governance" as a "reference group," rather than Western systems of government. Some recommended a "proletarian two-party or multiparty system," others the "separation of four powers: the legislative, the executive, the judicial, and the Communist party." To the general public, the most appealing defense of political restructuring was Wei Jingsheng's concept of the "fifth modernization" – democratization, defined as the prerequisite for implementation of the "four modernizations" program.[27]

In fact, the vocabulary of the opposition in the Soviet bloc also was Marxist at the onset (Ash 1990: 263; Taras 1991).

[23] The following is based on my survey of the twenty-two volumes of Chinese material stored in Harvard-Yenching Library.

[24] See Institute for the Study of Chinese Communist Problems (1980–85: Vol. 3, p. 55; Vol. 4, p. 64; Vol. 19, pp. 117–19, 123).

[25] See Widor (1981–84: Vol. 1, pp. 62–63).

[26] See Widor (1981–84: Vol. 1, pp. 53, 61, 619; Vol. 2, p. 489), and Institute for the Study of Chinese Communist Problems (1980–85: Vol. 18, pp. 210–11).

[27] See Widor (1981–84: Vol. 1, pp. 50–69, 78–83, 163, 360, 468–73; Vol. 2, pp. 105–09, 173–74, 202–06, 238–41, 315–16, 372–85, 434–443, 540–45), and Institute for the Study of Chinese

Wei's defense of democracy, like those by many of his comrades in the Democracy Movement, fell in line with the "Yan Fu argument," a utilitarian justification of individual liberties and democratic rights: They are desirable because they can elicit the individual citizen's creativity and energies to work for the nation as a whole, making China rich and powerful (Schwartz 1964; Schram 1984: 423; Nathan 1985: 4–5, 127–28). The same argument was commonly used in the Soviet Union in the early stages of Gorbachev's reforms (cf. Scanlan 1988: 45–46). In societies where the individualistic tradition is weak, justification of civil liberties has to begin with collectivist appeals.

4. In their demands for actualization of free speech as promised by the PRC Constitution, the radical MIs stressed that everyone should be granted the same right to free expression, irrespective of political attitude, that Criminal Law articles on punishment of dissidents should be eliminated, and that unofficial publications should be legalized.[28]

5. Many of the critics had arrived at fairly sophisticated analyses of the roots of bureaucratic domination in socialism. They argued that such roots were in the integration of political power and property control, by which the party-state had enjoyed organizational monopolization; in the unit system, in which the leader behaved like a feudal manorial lord, controlling resources indispensable to the employee's life; and in the system of cadre appointments. As long as these structural arrangements exist, official corruption and bureaucratic domination will continue, regardless of whether the Gang of Four or anyone else may be in power.[29]

6. Some MIs had been frequent visitors in the prison, and their narratives about the torture prisoners endured were extremely vivid and powerful. Protestors in the "April 5 Incident" when jailed were repeatedly beaten, and if they pleaded not guilty, their family members were brought for torture. Police in Shanxi went into the streets to make random arrests of pedestrians in order to secure manpower to construct their office buildings. Guards at the Beijing Second Prison used burning sticks to beat the homeless, and women prisoners were forced to eat food mixed with menstrual blood.[30]

Perhaps the most horrifying instance involved Zhang Zhixin, a party member

Communist Problems (1980–85: Vol. 1, pp. 68, 248; Vol. 4, pp. 91, 126–27; Vol. 8, pp. 309–15; Vol. 10, pp. 144–46; Vol. 13, pp. 36–37; Vol. 14, pp. 179–87; Vol. 19, p. 209).

[28] See Institute for the Study of Chinese Communist Problems (1980–85: Vol. 3, p. 45; Vol. 12, pp. 67–115; Vol. 14, pp. 124–27, 287–300), and Widor (1981–84: Vol. 1, pp. 49, 356; Vol. 2, pp. 396, 551–52, 561–67).

[29] See Institute for the Study of Chinese Communist Problems (1980–85: Vol. 1, pp. 83–84, 102, 226), and Widor (1981–84: Vol. 2, pp. 388, 444). In Gorbachev's Soviet Union, critical intellectuals applied exactly the same theory to analyze the Soviet system (Brumberg 1990: 164–65).

[30] See Widor (1981–84: Vol. 1, pp. 134–37; Vol. 2, pp. 185–91, 451), and Institute for the Study of Chinese Communist Problems (1980–85: Vol. 18, p. 244).

in Liaoning. In 1968–69, Zhang expressed reservations, at inner-party meetings, about Lin Biao's and Jiang Qing's doings during the Cultural Revolution, a right guaranteed to her by the party Constitution, but she was nevertheless jailed in September 1969. During imprisonment, she was handcuffed and fettered uninterruptedly for 570 days and for 10 days was forced to stand against a wall without rest. Early in 1975, Zhang was sentenced to death by Mao's nephew. Because the prison's authorities were afraid that at the place of execution she might shout protest slogans, on the eve of execution they had her larynx cut without anaesthesia. The radical MIs used Zhang's fate to illustrate that the inhumanity of the Communist prison was many times more than that of the KMT's one, described in Communist propaganda as the most brutal in the world.[31]

Zhang's case outraged the public's sense of humanity and justice more than anyone's mistreatment. Unlike most victims of the Mao regime, she was not an offspring of the "five black class categories" (the landlord, the rich peasant, the counterrevolutionary, the criminal, and the Rightist) but born of a "red" family; she joined the Communist movement when merely a teenager; she was not involved in any power struggle but was an ordinary office worker; she was full of revolutionary idealism and patriotism which were demonstrated by her speeches and writings in prison; she was a loyal wife and caring mother; and she had a beautiful and dignified appearance, which indicated, in the popular Chinese view, an inner moral quality of a high standard. The disclosure of Zhang's case, like the disclosure of the Soviet purges after Stalin's death, testified to the public that, under the "Great Leader," "innocence meant nothing; nationality meant nothing; Party membership meant nothing: justice was denied to all" (Rothberg 1972: 59).

7. Advocacy of human rights emphasized such rights in general, applicable for "the proletariat and revolutionary people" as well as for the "bourgeoisie and counterrevolutionary elements." Human rights so defined included not only the right to live but also rights to work, speak out, publish, and participate in state affairs.[32]

The third current that emerged in China's public life in the late 1970s and early 1980s encouraged by the rationalistic campaign was the younger generation's cry of its loss of faith in communism. This was reflected powerfully in the nationwide discussion, organized by the Beijing magazine *China's Youth*

---

[31]See Institute for the Study of Chinese Communist Problems (1980–85: Vol. 16, pp. 188–90, 273–312), and Widor (1981–84: Vol. 2, pp. 491–505).
[32]See Widor (1981–84: Vol. 2, pp. 421–24, 446, 635), and Institute for the Study of Chinese Communist Problems (1980–85: Vol. 14, pp. 149–50).

(*Zhongguo Qingnian*) from mid-1980 to early 1981, of the question "What is the ultimate meaning of life?"[33]

To the reporters of the magazine, neither the youth's disillusionment with nor its despair in the Communist system was new. In their daily contact with ordinary life, the reporters had long been touched by the general mood of youth, and they wanted to bring this crisis into the open. From mid-1979 to early 1980, they organized a dozen panels in factories, schools and colleges, and offices in the Beijing area, to air the problems Chinese youth faced. Some panelists could not help crying out during the discussions, saying that all their cherished ideals and values were smashed and that they simply did not know what they could rely on and where they should head. Two panelists in particular impressed the reporters: Mr. Pan Yi, a student at the Beijing Economics Institute, with a philosophical disposition, and Ms. Huang Xiaoju, a worker at the Beijing Fifth Wool Sweater Factory, with a literary disposition. Both were in their early twenties, and their views appeared representative of their contemporaries. The reporters asked each of them to put their thoughts into a candid "letter to the editor," then combined their letters into one, which was published in the May 1980 issue of *China's Youth,* under the pseudonym "Pan Xiao." The letter is worth quoting at length:

I am twenty-three. I should say that I am just beginning life, but already all of life's mystery and charm are gone for me. I feel as if I have reached the end. Looking back on the road I have traveled, I see that it was a journey from crimson to grey – from hope, to disappointment, to despair. When I began, the long river of my thought arose from a selfless source; now, at last, it has found its final resting place in the self.

I used to have beautiful illusions about life. In primary school, I heard the stories *How the Steel Was Tempered*[34] and *The Diary of Lei Feng,*[35] and although I did not fully understand them, the heroic acts they described excited me so much that I could not sleep for days. I even neatly copied Pavel's [the hero in the former book] famous words on the first page of my diary: "So live life that when you look back on the past, you will feel no regrets over having let the years go by, no shame at not having achieved anything . . ." When one diary ended, I copied the quote in the next one. This quote gave me so much encouragement! I thought: my father, mother, and grandfather are all Party members. Naturally, I believe in communism. Someday, I will join the Party too. I never had any doubts. . . . I began to develop my first and most beautiful views about life: Men live to make the lives of others more beautiful; men live, and so should have high ideals; when

---

[33] The following is based on Informant no. 22. Two reports exist in the English literature about the background of the letter; the one by Helen F. Siu and Zelda Stern (1983: liii–liv, 3–4) is much closer to the true story than the one by Peter J. Seybolt (1981: 3–4).

[34] A Soviet novel of the early 1930s by Nikolai Ostrovsky, which was translated into Chinese in the early 1950s and then became a classic for revolutionary moral education.

[35] Lei Feng was a soldier killed in an accident while on duty in 1963. Party leaders immediately made him a model hero and encouraged everyone to emulate his behavior. His diary, whose truthfulness has been questioned in China, was assigned by the party as a standard text for moral education in schools and units. The official campaign emphasized Lei Feng's determination to be a small, nameless, but useful "screw" in the machine of revolution (see Siu and Stern 1983: 5).

the Party and the people are in need, without hesitating, one should give one's all. I lost myself completely in a kind of ecstasy of self-sacrifice. . . .

But often, I felt a lurking pain, and it was this: the reality my eyes saw always sharply contradicted what my mind had been educated to accept. Soon after I entered primary school, the waves of the Cultural Revolution began and grew more and more terrifying. I witnessed the following: the searching of homes and seizure of property; violence; human lives disregarded; whole days when there was no talk, no laughter in my family; grandfather very carefully preparing for his self-criticisms; young people a little older than I swearing, gambling, and smoking all day; . . . I felt lost, because I began to realize that the world around me was not so beguiling as it had been portrayed in books. I asked myself, shall I believe in the books or my eyes? Shall I believe my teachers or myself? I felt full of contradictions. . . . My past education had endowed me with strange abilities: I had learned to close my eyes, to talk myself into believing things, to memorize Chairman Mao's words, to hide inside my own pure and elevated spiritual world.

Later, however, it didn't work. Life's adversities pounced on me. The year I was graduated from junior middle school, grandfather died. My warm, supportive family suddenly turned cold and cruel. We quarreled over money. My mother, who was working elsewhere, refused to support me any longer. I had to leave school, and was reduced to being a street youth. I felt as if I had been clubbed on the head. Heavens, if relationships among family members were like this, what about other relationships in society? [Later] I was given . . . a job in a small collective enterprise. . . .

I believed in the Party organization. Nevertheless, a complaint made to its leader blocked my entry into the Communist Youth League for years. . . .

I sought help in friendship. Once, however, I made a small mistake, and a good friend of mine went so far as to write up secretly all that I had confided in her and report it to the authorities. . . .

I sought love. I came to know the son of a cadre. His father had been persecuted by the Gang of Four, and they had been in a terrible situation. I rushed to the son with my most sincere love and deepest sympathy, soothing his wounds with my own wounded heart. . . . But I never thought that after the Gang of Four was smashed, his family would be reinstated, and from then on he would take no notice of me. . . .

I was devastated. For two days and two nights, I couldn't sleep or eat. I was angry, irritated. My heart felt ready to burst. Man, you truly revealed your vile, ugly face. Was this the intriguing mystery you wanted to show me?

Seeking the answer to the meaning of life, I observed people. I asked the white-haired old men, the inexperienced young men, the cautious masters in the factory, the farmers who rise in the dark to beat the dawn. . . . But not one of their answers satisfied me. . . .

I sought help from the treasury of man's wisdom. I read desperately, hoping to find comfort and explanations. I have read the social theories of Hegel, Darwin, and Owen. I have read the works of Balzac, Hugo, Turgenev, Tolstoy, Lu Xun, Cao Yu, and Ba Jin. But reading does not free me from my problems. These masters cut open layer after layer of human nature with pens like knives, enabling me to penetrate deeply all the ugliness of this human world. I am stunned to see how closely reality resembles what these masters described. It doesn't matter whether I immerse myself in books or return to reality, all I see are characters like Galathee [an evil character in Balzac] and Nekludov [an evil character in Tolstoy's *Resurrection*]. I lie in bed tossing and turning – thinking, furiously thinking, laboriously thinking. Gradually, I become calm, cool. Social Darwinism gave me a deep revelation: man is human! No one can escape life's underlying laws. In crucial moments, everyone chooses according to his instincts. No one can religiously follow the high morals and convictions he preaches. Man is selfish; there is no such thing as a selfless, noble person. The propaganda of the past was exaggeration or fiction. Ask the "great" saints, the distinguished scholars, the noble teachers, the "respected" propagandists. If they dare confront themselves, I dare ask how many of them can say they have escaped the underlying law of selfish struggle! In the past, I believed fanatically that "Man lives to make the lives of others more beautiful," and "Don't hesitate to sacrifice your life for the people." When I think of it now, it appears so ridiculous! . . .

I have come to understand this principle: whether one lives to exist or to create, everybody works for others by working for himself. It is like the sun giving off light: this is, first of all, an inevitable phenomenon of the activity of its own existence; its shining on the world is nothing but a kind of incidental result deriving from this. Therefore, I feel that if everyone strives to improve the value of his own existence, human society must move forward. This is, generally speaking, the law of man, and also a law of biological evolution – a law that no dogma can drown or deceive. . . .

People say the era is marching forward, but I cannot feel its strong arms; others say the world has a grand design, but I do not know where it is. Life's road – why is it getting narrower and narrower? I am already so tired. It is as if, were I to let out one more breath, it would mean utter destruction. I confess, I have gone secretly to watch services in the Catholic church. I have thought of becoming a nun. I have even thought of dying by my own hand. . . . My heart is so confused, so contradictory. (Siu's and Stern's translation, 1983: 4–9, with my alterations)

The response the letter generated was far beyond the editors' expectation. During the next seven months, more than sixty thousand letters came to the magazine, many cosigned by dozens or even a hundred of people (*China's Youth* No. 3, p. 16, 1981). In the long history of the magazine, the most letters received in response to an article had been about ten thousand in the early 1960s for "Lei Feng's Spirit." Of the sixty thousand letters, many were signed with pseudonyms, indicating the fear of official punishment (Informant no. 22); in the 1960s, when the press received letters expressing dissident views, the editors often sent those letters to the party bosses of the authors' units, causing severe consequences to the authors.

Nearly 10 percent of the sixty thousand incoming letters were critical of "Pan Xiao"'s attitude, seeing it as a reflection of "the beliefs of the exploiting classes" or as an attempt to "mix public welfare with self interests." (See, e.g., translations in Ownby 1985: 60–61, 63–67.) Another 10 percent or more not only agreed with "Pan Xiao"'s description and analysis of the social reality, but also with her way of coping with it (Informant no. 22). A letter from Nanjing complained:

China's writers and artists have portrayed so many model youths, but no one has truly spoken out the hearts of the young generation as Pan Xiao did. We are moved, but feel gloomy. Pan Xiao has, after all, something to pursue in literature. We have, however, nothing to engage in. . . . So many years have passed, no one ever dared to touch the pain of the youth. After the downfall of the Gang of Four, our moans are drowned by cheers. This does not mean that our fate has undergone fundamental change. (*China's Youth* No. 7, p. 18, 1980)

A Wuhan University student admitted:

In the past I believed in communism, and took as life's purpose the sacrifice of myself in order to secure the happiness of mankind. [After years of suffering] I finally discovered that lying, cheating, and flattery are the secrets of life, that selfishness is man's essence. . . . The individual is the center and foundation of the world. . . . This philosophy is perhaps greatly at odds with current ideology and morality, but it is one that has emerged from the painful experience of my own life. . . .

Last night while eating supper I heard over the university broadcasting system a song [that] contained four famous lines from *Lei Feng's Diary*, one of which was "Treat individualism the way the autumn wind sweeps away fallen leaves." I could not help but be alarmed. Sweep away individualism? Negate the individual? If this is a joke, it's not funny. . . .

In sum, according to man's basic nature, selfishness is that which is most sacred and inviolable, it is mankind's most elemental, most legitimate right. . . . Every social movement, including the Four Modernizations currently underway, should put living, feeling man at the first place. The movement is only the means; the self is the end. (Ownby's translation, 1985: 67–72, with my alterations)

A letter from Hangzhou warned:

Let it be noted: once we turn "public" and "private" into absolute antagonisms, then a handful of people's private interest can pass off as the public. This "public interest" is alienation, the inevitable result of the suppression of the majority's reasonable private interest. In a society that lacks democracy, it is particularly easy for a false "public" to replace the genuine "public," and this is perhaps one reason why those careerists who with all their might pursue their own private interests while throwing on a cloak of "public" especially enjoy fascist dictatorships. (Ownby's translation, 1985: 78–79, with my alterations)

About three-quarters of the letters responded with mixed feelings. Their authors hated to see "Pan Xiao"'s life end in tragedy and did not support her attitudes toward her future, believing them too despondent. They encouraged her to be self-respecting and self-confident, to try to seek new goals and love in life. On the other hand, these contemporaries of "Pan Xiao" confirmed that her portrayal of the social reality and of social relationships was true. Her feeling of having been cheated, abused, and abandoned, and her disillusionment, emptiness, and depression reflected exactly the mood of most Chinese youth (Informant no. 22). Of the 113 letters or excerpts published in *China's Youth*, most fall into this category, as the following examples show:

A Hubei CYL official: "Pan Xiao's letter could even arouse my great sympathy! Until I read the letter, I had been vague to myself. Now I am standing before myself, clear and without any disguises. As a matter of fact, it is not only I that can see a shadow of my own in Pan Xiao's life course, so do a vast number of other youths!" (*China's Youth* No. 6, p. 12, 1980)

A letter from a small town in Sichuan: "Pan Xiao said what everybody has on his mind and dares not to pour out. My friends and I admire Pan's candidness and courage and also commend the editors' courage. Exploration on the purpose and meaning of life is seen today as a scientific attitude of facing reality and seeking truth from facts. But who can guarantee that one day it will not be labeled as 'bringing shame to socialism, nursing a grievance against the society, and undermining the four modernizations program' so that you would be sent to jail, or to the countryside, to labor and reform your ideology?" (Seybolt's translation, 1981: 69)

A youngster from a county town in Henan: "For the first time I heard from someone else the song of my own heart. Though filled with tears and flames, the song sings the true feelings of my heart!" (Seybolt's translation, 1981: 17)

A young writer who had investigated the massacres in Guangxi and Hunan during the Cultural Revolution: "This generation of ours spent our early youth in a relatively stable society. With their exploits, heroes like Lei Feng . . . imbued our crystal-like hearts with the lofty and magnificent idea of 'revolution.' With great eagerness, we studied Mao Zedong Thought and were ready at any time to dedicate all we had to the Chinese revolution and the world revolution. When the Cultural Revolution got underway, our revolutionary enthusiasm erupted like a volcano. Swimming with the tide and obeying the orders issued by the proletarian revolutionary headquarters [of Chairman Mao], we plunged into the whirlpool of struggle. Finally, however, history mercilessly displayed before us the harsh reality. Confronted by the bloody facts, lies and deceptions fell one after another. The myth [about Mao Zedong Thought] exploded, and so did the deity himself. Ideals, life, hopes, and courage were all ruthlessly ruined." (Seybolt's translation, 1981: 24)

An official of the Shanxi Provincial Committee of CYL: "A letter written by an ordinary youth like Pan Xiao could generate reactions that were so rapid, deep, and extensive. Why? Only because she is candid? No. There are more profound and stimulating reasons here" [that is, Pan Xiao's attitude represents the unique quality of contemporary Chinese youths]: "they have seen through society"; "they have been discontent with the reality"; "they are eager for the value of the self." In short, they are displaying all the "reasonable self-consciousness and demands of the individual" that have been "wantonly suppressed by the propaganda and preachment of the past." (*China's Youth* No. 9, p. 18, 1980)

If monitoring the discussion, the editors of *China's Youth*, inspired by the campaign of "Seeking truth from facts," abandoned their established rules and did not cut sensitive and critical passages from the letters before they were published. The tone of these letters shocked the central leadership of the CYL. Hu Qili and several other leaders concluded that the discussion over the meaning of life sharpened what had been vague in the youth's minds, brought out what had been hidden, and made the public more sensitive to the negative side of PRC society. They worried that after the discussion, young people would be even less receptive than before to the party's instructions. To counter the pessimistic and dissenting attitude that dominated the discussion, the CYL Central Committee invited several OIs who were popular among the youth, among them Guo Luoji, Ruan Ming, and Li Honglin, to draw a conclusion from the discussion. The OIs, however, did not offer a rosy conclusion but, instead, drifted from the traditional line (Informant no. 22).

The message of the discussion in *China's Youth* was not unique. At that time, the early 1980s, the ruling elite learned of such feelings through other channels. On March 6, 1980, the *Workers' Daily*, the organ of the official trade union, published four letters from young workers that indicated the prevailing attitude among young members of the working class: nihilism from the bankruptcy of revolutionary ideals; cynicism from deep-rooted, recurring social problems, such as official corruption and special privileges; and strong indignation against the party-state for the irremediable losses the youth suffered during the Mao epoch. These letters, like the one by "Pan Xiao," generated great sympathy among young workers. As was routine, the official trade union reported this response to the higher authorities.

Meanwhile, reporters of the *Chinese Youth News* wrote in their internal publication, intended for the top leadership, about shocking cases of suicide among youths. The suicide rate was rising nationwide; sometimes more than ten young people took their lives in a suicide pact.[36] In late 1979, the CYL Central Committee published in an internal journal, *Research on the Youth*, a survey by the Student Council of Fudan University in Shanghai, conducted on the campus on September 25,[37] in which students responded to the question, "What worries you most now?" The leading answer (39.6 percent) was: "The present situation and the fate of our country and people" (*you guo you min*). In response to the question, "What is the number one problem confronting political developments in our country?" the leading answer (66.2 percent) was, "The inconsistency of official policies." To the question, "How likely is it that political figures of the type of Lin Biao and of the Gang of Four will rise again in our country within the next ten years?" 50.4 percent said "probable" and 39 percent "unavoidable." These gloomy answers clearly contradicted the then official claim that the political future of the PRC was bright and full of hope. Asked to assess "How long will it be before China can catch up with the United States economically?" 28.2 percent said "100 years," 24.6 percent "50 years," and still 13.6 percent "200 years." Few people seemed to credit the government's promise that China would achieve its goal of "four modernizations" by the early twenty-first century. To the question "What is your belief?" 25 percent responded "fatalism, religion, or capitalism," another 25 percent, "nothing," and 33 percent, "communism." The Fudan survey was one of the earliest of its kind in the PRC. Many of those questioned (including the author) were afraid that their handwriting might be identified by university authorities; taking this anxiety into account, the students' opinions were undoubtedly far more critical than their answers indicated.

---

[36] Quoted from Xing Pensi's internal report: "*Guanyu jinyibu kaizhan zhengli biaozhun taolun de wenti,*" October 1979.

[37] According to my own notes and the records of Xu Bangtai, one of the survey assistants.

Conclusion

The Dengist leadership's appeal to rationalism aimed primarily at the party-state bureaucracy, which had become fearful and intellectually ossified during Mao's reign. Its purpose was to put forward a new principle of legitimacy that would allow changes to be carried out in both the leadership and in policy. Deng and his allies tried to make the results of "doing" the standard for judging ways of "doing," thereby keeping Maoist creeds from affecting the formation of new policies, and rendering instrumental rationality self-justifying.

Progress in the rationalization of political life helped Deng and his allies consolidate their leadership and accomplish most of their immediate objectives. It also unleashed an uncontrollable backlash. The three currents led by the independent-minded OIs, the radical MIs, and the educated youth in general, although they differed in appearance, agreed in substance and all pointed to one fact: The roots of the tragedies of the Cultural Revolution were not only in Mao, Lin Biao, or the Gang of Four, but in the political and economic organization founded in China in 1949. To prevent the recurrence of these tragedies, and to make China into a modern industrial nation, fundamental structural changes were necessary. This mood, which penetrated every layer of the politically concerned Chinese population, was precisely what the Chinese authorities had termed "*san 'xin' weiji*": "the crisis of faith" – having lost faith in Marxism, Maoism, and communism; "the crisis of trust" – no longer trusting party-state officialdom; and "the crisis of confidence" – lacking confidence in the future of the socialist system and the official modernization program (Party Literature Research Center 1982: 354–56).

What China's ruling elite faced in the limited de-Maoization campaign resembled the problem the Soviet ruling elite faced in the de-Stalinization campaign. As a Soviet dissident put it, for the Soviet leadership, criticism of the dead leader's "personality cult" "had given answers to all the questions." But for the politically victimized, manipulated, but awakened, "the questions were only just beginning. We had just had time to be taught that communism was the world's most progressive doctrine and Stalin the incarnation of its ideas when presto, Stalin turned out to be a murderer and a tyrant, a terrible degenerate no better than Hitler! So what was the nature of the ideas that had produced a Stalin? What was the nature of a Party that, once having brought him to power, could no longer stop him?" (Rubenstein 1985: 7–8). One question inevitably led to another and finally to the one that pointed to the structural roots of the horrible past (Rothberg 1972: 42–43).

Lucian Pye (1986: 221–23) notes that Chinese political culture is characteristically hyperoptimistic and avoids systematic critical examination of the past. Pye's observation is superficial; he assumes what the CCP ruling elite publicly said was true, and neglects the attitudes of other elites in Chinese society.

What disturbed the CCP ruling elite most was that the independent-minded OIs and the radical MIs echoed each other (Informant no. 4; see also Deng 1984: 174, 236–39). The former had access to crucial institutional resources and could air their proposals from the official platform; the latter had great experience with grass-roots politics. The convergence of the two had the potential to split the party-state machinery and mobilize the urban population into active opposition.

This crisis, which obviously offered a serious challenge to the post-Mao ruling elite, also contained positive potential. The Dengist leadership's rationalistic appeal alone had not produced the crisis; late Maoist policies were equally – at the very least – responsible. The appeal created conditions for the exposure of the crisis. This national crisis mentality could be manipulated to the leading reformers' political advantage: In this situation, they could sell other power holders on their radical reform projects, and they could more easily overcome the resistance by vested interests to fundamental change. History offers many examples of the use of a sense of crisis to push forward great reforms, as in the cases of the Turkish reform (Lewis 1968), the Meiji reform (Duus 1976: 53–60), and the Gorbachev reform. Among the CCP ruling elite, some could see real possibilities for radical change. In a speech at the "Central Working Conference" of April 1979, Chen Yun clearly showed that leaders like himself well understood that great challenges and opportunities stood side by side. After characterizing two types of persons in China, the absolute pessimist who had lost all hope and the dedicated activist interested solely in exposing the regime's wrongdoing and incompetence, Chen asked:

Why do these two types of people exist? In my view, four reasons. First, they have understood what they didn't before, for example, that workers in foreign countries live a better life than Chinese workers do. To Chinese people, this fact alone can explain many things.

Second, they are no longer willing to listen to the empty words they have heard time and time again. For instance, you tell them: "The situation in China is getting better and better." But they still have to rely on ration coupons to buy food, and stand in long lines before stores. They cannot feed themselves with slogans.

Third, they don't want to be a sacrifice to ideals but a harvester of real benefits. "Communism likes a paradise." "Fine! Let the next generation enjoy it. I only wish my present life better."

Fourth, they are tired of waiting. They have already waited for thirty years [1949–79]. Now they are asked to wait for another thirty years. We even feel unhappy about this ourselves; so do they, of course. Furthermore, they want fair compensation. "For you officials, the sweet comes immediately after the bitter. Is it fair for we folks to stay in the bitter endlessly?"[38]

To cope with the strong resentment in society, Chen considered "three approaches":

Days ago I went to Jiuxianqiao [near Beijing] to speak with peasants and rural cadres. Then I invited several Fengtai [also near Beijing] workers to talk. In addition, I also talked with a number of high school and college students. Afterward, I become more confident about this viewpoint of mine: To cope with the problem, there could be three approaches.

The best way out [*shangce*] is to untie the knots from the roots. To do this, we must prepare to run the risk of losing power, and even get rid of the holy and inviolable symbol [of socialism]. As for the leadership of the Communist party, I'm afraid we can't attend to it much. But a policy so radical can get nobody's approval here. I won't talk about it anymore.

The second-best policy [*zhongce*] is reform, not thoroughgoing but moderate [*gailiang*]. Economic relations must be adjusted within a wide range. Minor operations should be made but on the condition that the existing political power structure must not be touched. For the time being, this approach can gain acceptance from more cadres, and is also more likely to yield quick results.

The unwise policy [*xiace*] is to preserve the status quo. . . . How long can it be preserved? Ten years? Eight years? Not for sure. But it should be no big trouble for three to five years. What about afterward? I'm afraid people of my generation can do little to help. We will rest underground by then.

Now let's study how to carry out operations within the frame of the second-best policy.

It is illuminating to compare Chen Yun's speech with the 1987 private memorandum by Mieczyslaw F. Rakowski, who became prime minister of Poland in fall 1988 (Ash 1990: 264). Poland, Rakowski said, had been living through an economic, social, and political "crisis" since 1980, and "we should not forget that basically symptoms of crisis are becoming apparent in all socialist countries." He went further to comment that "If one could transport a capitalist society into our everyday reality, it would very soon rise up in a revolutionary struggle" (ibid.: 280). According to Ash, the private statements of Hungarian Politburo members in the 1980s "reflect an equally striking realism in the diagnosis of the disease" (ibid.: 281). It is my observation that communism comes to its late, dying stage when not only the tiny, critical intelligentsia; not only the suffering ordinary citizenry; but also the empowered and privileged communist leadership loses confidence in the system. This is the unmistakable indication of the existence of a severe legitimacy crisis for a communist regime: Its leaders realize that truth and history are not on their side, and that they are defending a system that is doomed to fail.

[38] I heard Chen's speech from a Shanghai party official (Informant no. 23) in the winter of 1979. Afterward, I read the speech in the *Seventies* (Hong Kong) No. 4, 1980, and the printed text roughly corresponds with what I have heard. My translation is largely based on that text (pp. 74–75).

As is observed, since the late 1970s, the CCP ruling elite has indeed adopted the "second-best" approach: to undertake major reforms on the economic front and minor ones in the political domain, without touching the basic structure of the power system. The "four cardinal principles" that Deng Xiaoping issued on behalf of the ruling elite symbolized the conditions for permissible reforms in China.

Many observers, such as Stuart Schram (1984: 420–21), believe that some of Deng's harsh acts, like the declaration of the "four cardinal principles," were probably the result of "external constraints" – pressure from sources outside the reformers – rather than that of "internal constraints" – the reformers' own attitudes and preferences. These observers overestimate the difference between Deng and other hard-liners in the ruling elite on issues touching on the power structure. Although their positions on personnel appointments, economic policy, or foreign affairs may have diverged, on the crucial issue of the party's monopoly of political power their views were basically the same. In formulating and stressing his "four cardinal principles," Deng had no argument with other senior leaders at all.[39]

Earlier I have remarked that from the late 1970s to late 1980s there had been a consistent and remarkable growth in the collective self-consciousness of Chinese intellectuals as a politically awakened, independent social stratum with a unique role and responsibility. The three interconnected movements described here represented the starting point of that process.

The consequences that the Dengist leadership's rationalistic appeal invited exemplify the dilemma of legitimation faced by reformist regimes that struggle between ideological-institutional continuity and policy innovations. The devices reformers invent to gain legitimacy can only solve part of the legitimacy crisis by creating new problems, which will soon subject the reformist regime's authority to new challenges. In the rest of this book, we will see how the Deng regime was caught in this situation.

[39] As Ruan Ming relates (1991: 34–35), Hu Qiaomu played a key role in the making of the "four cardinal principles." Informant no. 2 noted that the older generation CCP leaders were all fond of the idea. Informant no. 4 observed that Deng had valued the party bureaucracy's domination over society in particular. Informant no. 24 reminded me of the great resemblance – in word as well as in spirit – between Deng's "four principles" and Mao's "six criteria" (national unity, socialist transformation and construction, the dictatorship of the proletariat, democratic centralism, the leadership of the CCP, and the unity of socialists and peace-loving peoples of all around the world; see Mao 1977: 412), and Lin Biao's "four points" (class struggle, the dictatorship of the proletariat, the primacy of politics, and the guidance of Mao Zedong Thought; see *Peking Review* No. 24, p. 13, 1966). All these informants attended the 1979 forum.

4

"Building socialist spiritual civilization" and the counterelite's response

This chapter is devoted to analyzing the official appeal to socialist morality and its consequences. It describes the sociopolitical background that explains why the Dengist leadership felt it necessary to put great efforts into a massive campaign called "Building a High Level of Socialist Spiritual Civilization" during the first half of the 1980s. It shows how the Dengists' carefully formulated dual-traffic policy, as represented by the appeal to socialist morality, was attacked from both sides.

The hard-liners in the military and party establishment were angry about the Dengist leadership's partial concessions to the functional requirements of modernizing China, for example, opening to the outside, stress on the development of science and education, and respect for technical personnel. They worried that the partial concessions would lead to total decay of the structural uniqueness of Chinese communism.

The counterelite opened fire on the dual-traffic policy from the opposite direction. It was angry about the Dengist leadership's retreat from the commitment to "material civilization" – that is, to modernizing China – and protested that preservation of "socialist uniqueness" could only suffocate the vitality and dynamism recently regenerated in Chinese society through openness. It therefore strove to remove from the official agenda all ideas and policies incompatible with modernizing China.

This chapter aims to demonstrate that the Deng regime's second major device of political legitimation, like its first one, created more predicaments than conveniences for itself.

Background: increasing knowledge of the outside

The movement to "emancipate the mind" launched by the Dengists in the late 1970s encouraged the de-ideologization of public life, meaning the rapid attenuation of the impact of communist ideology on all aspects of society. The crisis of faith, trust, and confidence as portrayed in Chapter 1 exhibited this tendency.

At this time, Chinese society began to have multiplying opportunities to know the outside world, and thereby the effects of horizontal comparison entered the political processes. The following were the main channels that contributed to the Chinese's world awareness.

First, the circulation of the internal daily *Reference News* (*Cankao Xiaoxi*)[1] was expanded in the late 1970s, from "for state cadres only" to "for all cadres, state employees, and university students." This means that legally the daily became accessible to all professionals, urban workers, students in higher educational institutions, urban and rural party officials, and army officers, together making up almost 20 percent of the population.

The contents of the *Reference News* were Chinese translations of news and comments in the foreign media (e.g., the *New York Times,* Reuters, and *L'Express*), covering international events, China's domestic issues (the politically most sensitive parts were omitted, e.g., the internal conflict within the PRC leadership), and major developments in foreign business, industry, science and technology, culture, law, and social life. Subscriptions to the daily reached its peak in the early 1980s, at about eight million per year (Informant no. 31), surpassing all other newspapers in the country. According to the author's observations in various places and institutions during 1978–81, each copy had multiple readers, especially among educated urban workers.

Second, the legal and technical obstacles to listening to foreign radio broadcasting were largely removed. During the Maoist regime, the government systematically jammed foreign radios and punished listeners severely.[2] After Mao's death the government stopped the jamming and the punishment of listeners, tens of millions of people throughout the PRC turned to the Voice of America, the British Broadcasting Company, the Voice of Free China (Taiwan), and other outside sources for news. Even party officials often cited what they heard from the VOA or the BBC to support their arguments at formal mass meetings. In the meantime, more, cheaper, and better radio sets became available on the market:

---

[1] On this daily, see Michael Schoenhals (1985) and Fox Butterfield (1982: 389–90). But Butterfield's judgment that "any Chinese can subscribe" to it was incorrect. Formal restrictions on subscription existed, albeit in practice most urban citizens had access to it after Mao's death.
[2] During the Cultural Revolution, the penalty became severer than before. Late in 1966, under Xie Fuzhi and Kang Sheng, two radical Maoists in charge of the police, a document entitled *Guanyu Wuchanjieji Wenhua Dageming zhong jaqiang gongan gongzhou de ruogan guiding* (Several rules on strengthening public security work in the Great Proletarian Cultural Revolution) was prepared. In January 1967, the document was issued and put into effect by the regime, and known as *Gongan Liutiao* (Six articles on public security). Under it, many people who listened to foreign stations were imprisoned and some even were executed if they not only listened to the broadcasting but also spread the news. In February 1979, the document was declared void by the government.

in 1978, fewer than 8 radio sets per 100 people; in 1983, 20 radio sets; and in 1986, about 25 sets (*China Statistical Yearbook* 1982: 508; 1987: 634).

Third, the translation business was flourishing and translated books were increasingly available to the general public. During the Maoist reign, China had a nationally coordinated translation project in which influential writings published abroad in the social sciences, military studies, the humanities, and literature (especially biography) were promptly and systematically translated into Chinese. But since they were defined as "bourgeois [i.e., the Western] and revisionist [i.e., the Soviet and East European] propaganda," those translations were printed in a very small number of copies, and principally for the reference of party-state officials and OIs who assisted party leaders in fighting foreign ideas; the general public was excluded from the readership.[3]

After Mao, restrictions on the circulation of previously translated books – for example, Sartre's works on existentialism and Churchill's and Nixon's autobiographies – were gradually relaxed. Publishers were permitted to make huge reprints; libraries were able to order them and lend to regular readers; individuals of selected social categories, such as high school and college teachers and university students, were allowed to purchase them on their own.

More important were the newly founded translation projects starting in the late 1970s. In response to the great demand in the educated population for knowledge about the outside, most major publishing houses set up ambitious translation projects: The editors were as eager to know the outside as the readers were, and were excited about the new opportunities to make their publishing houses influential and profitable.

The party-state organs on cultural affairs attempted to regulate this flourishing business by forming a centralized system in 1981 to "decide what titles [in the social sciences] are suitable for translating and which publishing houses should get the assignment" but failed to do so, because publishing institutions engaged in this business were too numerous to supervise.[4] Table 3 shows that since 1978 the publication of translations on social, economic, and political subjects from major foreign languages increased dramatically.[5]

---

[3]According to the sensitivity of the subjects, covers of those translated books were printed in different colors (e.g., dark grey, light grey, yellow, white), with the darker cover signifying the more sensitive subject. The lowest hierarchical level to which those books were circulated was county governments.

[4]Based on Informant no. 32. But this person also admitted that most publishing houses would not go far enough to offend the central authorities by releasing sensitive titles; they usually cooperated with the rule of "internal" versus "open" classification, that is, placing the more sensitive titles in the category of "internal circulation only" – for selected social categories and institutions – and the less sensitive ones in that of "open circulation."

[5]The two setbacks in 1982 and 1985 were apparently caused by two official campaigns, the battle

Table 3. *Publication of translated books (1978–85)*

Source	1978	1979	1980	1981	1982	1983	1984	1985
Communist Europe	9	28	71	88	76	113	134	90
Noncommunist Europe	25	44	86	103	105	105	113	105
United States	5	33	76	67	76	85	112	109
Japan	4	10	35	49	52	39	72	71
Other Noncommunist countries	1	9	17	75	47	111	95	116
Total	44	124	285	382	356	453	526	491
As of 1978	100%	282%	648%	868%	809%	1030%	1195%	1126%

Sources: Quanguo Zong Shumu (Books in print: a general index) 1976–1984 (Beijing: Zhonghua Shuju, 1985); *Zhongguo Guojia Shumu* (A national index of books) 1985 (Beijing: Shumu Wenxian Press, 1987).

When reading this table, notice that the two sources on which it is based do not count the many translations published in the "internal circulation" category, and that many translations from the European Communist countries were in fact the Soviets' and the East Europeans' introductory writings on Western ideas and societies: Chinese publishers used this politically safer channel to pass on information about the West to the public. In estimating the magnitude of Western influence on the educated Chinese, we must take these two factors into consideration.

Another important channel through which the educated Chinese learned of the outside was periodical publications and newspapers carrying translations and introductory writings about foreign things. After Mao's death, new magazines and journals sprang up like mushrooms after rain (see Table 4).

Of the periodical publications, those that specialized in publishing translations (see Table 6, the appendix to this chapter) were particularly instrumental in spreading foreign ideas. Designed to inform educated Chinese of popular culture and social trends, or of the latest books, essays, conferences, and discussions in the fields of social and cultural studies in foreign countries, most of these periodicals were available in public and college libraries, and some were open to private subscriptions.

Still another channel through which the Chinese learned of the outside was Chinese visitors' reports. After Mao's death, more officials and elite intellectuals had chances to visit foreign countries. Upon returning home, the visitors were

against "bourgeois liberalization" in 1981 as symbolized in the attack on the movie *Unrequited Love* made by Bai Hua et al. (see Chapter 5), and the Anti–Spiritual Pollution Campaign in 1983–84. Because the publishing cycle in China was very slow, the impact of such campaigns on the publishing industry became visible in the next year's statistics.

Table 4. *Growth of periodicals in China (1977–87)*

Year	Number of periodicals	Total copies (millions)	As of 1977
1977	628	560	100%
1979	1,470	1,180	211%
1981	2,801	1,460	261%
1983	3,415	1,770	316%
1985	4,705	2,560	457%
1987	5,687	2,590	463%

Source: Zhongguo Chuban Nianjian (China's yearbook of publishing) 1989 (Beijing: Commercial Press, 1989).

often asked by their colleagues to present what they had seen, heard about, and thought of during their trips. In oral reports, they were more willing to tell the story in an informative and direct manner than in their formal writings,[6] and their talks were often recorded by organizers of such meetings and then distributed, through informal or official networks, to a wide range of institutions as "information for internal reference only," reaching hundreds of thousands of people.

Among these visitors' reports, Huan Xiang's and Wen Yuankai's perhaps were the most influential. In April 1979, Huan, who just left the post of ambassador to the European Community, gave a talk in Beijing to an audience of officials and intellectuals. Huan detailed economic growth in Western European countries during the 1960s and 1970s and the accompanying changes in the social structure and way of life in these countries. For example, advances in technology gave rise to a white-collar middle class and caused the traditional working class to diminish, and the combination of parliamentary politics and a welfare system eroded the foundation of class struggle in advanced industrial societies.

Audio tapes and written records of Huan's presentation were passed down even to the county level. Local party leaders, regular office workers, teachers,

[6] Even Deng Liqun fell into this behavior pattern. In his oral report on his 1979 visit to Japan given to the social science circles in Beijing, Deng favorably portrayed Japan's economy and society: workers' and farmers' high incomes; workers' participation in management and identification with their companies; a well-balanced industrial structure; a good social welfare system; wise economic planning by the government; and admirable "mood of society" and "spiritual and moral quality" of citizens. Deng admitted that in these respects capitalist Japan did much better than socialist China. He even went so far as saying that he had found "some features of communism" that Marx dreamed of in the Japanese socioeconomic structure.

Deng's report became widely known in the capital and other major cities, and then appeared, in a modified form, in the monthly *Jingji Guanli* (No. 3, pp. 1–9, 1979). During the Anti–Spiritual Pollution Campaign, when Deng made a harsh criticism of intellectuals who praised capitalism over socialism, many intellectuals in the CASS and provincial academies took out his report and made fun of him.

and college students all got the chance to listen and read.[7] The capitalist world Huan described was so different from what the Chinese had been told about in the official media and classroom, and they were astonished by the prosperity in the West.[8]

Wen's reports were even more popular than Huan's. Unlike Huan, Wen focused on the ways of doing things and the details of daily life in the West, Hong Kong, and Japan: how fast people walked, spoke, and greeted each other; how quickly a business deal could be made on the spot; how customers were treated in stores; how individual rights and privacy were respected; how easy it was to make telephone calls from country to country, get cash from automatic money tellers, and do shopping through mail-order companies and in super-markets; how laboratories were equipped and operated; how companies valued talented experts; and how open competition for scholarships was practiced. When talking about these details, Wen never forgot to make contrasts with China, inspiring his audience to look critically at everything in their own society.

Moreover, Wen took advantage of his status as a known chemist and lectured the audience about the ongoing technological revolution in the capitalist world. He warned his fellow countrymen that if they failed to make sweeping changes in their mentality and in the ways that China's economy and society were managed, the Chinese would inevitably be enslaved by the advanced nations.

From 1980 on, Wen was invited by youth organizations and work units to give talks all over the country.[9] His reports were printed in hundreds of thousands of copies and even used as study material for youth in several provinces.[10]

To the ordinary Chinese who had been isolated from the rest of the world for so long, such eyewitness reporting was truly a remarkable process of national education. The shocking and eye-opening effect was very much like the impact on the Japanese of Iwakura Misson's reports. In 1871, Japan sent a team of observers to the West. During the next two years they kept reporting to their countrymen the power and wealth of the industrial West. For the first time, the Japanese became aware how far ahead of them the "Western barbarians" were,

---

[7] Personal observations in Anhui, Jiangsu, and Shanghai.

[8] It is no accident that Huan later became a major figure backing the *World Economic Herald*.

[9] When Wen was invited to talk to the students and faculty at Fudan University, Shanghai, in 1981, which the author attended, students who came from many other places said that Wen had already visited their home provinces.

[10] For example, one of Wen's speeches, *China's Megatrend* published by the Shanghai People's Publishing House in 1984, had 300,000 copies for the first printing. Another one of his speeches, *The Dawn of the Reforms* by the Shanxi People's Publishing House in 1984, was printed in the same quantity for the first printing and was assigned by the provincial authorities as "young workers' study material." Wen was put under house arrest, because of his involvement in the Democracy Movement, for many months after the spring of 1989.

and this awareness contributed immensely to the Japanese determination to change their society (Duus 1976: 82–90).

Last but not least was the contribution of tourism. During the last years of Mao's reign, except for a few "guests of the state," almost no outside visitors were present in Chinese society. After Mao's death, tourists came to China in the number of millions every year (Table 5).

Of the millions of foreigners (i.e., nonethnic Chinese), about three quarters came from industrialized capitalist countries. From these tourists' clothes, luggage, facial expressions, and way of talking, the average Chinese who never had a chance to see the outside world now could imagine the quality of life and the degree of individual freedom in capitalist countries.

In this respect, post-Mao China shared similar experiences with the post-Stalin Soviet Union. In 1957 the International Youth Festival was held in Moscow for the first time, bringing thousands of young Europeans to the city, which had been isolated by the Stalin regime from the outside for decades. A young Russian, who later became a dissident, remembered "following a group of young Scandinavians about the city. He never spoke to them, but by their clothes and demeanor he recognized a sense of personal freedom and nonchalance that his own generation, born after the Revolution, lacked completely" (Rubenstein 1985: 13).

To the PRC residents, the contrast between themselves and the Chinese visitors from outside the PRC was even more irritating. As Table 5 indicates, each year millions of ethnic Chinese visited the mainland (many were frequent visitors), mostly from Hong Kong and Taiwan, the two places the Communist party used to describe as the "hells on earth," because they were ruled by a colonial government and the "reactionary KMT."

The ethnic Chinese tourists had more freedom than Westerners when traveling in China: They spoke local dialects, had relatives somewhere, and hence could reach various levels of society. When returning to hometowns or ancestors' villages, they normally brought expensive gifts for their relatives. They would also, of course, tell stories about their lives and the general situation overseas. The PRC residents could not help but question: "Who lives in the hell? They or we?"

In brief, when the Deng regime opened China's door to the outside, the Chinese people were already disillusioned with communism owing to their suffering in the past. The "opened door" contributed to the political process by providing Chinese citizens with reference groups that could be compared to their own system and considered as alternatives to it.

This effect can be discerned from the following questions that people raised

Table 5. *Development of tourism in China (1978–88) (thousands)*

	1978	1980	1982	1984	1986	1988
Total number of tourists	1,809	5,703	7,924	12,852	22,819	31,695
Foreigners	230	529	765	1,134	1,482	1,842
Chinese from Hong Kong, Taiwan, and Macao	1,562	5,139	7,117	11,670	21,269	29,773
Ethnic Chinese from other countries	18	34	43	48	68	79
Of foreigners, % of those from industrial democracies	N/A	N/A	75%	76%	74%	72%

Sources: China Statistical Yearbook 1985: 504; 1986: 536; 1989: 650.

at political meetings. As discussed in the appendix to this book, these questions have been "smoothed over" considerably by the collectors.

Questions common among soldiers and army officers were:

Why is it that our people's living standards have been improved so slowly? Does the reason lie in the socialist system? . . . In some capitalist nations, science and technology are advanced and the economies are highly developed. Can we say that these facts demonstrate that capitalism is not decaying but superior to socialism? (PLA Publishing House Q & A Editorial Group 1984: 3, 6)[11]

Among civil servants, workers, professionals, and university students, the same questions were put more sharply:[12]

Our country's level of economic development and science-technology are far behind capitalist countries'. Since we admit that practice is the sole criterion for testing truth, and that practice of production is the basic form of human practice, we should admit logically that socialism is indeed inferior to capitalism. (Zhang Yi 1989: 16)

In capitalist countries, workers' living standards have been gradually improved with the evolution of capitalism. . . . In the face of this reality, how can the Marxian theory of pauperization [i.e., workers are getting poorer and poorer under capitalism] hold? With

[11] The editor of this question and answer material noted that the questions collected therein had been raised in political meetings in the grass-roots units of the PLA since 1979 (PLA Publishing House Q & A Editorial Group 1984: ii).

[12] The editor of this question and answer material explained in the preface that: "The questions here have been put forward by cadres, workers, and university students at dialogue meetings. Some panelists did not dare to speak out publicly, so they told me their true opinion in private conversations. Most of these questions have been raised again and again over the years, and bothered us" (Zhang Yi 1989: 2).

In comparing the questions collected by Zhang with those by the Shanghai Municipal Commission for Education and Public Health (1987), one finds a great resemblance, which indicates the representativeness of these opinions.

improvement in their quality of life, how is it possible that the proletariat still want to make revolutions? (ibid.: 30)

As to the question of democracy, soldiers and army officers wondered:

In the past, there has been very little democracy in our country. What was the reason? Caused by the people's democratic dictatorship [the code for the communist system of government]? (PLA Publishing House Q & A Editorial Group 1984: 54)

In the civilian sectors of the population, the question was formulated in this way:

Why is it that we get this feeling: Bourgeois democracy is said to be phony, but in practice it appears to be real; socialist democracy is said to be real, but in practice it appears to be phony? We can hardly accept the saying that bourgeois democracy is for the minority of exploiters. But it is very easy for us to accept the saying that socialist democracy is not as good as bourgeois democracy. . . . Capitalist countries legally allow communist parties to exist, the proletariat to publish progressive things like Marx's *Capital,* and citizens to protest in the streets and condemn presidents. But in our country, reactionary parties are not allowed to exist and reactionary journals are not allowed to publish. In this regard, our democracy is not as extensive as bourgeois democracy. (Zhang Yi 1989: 223, 226)

The preceding material reflects the state of mind of the citizenry in general. Among university students, Western influence took a rather sophisticated form. During the 1980–81 academic year, the Shanghai Municipal CYL Committee conducted a survey at several universities, and concluded that while Marxist and Maoist teachings were openly mocked at "political and ideological education" classes, modern Western philosophies, mainly existentialism, Freudianism, and Nietzscheanism, and Christianity were the concepts that Chinese university students were most interested in.[13]

In the report the Shanghai CYL Committee sent to the central authorities in Beijing, this trend was labeled as "the second shock to Marxism and socialism" (the first was the crisis of faith, trust, and confidence). Understandably, the report caused a great concern among the ruling elite.[14]

Western influence on university students was not limited to Shanghai. In a survey conducted by sociologists in January 1983 at seventeen universities in

[13] I came to know the survey and the party leadership's reaction to it in the fall of 1981, and was informed by a party official working at a Shanghai university. Then I went to the Shanghai Institute of Foreign Languages, the Shanghai University, the Huadong Normal University, and Fudan University to talk to upper-class undergraduate students and graduate students, and the survey message was basically confirmed. The material collected by Zhang Yi (1989: 262–65) also shows the prevalence of the trend among the best-educated in other parts of the country.

[14] Starting in late 1981, the PCPD, the Ministry of Education, and the CYL Central Committee arranged for a group of writers to attack modern Western philosophical trends and suppress their influence, see articles published in *China's Youth* (No. 1, 1982), *Philosophical Studies* (Nos. 2 and 11, 1982), *Wenhui Bao* (June 18 and November 17, 1982), *Study and Think* (No. 7, 1982), *Red Flag* (No. 23, 1982), etc.

Beijing, Tianjin, Shengyang, and Dalian,[15] the respondents expressed a "philosophy of life [*renshengguan*]" sharply contradictory to the party-state's instruction. When asked to mark his or her number one expectation from a list, those choosing "to join the party or the CYL" counted only 5.5 percent, far less than those choosing "to raise my professional skills" (50.4 percent), "to succeed in entrance examinations for graduate schools" (10.1 percent), "to have a colorful leisure time" (9.9 percent), or "to make friends" (8.6 percent). Forty percent of the respondents believed that "communist ideology contradicts the selfish nature of human beings and therefore is unworkable," that "communism lacks positive proof from the realities," and that "communism is irrelevant to me."

The appeal to socialist morality

What I have described clearly indicates that the Chinese Communist regime faced a serious challenge to its moral and political authority from within the educated population, especially the youth. The ruling elite was deeply disturbed by two mutually reinforcing trends in Chinese society in the early 1980s: the disillusionment with the system at home and the interest in foreign ideas and government models. To counteract the challenge to its legitimacy, the party leadership began a campaign to "build socialist spiritual civilization" in the early 1980s.[16]

In December 1980 when the party's Central Committee held a working conference, the issue of how to build "socialist spiritual civilization" was a major topic. In his keynote speech at the meeting, Deng Xiaoping gave an authoritative explanation of the official campaign:

[15]The survey was done by Zhao Zixiang et al. and reported in *Shehuikexue Zhanxian* No. 1, 1984, under the title "*Guanyu Daxuesheng de Renshengguan Zhuangkuang he Tedian de Yanjiu.*"
[16]The term "socialist spiritual civilization" was used first in Ye Jianying's speech at the rally celebrating the thirtieth anniversary of the founding of the PRC (*People's Daily* September 30, 1979). But it did not receive much attention until late 1980. In December, Li Chang wrote to the party-state leadership to express his worry over the post-Mao tendency to "neglect the role of spiritual values." He suggested that the general goal of the party and the nation should not be defined as the attainment of "four modernizations" only, but must include the "construction of socialist spiritual civilization" as well. He recommended this goal because after the Cultural Revolution, "feudal and bourgeois ideologies and colonial mentality" spread widely in the party, and "party members and the general population are somewhat lax in ideology" (*Banyuetan* February 10, 1981).

The notion of "spiritual civilization" and its counterpart, "material civilization," were the products of a debate in China on the conflict between the East and the industrial West during the first decade of this century. On the origins and usages of these two notions, see Su Shaozhi and Ding Xueliang: "China and the Making of the New, Socialist Spiritual Civilization," a research report for the United Nations' Educational, Scientific and Cultural Organization (*Selected Studies on Marxism* No. 1, 1984). Roughly speaking, "material civilization" in modern Chinese means the way and state of material life and, correspondingly, "spiritual civilization" means the way and state of intellectual and spiritual life (cf. Wiener 1973: Vol. 1, pp. 613–21, for discussion on the Western usages of "civilization" and "culture").

The socialist China we are building should have a high level of material civilization as well as a high level of spiritual civilization. When I speak of a high level of spiritual civilization, I refer not only to education, science, and culture (which are of course indispensable) but also to communist thinking, ideals, beliefs, morality and discipline, as well as a revolutionary stand and revolutionary principles, comradely relations among people, and so on. (Deng 1984: 348, with my editing)

Over the next two years, the regime invested great efforts in popularizing the program. In early 1981, the military leadership took the lead to start a campaign in the army known as "Four haves, three stresses, and two defy's" – "To have lofty ideals, moral integrity, knowledge, and a strong physique; to stress appearance and bearing, manners, and sense of discipline; and to defy hardships and sacrifice" (Deng 1984: 416). Meanwhile, the PCPD and the Ministries of Public Security, of Education, of Culture, and of Public Health, with the assistance of trade unions and student and women's organizations, pushed forward a similar program among the urbanites. A year later, the party's Central Committee and the State Council decided that from 1982 on March would be "the month of civilization and manners," during which campaigns to breed communist values and decorum should be intensified (Party Literature Research Center 1982: 1285–98).

The techniques the regime used in the campaign were typical of Chinese Communist politics: to impress and mobilize the masses with easily remembered slogans. By repeating these simplified slogans, the regime aimed to make party policies and officially sanctioned norms part of the popular culture, and eventually to integrate them into people's subconsciousness. Such techniques had been used over and over again in earlier campaigns, such as the "Three-Anti and Five-Anti movements" of 1951–52 (Schurmann 1968: 315–27) and the Cultural Revolution (Lee 1978).

Why did "building socialist spiritual civilization" suddenly acquire a position in the regime's agenda parallel to that of "attaining four modernizations"? Party leaders later gave further explanations. As Hu Qiaomu acknowledged:

To resist the erosive influence of bourgeois ideology, we cannot rely on the policy of "distribution according to work" only. Because our country is large and poor and has a huge population, even after our GNP multiplies twice and tops the world, our per capita income will be still far below those of the advanced capitalist countries. Therefore, we must rely mainly on Communist ideology to battle the erosive influence of bourgeois ideology. (*People's Daily* September 24, 1982)

In a document prepared by Deng Liqun's Policy Research Center, the rationale was elaborated in this way:

If we do not develop socialist spiritual civilization . . . , and if we see socialism only as a course to accumulate wealth and improve the conditions of production and living standards, we will be caught in an extremely one-sided understanding of socialism and direct the people's attention exclusively to the construction of material civilization or even the pursuit of material interests. Letting things go this way, we will be unable to orientate the modernization program to the socialist direction. Our socialist society will lose its ideal and goal, develop lopsidedly, and deteriorate. (Party Literature Research Center 1985: 622)

It is clear that "building socialist spiritual civilization" was added to the official scheme of national goals mainly because the existing system would have lost its raison d'être if the regime set up national goals in such purely instrumental terms as those of the modernization of industry, agriculture, defense, and science and technology. For in every *measurable* respect, the performance or, to use the official code, "practice" of the Chinese Communist system was far poorer than that of capitalism in the West, Japan, Hong Kong, and Taiwan. "To catch up with foreign countries in economic and technological modernization, you must adopt the universally workable economic and political institutions!" – This was precisely the demand that the general public posed to the ruling elite, as seen in the question and answer material and surveys cited earlier.

Huntington (1991: 258–59) points out that "performance legitimacy plays a role in democratic regimes, but . . . it is secondary to procedural legitimacy." If a democratic system experiences a legitimacy crisis, it can renew itself through the process of elections. In contrast, "the legitimacy of authoritarian regimes (including, in the end, communist regimes) came to rest almost entirely on performance." If they fail to deliver what they have promised, for example, a high rate of economic growth, there exist no mechanisms of self-renewal for these regimes, and they will face the total erosion of their legitimacy.

The PRC ruling elite clearly understood this danger. "Building socialist spiritual civilization" was thus designed to deemphasize the issue of performance in regime legitimation. Entirely resting on performance legitimacy rendered the Communist system vulnerable to the popular push for sweeping change in every aspect of the existing order. The ruling elite wished to control change by excluding two important spheres, the political and the moral, from change.

In formulating the socialist-moral appeal and planning the program, the ruling elite drew inspiration mainly from two predecessors – China's conservative reformers of the late nineteenth century and the Soviet leadership of the 1960s and 1970s.

In the late nineteenth century, when China encountered its greatest crisis in its contact with the industrial West, cries for fundamental changes arose from a group of Western-influenced intellectuals but met strong objections from the powerful imperial bureaucracy. Gradually, some moderate scholar-officials began to acknowledge the superiority of the West in producing wealth and power but still maintained the superiority of the Chinese in moral values. They developed a theory to advocate moderate modernizing movements to respond to the Western challenge, known as *Zhongti Xiyong* (Chinese learning as essence and Western learning as utility) – that is, to manage the state and society in light of the Chinese classics but to adopt Western techniques to make the country rich and powerful (Teng and Fairbank 1979: 183; see 50–186 of this collection for more details). As Joseph Levenson (1965: 69) notes, this prescription has never lost its appeal since it was expressed.

After Ye Jianying first mentioned "socialist spiritual civilization" in October 1979, the Institute of Information in the CASS began to publish systematically, in its internal as well as open journals, translations of Soviet literature on "the development of socialist spiritual culture," "the making of new socialist man," and "the perfection of the socialist way of life."[17]

The reasons the Soviet regime was interested in these theories were that, first, Soviet society faced serious problems such as alcoholism, family crises, juvenile delinquency, and the reemergence of religions. The regime needed certain frameworks to deal with these practical issues. Second, being aware of Western sociology on the "welfare state," "mass consumption society," and "quality of life," Soviet leaders felt it necessary to have conceptual weapons to counter these "bourgeois ideas" and convince Soviet citizens of the superiority of communist society (see Soviet official statements on this matter in Saikowski and Gruliow 1962: 104; Hodnett 1974: 246; and *Current Soviet Policies VIII* 1981: 23). The Chinese ruling elite was very impressed by Soviet experience in this respect.[18]

Tension between "material" and "spiritual civilization"

There is no evidence that the socialist-moral appeal has helped the Communist regime to repair its legitimacy. Soon after the campaign to "build socialist spiritual civilization" was started, there was a popular saying among urban Chinese satirizing the official effort: *Wuzhi bu gou, jingshen lai cou* (When the material is in short supply, the spiritual is used to make up for it). In the question and answer material, a sort of public opinion poll, many questions were directed against the regime's attempt to reinforce the influence of communist values and Marxist principles in public life. For instance, soldiers and army officers asked, "Why does our 'four modernizations' program have to be guided by Marxism, Leninism, and Mao Zedong Thought? Without the guidance of these ideologies, capitalist countries have achieved modernization. Haven't they?" (PLA Publishing House Q & A Editorial Group 1984: 16). The civilian version of that

[17] Based on my survey, during 1982–84, of the institute's publications, mainly *Guowai Shehuikexue Dongtai*, *Guowai Shehuikexue Cankaoziliao*, and *Guowai Shehuikexue*.
[18] On post-Mao Chinese leaders' increasing interest in Soviet experience, see Gilbert Rozman (1987).

statement was: "Taiwan does not take Marxism as its guide but its per capita GNP exceeds ours. Why should we insist on having Marxism as our guide?" (Zhang Yi 1989: 259; see a similar statement in Shanghai Municipal Commission for Education and Public Health 1987: 178).

University students made an interesting comparison between what the Communist regime promoted and what it suppressed in the campaign to "build socialist spiritual civilization": "It is said that Marxism is truth, but we are not interested in it. It is said that Sartre's and Freud's stuff are not truth, but we are however interested in them. Is that strange?" (Zhang Yi 1989: 264).

It must be made clear that the Dengists' purpose for the campaign was not exactly to put the modernization program under the strict guide of Marxism and Maoism, as the official rhetoric stated. The real purpose was to match "material civilization," namely, the modernizing effort, with "socialist spiritual civilization," thereby keeping a delicate balance between the changes they pursued in "hardware" (i.e., the economic domain) and the continuity they wished to preserve in "software" (i.e., the political domain). But this device of maintaining regime legitimacy and stability in a changing environment proved extremely difficult to implement. The internal contradictions in this "dual-traffic" policy were immediately brought out by competing political and social groups.[19]

A group of political leaders in the army was the first to transform this policy into a political struggle, known as the "Zhao Yiya incident." On August 6, 1982, the CCP Central Committee held a plenum, announcing the Twelfth Party Congress to be open on September 1. In mid-August, an almost-final version of party chief Hu Yaobang's keynote speech to the scheduled congress was circulated at higher levels of leadership. Following Deng Xiaoping's formula, Hu Yaobang (1982: 40) elaborated that "socialist spiritual civilization consists of two aspects, the cultural and the ideological." Whereas the ideological aspect by definition has "class character" (i.e., is extremely partisan) and defers to Communist ideals and party discipline, the cultural aspect is, relatively speaking, politically neutral.

It refers to the development of undertakings such as education, science, art and literature, the press and publishing industries, broadcasting and television facilities, public health and physical culture, and libraries and museums, as well as the raising of the level of general knowledge of the people. It is an important requisite both for the building of a material civilization and for the raising of people's political consciousness and moral standards. (Hu Yaobang 1982: 40, with editing)

In view of the habitual practice of antiintellectualism in party officialdom, for example, "underestimation of the importance of education, science, and culture

---

[19]The following is based on Informant no. 6. This important incident has received only marginal attention in Western scholarship (see Ginsberg 1984: 46 and Schram 1984: 434).

and discrimination against intellectuals," Hu expressed a strong commitment to the development of education and the cultural enterprise (ibid.: 41). He announced that in reforming the bureaucracy, the party leadership would ensure that the newly recruited or promoted must be – in addition to politically acceptable – younger, better educated, and professionally competent (ibid.: 70).

On August 28, 1982, just four days before the scheduled party congress, the military establishment's mouthpiece, *Liberation Army Press,* printed a major article by Zhao Yiya, its deputy editor in chief and a member of the leading organ in charge of political affairs in the army. Entitled "Communist Ideology Is the Core of Socialist Spiritual Civilization," the article made two strong arguments against Hu.

First, Zhao insisted that not only the ideological aspect of "spiritual civilization" has class character, but that the cultural aspect does as well. Furthermore, Zhao contended that like "spiritual civilization," "material civilization" also has class character. For example, the automation technology in capitalist society is of capitalist nature – it is used for the bourgeoisie's class interest. Here Zhao simply disparaged Deng, who repeatedly pronounced:

We cannot say that everything developed in capitalist countries is of a capitalist nature. For instance, technology and science – including its branch industrial management – that have been developed in capitalist countries will be useful in any society or country. We intend to acquire advanced technology, science, and management skills to serve our socialist economy. And these things as such have no class character. (Deng 1984: 333, with editing)

By attaching a class label to every sphere of culture and civilization, Zhao uprooted the rationale of the open-door and reform policies: Why should socialist China learn from capitalist nations, since everything over there is of a capitalist nature? By virtue of their "proletarian nature . . . our party, our army, our country, and our society are the most progressive and hence the most 'civilized' in the world" (*Liberation Army Press* August 28, 1982). According to this assessment, the post-Mao course of learning from advanced industrial nations was truly "a great leap backward."

Second, Zhao fiercely attacked the Dengist formula that educational attainments and professional competence should be an important factor in bureaucratic recruitment and promotion. In his report, Hu quoted Deng's famous saying that set up four standards for the official training program – "lofty ideals, moral integrity, general education, and a sense of discipline." Zhao omitted "general education" and challenged Deng's claim:

Someone said that without a certain level of general education, one can hardly have lofty ideals and moral integrity. This saying is wrong. . . . In the West, many individuals have diplomas and degrees but act as lackeys of the bourgeoisie . . . In contrast, Lei Feng [see Chapter 3] and numerous unknown heroes in our revolutionary ranks have very little education, but their lofty ideals and moral standards deserve to be emulated by all of us. (*Liberation Army Press* August 28, 1982)

Zhao's polemic article was immediately reprinted on the Shanghai-based *Jiefang Daily,* by the directive of Chen Yi, a party secretary and propaganda chief in the Shanghai Municipal Party Committee, who once was a division director of the army's General Political Department and had strong connections with the military establishment.

Earlier I argued that to the politically concerned population, including the huge number of government employees working in the state machinery, the top leadership's political appeals matter in two senses: These appeals induce them to believe the worthiness of the existing order to be recognized, and these appeals also indicate policy directions that will affect their ideal or material interests. This second aspect is particularly true in communist systems, where differences over concrete policy issues cannot be addressed to the public in a simple and direct manner but instead have to be played out through highly symbolic and abstract codes of communication. To the outsider, such codes are merely "ideological stuff," meaning rhetoric that is out of touch with real life and that nobody truly believes in. But to those living in the system, such codes tell who is fighting against whom for what.

In the case under discussion, the debate over "spiritual civilization" was a struggle over the meaning of socialism in the circumstances of opening and reform: If China must be opened to the capitalist world in order to modernize itself and should reform its economic system in line with market principles, then why should the socialist political and normative order be preserved?

In the meantime, the debate was also a struggle over concrete issues: Those placing emphasis on the political dimension of "spiritual civilization" wanted to keep China a Maoist state, with strict party-state control of society, no economic liberalization, no contact with the outside, no professionals in officialdom, and no freedom for intellectual life. On the other hand, those putting weight on the educational and cultural dimension of the notion intended to push China in the opposite direction: more money and freedom for education, science, and cultural enterprise; enhancement of intellectuals' social status; the autonomy of society vis-à-vis the party-state; and unrestricted personal and intellectual exchange between China and the capitalist world. The Dengist leadership, however, attempted to keep a balance between these two sides.

Understandably, Deng and his comrades were shocked by the attack launched by the *Liberation Army Press,* which opened fire on major reform policies on the eve of a party congress, clearly indicating that it was aimed to bring about change both in policy and personnel. In September, Deng removed Politburo member Wei Guoqing from chairmanship of the PLA's General Political Department and had the *Liberation Army Press* publish a self-criticism (September 27, 1982), which admitted that the publication of Zhao's article was evidence of persistent influence of "leftism," that is, Maoist radicalism, among military and party officials.

Some members of the counterelite, especially those in the CASS and the *People's Daily,* saw an opportunity in the clash between the Dengist leadership and the hard-liners. They attempted to launch a counterattack on the hard-liners and further push the leadership to abandon the campaign to build "spiritual civilization." But, fearful of offending the military establishment too much, Deng kept other newspapers from attacking the *Liberation Army Press* (Informants nos. 6 and 24). Determined to maintain the dual-traffic policy, the leadership refused to cancel the campaign, even though the leadership itself was hurt by that campaign.

The Dengist leadership's handling of the "Zhao Yiya incident" did not, however, stop the attempt from within the party establishment to alter the dual-traffic policy. One example of this challenge came in the spring of 1983: With the endorsement of Chen Yun and Peng Zhen, the PCPD and the Policy Research Center of the party's Central Secretariat initiated a national indoctrination program known as "Hold High the Banner of Communism." The outline for this program, entitled "Communism as Practical Activity and as Ideological Education" (*Sixiang Zhengzhi Gongzuo Yanjiu* No. 2, 1983), was issued to all party cells and work units. State employees, especially party members, were urged to apply the outline to their work.

The outline warned the whole party that since the policy of economic reform and opening to the outside was enacted, capitalist influence in China had been increased (section 3). The "purity of communism can be saved" only by building a "socialist spiritual civilization" that takes communist ideology as its core (sections 6 and 14). A central element in that ideology is "the attitude to work": Communists should not work for money, so that "the currently emphasized policy of distribution according to work must not be regarded the highest revolutionary value" (section 8). Party members "should oppose the erroneous trend '*yiqie xiang qian kan*' [always think of money]" (section 4).

As mentioned in Chapter 3, the policy of "distribution according to work" (i.e., material incentives) was the chief measure the Dengists introduced in the economic reforms. It was the rationale the Dengists used to defend the "household responsibility system" in agriculture and the wage differential and bonus system in the industry.

The outline also complained of Deng Xiaoping's and Zhao Ziyang's tactics for justifying the semicapitalistic economic reforms. Highly controversial measures were often labeled "socialist," for example, "the socialist individual economy," "socialist markets," and "the socialist system of responsibility." "We must not label things that are definitely capitalist as noncapitalist," protested the outline. "We must not label things that are definitely nonsocialist as socialist" (section 5). Commenting on the post-Mao reform allowing limited liberalization in the economy and limited relaxation in political life, the outline cautioned reformist leaders in the party:

> Never trade our great course for temporary results. . . . Never sell the proletariat's principal interests for real or conceived small gains. The pragmatic measures we have taken to solve day-to-day practical issues are after all for the realization of the great ideal of communism and should never deviate from it. To carry out reforms we have to make necessary concessions, but we must keep ourselves clear-headed. (section 14)

Having failed to launch a counterattack on the hard-liners during the "Zhao Yiya incident" and undo once and for all the program of "building socialist spiritual civilization," the counterelite, mainly critical CIs and independent-minded OIs, engaged in a long battle. Those involved were for the most part members of national and provincial institutes for social and cultural studies; people working for the mass media; and junior professors, graduate students, and upper-class undergraduate students at universities. They organized activity primarily through semiofficial and official institutions,[20] with their statements being printed in "cliquish journals," semiindependent newspapers, professional journals, and the official press. This pattern was typical of nonconformity and

---

[20]The major events included several panel discussions organized by the Institute of Marxism, Leninism, and Mao Zedong Thought in Beijing in November 1982, with more than sixty people attending; discussions on "Western material civilization versus Eastern spiritual civilization" initiated by the Editorial Committee of the Wuhan-based *Youth's Forum* during late 1984 to late 1986; a conference held in Fuzhou on "Problems Regarding the Construction of Spiritual Civilization in the Urban Areas" in November 1985, jointly organized by the Provincial Academies of Social Sciences of Hubei, Sichuan, and Fujian; a symposium on "Reforming the Economic System and Building Socialist Spiritual Civilization" sponsored by the Chinese Society of Scientific Socialism and its Beijing branch in December 1985, where more than fifty panelists presented their papers; a meeting with about seven dozen participants, co-initiated by the *Guangming Daily*, the Chinese Society of Scientific Socialism, and the Institute of Marxism in February 1986 in Beijing; a seminar on "Theories of Reform under the Current Circumstances" in May 1986 in Shanghai, sponsored by the Municipal Party Propaganda Department and the Shanghai Social Sciences Association; a workshop on "Youths, Reforms, and Spiritual Civilization," which was made possible by the Research Center of the CYL Central Committee in July 1986; a conference on "Developing the Socialist Commodity Economy and Building Socialist Spiritual Civilization" hosted by the Guizhou Provincial Economics Association in the city of Guiyang in August 1986; during the same month a conference held in Jinan by the Shandong Provincial Society of Scientific Socialism; again during the same month a symposium hosted by the Shanxi Provincial Party Propaganda Department in Taiyuan on "Reforms and the Development of Spiritual Civilization," in which more than one hundred people participated; and in December 1986 a national conference on "Urban Communities and Spiritual Civilization" took place in Chongqing, with two hundred or more delegates attending. (Data about these meetings were provided by members of the Chinese Society of Scientific Socialism.)

opposition in post-Mao China and explains why the notion of institutional para-sitism, rather than that of civil society versus the state, is more appropriate in such circumstances.

Some members of the counterelite, usually the older ones, employed a strat-egy similar to the hard-liners' – to use one half of the dual-traffic policy to kill the other. The younger members took an almost frontal attack on the campaign to "build socialist spiritual civilization." Let me cite a few examples to illuminate each of these undertakings.

In response to the military and party hard-liners' outcry, many intellectuals contended that to expose China to the outside did not impair, but instead helped, the growth of "spiritual civilization" in China. As the hard-liners' attack focused on the southeastern region where contact with the capitalist world was intensive, the counterelite cited progress in that region to fight back. In the fall of 1982, an investigative report on life styles in Guangzhou (Canton) stated that "spiritual civilization" there was healthy:

> The appraisal that opening to the outside can bring only negative effects to spiritual civilization is unfounded. The capitalist world's education, science, and technology con-tain many things that we should absorb and make use of. . . . Even in the ideological and moral sphere of the capitalist world, which has strong class character, things can be transplanted into our country through critical selection. (*Guangming Daily* October 25, 1982)

Here the intellectuals attempted to depoliticize the notion of "spiritual civili-zation" and make it a denotation of things with universal values as opposed to the regime's denotation of the term, which meant communist attitudes.

Immediately after the Anti–Spiritual Pollution Campaign of 1983–84 that targeted foreign influence, members of the Institute of Juvenile Studies in Beijing went down to Xiamen (Amoy) and used their survey to refute the charge that "opening to the outside causes spiritual pollution."[21] They argued that the moral state and "spiritual quality" of the youth in Xiamen were far better than before, because openness exposed them to cultural heritages of not only Chinese civilization but of all civilizations (*Hebeidaxue Xuebao* No. 2, pp. 1–7, 1984). Reports on the beliefs and life-styles of the youth in Guangzhou (*Guangzhou Yanjiu* No. 4, pp. 18–22, 1984) and Shenzhen (*Zhongshandaxue Xuebao* No. 3, pp. 62–66, 1986) by two groups of sociologists made the same statement.

A commentary in the *Guangming Daily*, which was based on the speeches

---

[21] Soviet Communists used the term "ideological AIDS" to denote political trends that they disliked (Brovkin 1990: 252).

that the official and cultural intellectuals aired at many meetings during the mid-1980s, well represents this moderate strategy: The notion of "socialist spiritual civilization" was not directly attacked but was skillfully transformed into a noncommunist concept.

> Socialist spiritual civilization can and has indeed absorbed certain progressive ideas and moral values from capitalist societies, for instance, respect for knowledge and experts, the idea of efficiency, consideration for others, care about public health and environments, and stress on politeness and decorum, etc. (*Guangming Daily* June 30, 1986)

In another commentary in the *Guangming Daily* (November 19, 1986), the fruits of "capitalist spiritual civilization" that China's "spiritual civilization" should adopt included the values of "freedom, democracy, equality, and humanism."

The radical members of the counterelite instead contended that to build "socialist spiritual civilization" and to build an efficient market economy were in conflict. Xing Kuishan, director of the Research Center of the CYL Central Committee, remarked that some people used the moral standards of yesterday to judge the economic conduct of today. "This 'ethics-centered' attitude runs counter to the modernization enterprise. It must be remembered that doctrines that sound good morally can be disastrous economically, such as egalitarianism" (*Chinese Youth News* August 14, 1986). To Cai Chongguo, an editor of the *Youth's Forum* and a junior professor at Zhongnan Caijing University, the appeal to morality was the return of Mao's cultural revolutionary policy. He warned: "Those 'revolutionaries' who specialize in enhancing people's moral standards look 'lofty.' . . . But their preaching for asceticism and 'selflessness' often is a mask to cover their ultraselfishness, autocracy, and desire for political and economic monopoly" (*Youth's Forum* No. 6, pp. 12 and 21, 1986).

The counterelite's critique of "socialist spiritual civilization" as impairing economic reforms centered around the saying of "think of money" [*xiang qian kan*]. In the circles of reformist economists, this popular saying was interpreted as the embodiment of efficiency and market economics. The PCPD's outline of 1982, as cited before, singled it out as a target. In defiance of the PCPD's authority, the *Chinese Youth News* published an article on August 9, 1983 by Zhang Weiyan, a graduate student in economics, to defend the saying. In Zhang's view, money in the modern economy is the reward society gives to those who have made contributions to the social system. "'Think of money' should be an essential element of businesspeople's professional ethics in a socialist society. If the producer does not think of money, how can he possibly know the needs of consumers? How can the national income be maximized and the state, the collective, and the individual all benefit?"

In late 1983 and early 1984, Hu Qiaomu, Deng Liqun, and even Deng Xiaoping himself,[22] who was apparently pursued by the two to do so, condemned the editors of the *Chinese Youth News* and writers like Zhang for their promotion of the idea "think of money." But soon the intellectuals made a comeback. For instance, in the spring of 1985, the Shanghai-based journal *Social Sciences* published an essay by Zou Dongtao, a graduate student. He rejected the critics' interpretation of the "think of money" phrase and blamed them for equating "the commodity [read: market] economy mentality" with making money by illegal means. While the latter should be opposed, the former was in concord with the progressive course of economic restructuring (*Shehuikexue* No. 4, pp. 14–16, 1985). About a year latter, at the Taiyuan conference on "Reforms and the Development of Spiritual Civilization," Yu Guangyuan as the keynote speaker told the 100-plus participants that the argument Hu Qiaomu used in his preaching for communist ideals, "principles of the commodity economy should never be allowed to apply to interpersonal relations," was in fact an expression quoted from the Gang of Four (*Jingji Ribao* September 13, 1986).

The radical members of the counterelite noted that the core of the Communist regime's "socialist spiritual civilization" formula was that "socialist China is inferior to the capitalist West in material civilization, but superior to it in spiritual civilization." This apology, the *Youth's Forum* pointed out, was a dressed-up version of the *Zhongti Xiyong* (Chinese things as essence and Western things as utility) of the late nineteenth century. Since that time, whenever China was challenged by foreign "progressive trends" and Chinese reformers rose up to push for change, defenders of the old order have always come out shouting "Chinese moralities are better than Western ones." (See *Youth's Forum* No. 5, pp. 155–56, 1985; No. 6, pp. 60–70, 71–83, 1986.) "Socialist spiritual civilization" was in fact a Marxist version of *Zhongti Xiyong* and was intended to demoralize Chinese people longing for fundamental changes in their social environment, according to many of the participants in a Shanghai conference sponsored by the Municipal Party Propaganda Department and the Shanghai Social Sciences Association in May 1986 (*People's Daily* July 29, 1986). The *World Economic Herald* (December 15, 1986) made the charge against the regime's apology in such a manner:

"The West is stronger in material civilization, the East is stronger in spiritual civilization" and "China is poorer physically but richer morally" are artificial myths. Since we began using this shield . . . , our backwardness and benightedness have all "disappeared." It

[22] Deng Xiaoping's statement can be found in Deng (1987: 32). Hu Qiaomu and Deng Liqun made attacks in their speeches that were then issued as "study material" for universities and research institutions.

seems that an economically very poor developing country, which bears strong feudal [read: despotic] elements in every respect, can be almost perfect in its social and value system. This is really an Oriental myth of the A-Thousand-And-One-Nights style! . . . We should instantly awake from this deceitful illusion of "sniritual civilization superiority."

From the "Zhao Yiya incident" until 1987 when other political arenas became available (see the subsequent chapters), fighting between those who wanted to develop education, science, and culture through international exchange and those who wanted to strengthen the Communist normative order by excluding China from foreign influence continued both within the ruling elite and between the counterelite and the ruling elite. To be sure, the fighting on these two fronts had very different natures. The argument within the ruling elite was over which side of the "two civilizations" should be given more weight, the "socialist spiritual" or "material," but the argument between the counterelite and the hard-liners in the ruling elite was over which side should give way to the other when they came into conflict.

Having gradually realized that "socialist uniqueness" embodied in "socialist spiritual civilization" was indeed counterproductive to the growth of "material civilization," Hu Yaobang, Wan Li, and Hu Qili, with the assistance of new propaganda chiefs Rui Xingwen and Zhu Houze, managed to pass a document, entitled "The CCP Central Committee's Resolution on Guiding the Construction of Socialist Spiritual Civilization" (*People's Daily* September 29, 1986), at a party plenum in September 1986. In this document the crucial statement that "socialist spiritual civilization takes communist ideological principles as its core" was thrown away, and emphasis was given to educational development and cultural change essential to the market-oriented reforms. Yet, after Hu Yaobang was removed from the post of party chief and Zhu lost the propaganda directorship owing to the student demonstrations in late 1986, Peng Zhen and Hu Qiaomu restored the statement and gave it special weight (see *People's Daily* January 7 and 15, 1987).

The Dengists added "socialist spiritual civilization" to the official agenda in order to keep China's economics and politics proceeding along two separate tracks without mutual interference. It turned out that this device did not solve the problem but made tensions between the two sides severer. The Dengists' formula of "building two civilizations" was introduced as a compromise measure, but instead of being pacified, each group, the party-military hard-liners and the counterelite, took half of the formula and ran with it in opposite directions.[23]

This case typifies a predicament common to many communist regimes. Without altering the basic structure of the political system, they wanted to uncouple

[23]I am indebted to Rachael Winfree for suggesting that I make this point explicit.

economics from politics. However, as centralized bureaucratic structures whose raison d'être is sanctioned by a unified politicoeconomic ideology that cannot be disconnected, communist systems have demonstrated a low capacity for allowing subsystems to run in accordance with contrary principles. Any major changes in the economic domain immediately lead to the negation of the justifying principle of the entire communist order. In Chapter 6 we will see more evidence on this matter.

Conclusion

The Dengists' socialist-moral appeal was a response to the public's disillusionment with the Communist system and its cry for remodeling home political and economic institutions after foreign examples. The target audience was the better-educated sectors of society, who, owing to access to information from abroad and their ability to make horizontal comparison, were especially cynical and critical.

The sociological literature on "reference groups" (see Urry 1973 for a comprehensive review) can help us fathom how comparison works to accelerate the crisis of legitimation and to foster political instability. The most distinctive contribution of reference group theory is the insight that "men may shape their attitudes by reference to groups other than their own and may shape their self-evaluations by the choice of unusual points of social comparison" (Sills 1968: Vol. 13, p. 354). Such comparisons often generate, or reinforce, an individual's sense of relative deprivation (Stouffer et al. 1949).

Several points in the reference group theory are especially relevant to the situation examined in this work. First, for some individuals, the number of remote groups with which they make comparison is very small; but for some others, the number could be much bigger. The latter type of individual is called rich in "imaginative sociability" (Sills 1968: Vol. 13, p. 356). They are in possession of a multiplicity of reference groups, each serving as a specific point of reference against which they appraise a certain dimension of their own situation (Hyman 1942; Stouffer et al. 1949; Turner 1955).

It has also been noticed that, in the process of selecting comparative reference groups, individuals tend to follow what Ralph Turner (1955) terms the "relevance principle": Social objects are chosen on the basis that a certain affinity exists between the selector and the selected. In other words, the selected objects must be relevant to a particular aspect of self-evaluation. In many cases such affinity or similarity is more imagined or perceived than actual (Merton 1957: 242–43).

In the case under study, members of the Chinese counterelite can be said to possess rich imaginative sociability. They have compared their country with the

West (especially the United States), with Japan, and with the four little dragons (especially Taiwan). Their ability to select such a diversity of comparative reference groups can be explained by a contextual factor: the multifaceted nature of their home country. China used to be the richest and most powerful country on the earth for centuries (see Kennedy 1987 for a comparison of the great powers in history), and the collective memory of this fact is still vivid in the minds of the better-educated Chinese. So it was appealing to Chinese intellectuals to compare their country with today's "rich and powerful" nations.

China's size and feeling of self-importance parallel America's. This similarity led the Chinese counterelite, in appraising China's status in the international community, often to look at the United States. On the other hand, China and Japan and the four little dragons have cultural and racial affinities. The mainland Chinese were naturally inclined to choose these noncommunist East Asian neighbors as their comparative reference groups.

Such comparisons become more effective in generating disillusionment and discontent with the home government when more variables are under "control" in the comparative process, much like in a laboratory experiment. This and the following chapters show that, to PRC residents, developments in Taiwan have carried a special weight. In the comparison between the PRC and Taiwan, all the cultural and ethnic variables were "controlled": Both sides had a Chinese population and a Chinese regime.[24] If one side could have a capitalist system and had made it work well, why not the other side? As PRC citizens in the 1980s were more and more aware of economic prosperity and political liberalization in Taiwan, they became increasingly intolerant of the pace of change in their own society.

The campaign to "build socialist spiritual civilization" was proposed to curb this popular attitude. As a strategy of regime legitimation, the Dengists' appeal to socialist morality differed from their appeal to rationalism in important ways. While the latter was designed to sanction changes that strayed from the Maoist policy, the former was designed to defend the political features of Leninist socialism in general.

Therefore, in the appeal to rationalism, stress was placed on morally neutral, universally applicable instrumental rationality. In the campaign to "build socialist spiritual civilization," the emphasis was shifted toward the "socialist uniqueness," to use the socialist Chinese *ti* (essence) to counterbalance the sociopolitical ramifications of the capitalist Western *yong* (utility), thereby drawing a line between what was subject to Western borrowing and change, and what was not.

---

[24] It follows that, to PRC citizens, the Hong Kong comparison was not as meaningful as the Taiwan one, for Hong Kong has attained prosperity under a foreign, colonial government.

When making the appeal to rationalism, the Dengist leadership was primarily concerned about its authority over the party-state bureaucracy. It was those in positions of power who questioned the legitimacy of the reformist leadership and its new policies. However, when making the appeal to socialist morality, the Deng regime was mainly concerned about its legitimacy in the eyes of the governed: It was they who questioned its right to rule. Thus, during the late 1970s and mid-1980s, there was a shift of emphasis in the politics of legitimation in China – a shift from the emphasis on legitimation within the government to legitimation among the well-educated and influential sectors of society. In the following chapters, we will see that the emphasis alternated between the two during the course of reform.

Such shifts exemplify the dilemma of legitimation typical of communist regimes in transition: They have to solicit not only the traditional power centers for recognition and support, but also the influential groups in society for recognition and cooperation. To keep political power and attain socioeconomic objectives, communist regimes have to fight a two-front war to win legitimacy. This is why, as I have argued earlier, it is a mistake to pay attention only to top political leaders and the issue of political survival when studying regime legitimation in late communism.

Appendix

Table 6. *List of periodicals specializing in publishing translations*

Title	Location	Founding year	Subscriptions
Zhexue Yicong	Beijing	N/A	13,000
Guowai Shehuikexue	Beijing	1978	10,000
Guowai Shehuikexue Cankaoziliao	Beijing	1979	N/A
Guowai Shehuikexue Dongtai	Beijing	1979	5,000
Guowai Shehuikexue Zhuzou Tiyao	Beijing	1980	N/A
Guowai Shehuikexue Lunwen Suoyin	Beijing	1980	3,000
Guowai Shehuikexue Kuaibao	Beijing	1983	1,350
Makesizhuyi Yanjiu Cankaoziliao	Beijing	1979	6,000
Kexue Shehuizhuyi Cankaoziliao	Beijing	1979	3,000
Guowai Zhengzhixue	Beijing	N/A	3,500
Meiguo Yanjiu Cankaoziliao	Beijing	1981	1,740
Shijie Zhongjiao Ziliao	Beijing	N/A	5,000
Shijie Lishi Yicong	Beijing	N/A	N/A
Shijieshi Yanjiu Dongtai	Beijing	N/A	6,600
Jingjixue Yicong	Beijing	N/A	10,000
Shijie Jingji Yicong	Beijing	N/A	N/A
Jingji Yanjiu Cankaoziliao	Beijing	1979	11,000

Table 6 *continued*

Title	Location	Founding year	Subscriptions
Guowai Jingji Wenxian Zhaiyao	Beijing	N/A	N/A
Faxue Yicong	Beijing	1979	10,000
Minzu Yicong	Beijing	N/A	4,000
Kexue yu Zhexue	Beijing	N/A	7,000
Kexue dui Shehui de Yingxiang	Beijing	N/A	4,000
Zirankexue Zhexue Wenti Cong5an	Beijing	N/A	12,000
Duiwai Xuanchuan Cankao	Beijing	1979	16,000
Bianyi Cankao	Beijing	1980	N/A
Haiwai Wenzhai[a]	Beijing	1984	300,000
Jingji Shehui Tizhi Bijiao	Beijing	1985	N/A
Su Dong Wenti Yicong	Beijing	1985	N/A
Guowai Shehuikexue Xingxi	Beijing	1988	N/A
Xiandai Waiguo Shexue Shihuikexue Wenzhai	Shanghai	N/A	10,000
Guoji Wenti Ziliao	Shanghai	1983	22,000
Shijie Jingji Wenhui	Shanghai	N/A	9,400
Shijie Kexue Yicong	Shanghai	N/A	N/A
Meiguo Kexue Xingwen	Shanghai	N/A	N/A
Shijie Zhichuang[a]	Shanghai	1979	320,000
Guowai Shehuikexue Xueshu Qingbao	Harbin	1980	N/A
Yanjiu yu Jijian	Harbin	1984	1,500
Guowai Shehuikexue Qingbao	Shenyan	1978	N/A
Kexue[b]	Congqing	N/A	N/A
Guowai Shehuikexue Qingkuang	Nanjing	1981	N/A
Jingji Ziliao Yicong	Fujian	N/A	6,000
Duiwai Jingji Ziliao	Fujian	N/A	600
Huaqiao Shijie	Fujian	1985	N/A
Qingnian Bolan	Fujian	1985	N/A
Shehuikexue Yanjiu Cankaozhiliao	Chengdu	1979	N/A
Wenhua Yicong	Tianjin	1980	20,000
Waiguo Wenti Yanjiu	Chang-chuan	1980	1,000
Xiandai Riben Yanjiu	Chang-chuan	1982	3,000
Xiandai Zhexue	Guang-zhou	1985	7,000
Duzhe Wenzhai[a]	Lanzhou	1983	300,000
Guowai Jingji Yicong	Huhhot	1983	N/A

[a]These three carry nonscholarly material. In China of the 1980s, there were many more translation magazines of popular nature. These three were the best known.
[b]Philosophical discussions often appear in this journal.
Sources: Zhongguo Chuban Nianjian (China's yearbook of publishing) 1980 (Beijing: Commercial Press, 1980); *Zhongguo Baokan Minglu* (A title index of Chinese newspapers and magazines) 1984 (Beijing: Xinhua Press, 1985); *Zhongguo Dangdai Baokan Zonglan* (A general survey of contemporary Chinese newspapers and magazines) 1987 (Harbin: Heilongsiang People's Publishing House, 1988).

5

Two contending patriotic campaigns

This chapter is about patriotism as a two-edged sword in the politics of legitimation in post-Mao China. We shall see, on the one hand, how the Communist
ruling elite made an appeal to patriotism in the hope of bolstering popular
support for the regime. We shall also see how the counterelite appealed to
patriotism in an attempt to mobilize popular resentment against the regime.
The ruling elite's effort to appeal to patriotism was made necessary precisely
because there had already been a crisis of confidence in the Communist system,
and the government's socialist-moral appeal had failed to produce positive results. But it turned out that patriotism, which had been the regime's strong
legitimating instrument, became in the hands of the counterelite a powerful
tool for criticism of, and protest against, the Communist regime.

Background: the failure of the regime's earlier legitimation device

The Communist regime turned to patriotism in response to two sociopolitical
shocks. One might be called the *"Unrequited Love* shock," the other the "Fang
Lizhi shock." The first refers to middle-aged intellectuals' resentment and indignation as a result of their experience under Communist rule. A great number
of them had been the Communist party's allies when it fought for survival
during the Japanese invasion and the civil war in the 1930s and 1940s. When the
KMT regime retreated to Taiwan in 1949, the majority of the intellectuals
refused to go with it and chose to stay on the mainland, hoping to work with the
new regime to build a democratic and prosperous China, as the Communists
promised. Some of the intellectuals gave up comfortable lives and bright professional futures abroad and returned to the PRC in the early 1950s, in response to
the government's call to "revive the Chinese nation," and were willing to bear
any hardship for that glorious cause.

It turned out, however, that the Communist regime broke its promise soon
after taking power and made the intellectuals – the leading social force in

criticizing official corruption and incompetence – a major target of political purges. After Mao's death, Bai Hua, a writer in the army, was one of the first established intellectuals who dared to pour out the feelings of being betrayed and abused that were prevalent in the intellectual strata.[1] In his screenplay *Unrequited Love,* published in the fall of 1979,[2] Bai told a story about a fictional character, who was once an anti-KMT activist and later a well-known painter in the West. Shortly after the PRC was founded, the painter and his wife, overcoming tremendous obstacles, returned to their motherland. During the Cultural Revolution, the painter was regularly beaten and his family was thrown out of its home. His daughter tried to leave China with her fiancé who was a foreign citizen. But the father opposed their emigration and the daughter replied, "Dad, I'm going with the man I love. I love him and he loves me. . . . Dad, you love our *guojia.* . . . Does this *guojia* love you?" (Bai Hua 1981: 83).

Here Bai deliberately used the word *guojia,* meaning "state" or "country" in Chinese, instead of *zuguo,* meaning "motherland." Later he explained:

I consciously chose the word *guojia* at that time, mainly because I felt that "motherland" and "state" were two different concepts and we must not mix them up. Did the state love Zhang Zhixin? [Of Zhang's tragedy see Chapter 3.] It was precisely in the name of the state that the Gang of Four had her executed. (*Nineties Monthly* No. 1, p. 90, 1988)

The painter stayed in China and encountered more persecution. He was hunted by the police, had to hide in desolate marshes, and eventually starved to death in a snow storm. In the last scene, a helicopter goes in search of him:

The helicopter slowly descends. . . .
A question mark lies on the ground, becoming bigger and bigger. . . . In the very last stage of his life, the painter used his body, with his remaining strength, to engrave a huge question mark on the pure white snow. The final dot in the question mark is his frozen body. (Bai Hua 1981: 94; with my alterations in the translation)

A few months later, a film was made of Bai's screenplay. After Liu Baiyu, director of cultural affairs in the PLA's General Political Department, made a report about this highly political work to the top leaders, Deng Xiaoping and his colleagues ordered a screening. Many became angered and told the department to lead a national condemnation of the film.[3]

---

[1] To sense this feeling one might read Liu Binyan (1990) and Anne F. Thurston (1987).

[2] On this play and its political significance, see Goldman et al. (1987: 183–232). From the literary point of view, the play is not a fine work. But as Joshua Rubenstein (1985: 9–10) has observed of influential writings in the de-Stalinization campaign in the Soviet Union, a literary work's "literary merits and weaknesses were of little importance next to the picture of life that readers recognized."

[3] On the top leaders' condemnation of the film, see Party Literature Research Center (1982: 877–951). My narration of the role of the PLA's General Political Department in this event was based on Informant no. 33.

Another sociopolitical trend causing the ruling elite to turn to patriotism for help was the increasing use of foreign models to criticize the government, and the educated youth's clamor for change, a phenomenon discussed in the preceding chapter. This trend had its powerful expression in the nationwide student protest of late 1986, intellectually stimulated largely by Fang Lizhi (Schell 1989: 211–46). From 1985, Fang had been invited to talk to university students in Anhui, Shanghai, Zhejiang, Beijing, and elsewhere about political reform and intellectuals' role in changing China. His speeches were recorded and spread by students to almost every major campus across the country (see the collections in Fang Lizhi 1989 and 1991). In those speeches, Fang enthusiastically advocated "all-around Westernization" as a prescription to rescue China. "By 'all-around Westernization,' I mean thorough and comprehensive openness," elaborated Fang. "For taken as a whole, our culture has been far behind the world's advanced cultures, far behind not in one respect but in every way." Fang explained that his concept of culture is broad, including the polity, economy, science, and education.

What should we do in the face of this situation? We of course should have thorough and comprehensive openness. . . . Let the advanced cultures from all over the world come and shake us, shaking every aspect of our society. . . . Through this process, good things in our society will be saved and bad things eliminated. (Fang Lizhi 1989: 4, 10; see also Schell 1989: 218–19)

In the student movement of late 1986, which originated in the city of Hefei, where Fang worked as vice-president of a major university, and instantly spread to other cities, we can see clearly the marks of Fang's "all-around Westernization" approach – using foreign institutional models and political values to attack the Communist structure in China. These are some of the slogans and wall posters present in the movement:

Government of the people, by the people, and for the people.

I have a dream, a dream of freedom. I have a dream of democracy. I have a dream of life endowed with human rights. May the day come when all these are more than dreams.

In the United States there is the "false freedom" to support or not to support the Communist party. In our country we have the "genuine freedom" of having to support the Communist party. In the United States there is the "false freedom" of the press. In our country we have the "genuine freedom" of no freedom of the press.

Give Me Liberty or Give Me Death!
                                            (Schell's translations, 1989: 213–14, 225, 236–37)

A variety of "question and answer" material also reflects the popularity of this "Western institution-borrowing" attitude among other educated social sectors.

Are there any things better in our system of people's congresses in comparison with the Western parliamentary system? (Shanghai Municipal Commission for Education and Public Health 1987: 79–80)

Without checks and balances, power will corrupt. A multiparty system and the separation of powers can keep corruption from occurring. Why do our newspapers describe these as "bourgeois things"? Why we are not allowed to try these? (Zhang Yi 1989: 227)

The official appeal to patriotism

During the early 1980s, in response to the *Unrequited Love* type of sentiment, party cells often used this saying to describe the state-citizen relationship and appease those mistreated under Communist rule: "Children wouldn't blame their moms even if they were wrongly beaten by their moms."[4]

After the student movement of late 1986, this saying was once again used by party leaders to justify their absolute authority over the students. When commenting on the regime's harsh reaction to the student demonstrators, Bo Yibo, vice-chairman of the party's Central Advisory Committee, said: "The relationships between the Communist party and the students are exactly the same as those between father and son. It doesn't matter if the father wrongly punishes his son."[5]

In response to the criticism that Communist politics and the state's mismanagement of the economy had long kept China as one of the countries with the lowest per capita GNP in the world, the regime appropriated a folk adage, turned it into a slogan, and directed party cells to use it in indoctrination: "A son doesn't dislike his mother because of her bad looks; a dog doesn't dislike his home because it is poor. China is your motherland; no matter how backward she is, she is your great mother who gave birth to you and raised you." (See *People's Daily* March 19, 1981.)

In accordance with the directives of leaders such as Deng Xiaoping (1984: 369–70, 396) and Wang Zhen (*People's Daily* July 10, 1982), the regime began to put great effort into patriotic campaigns in the early 1980s. In October 1982, the central party organs embarked on a long-run undertaking called "Three Loves": "Love the party, love socialism, and love the motherland" (*People's Daily* October 9, 1982). In July 1983, the PCPD and the party's Central Secretariat's Research Center formulated a comprehensive action program for patriotic campaigns (*People's Daily* July 16, 1983), which set up concrete plans for the television, movie, publishing, and tourist industries; elements of the program included how to make television programs and films out of "the Chinese heroic struggle against Western and Japanese imperialism"; how to highlight in daily

---

[4] Personal observations in Anhui and Shanghai in 1978–82.
[5] Quoted from a letter written by a Beijing student. See also *China Spring* No. 2, p. 20, 1987.

television shows "the party's great achievements in leading the motherland to become modern"; and how to portray that "model Communist members are Chinese patriots of the best type."

Soon the trade unions and pubuic libraries and the club system formed their own measures to implement the patriotic action program (*New China News Agency* July 24, 1983). Meanwhile, the Ministry of Education dictated that all schools add "patriotic content," such as the institution of the daily raising of the national flag and the singing of the national anthem, to the curriculum and extracurricular activities (*Zhongguo Jiaoyu Bao* August 25, 1983).

After the student movement of late 1986, senior leaders Wang Zhen, Bo Yibo, Song Renqiong, Hu Qiaomu, and Deng Liqun urged that these projects be strengthened and that traditional and popular artistic means be used to win the hearts of educated youth, keeping them from being seduced by the "all-around Westernization" trend (*People's Daily* December 29, 1986, and February 18, 1987; *Zhongguo Jiaoyu Bao* February 7, 1987).

In the regime's patriotic appeal there was an internal tension. On the one hand, the party leaders clearly saw that with communism and Marxism bankrupt, patriotism became the only symbol capable of integrating political society. As a party document acknowledged:

Among patriotism, collectivism, socialism, and communism, patriotism has peculiar features and functions. Linked with age-old historical traditions and backed strongly by public opinion and social psychology, patriotism can easily be comprehended by, and gain acceptance from, the broad masses who differ in family origin, life experience, vocation, ethnic category, age, educational attainment, and level of political awareness. Patriotism is the banner of greatest appeal. (*People's Daily* July 16, 1983)

Despite this understanding, the Communist ruling elite was unwilling to treat patriotism – loyalty to the Chinese nation – as an independent, self-sufficient value, but tried to make it an intermediate value and use it to bolster support for the state.[6] Deng Xiaoping (1984: 369–70) resentfully remarked: "Someone has said that not loving socialism isn't equivalent to not loving one's motherland. Is the motherland something abstract? If you don't love socialist New China led by the Communist party, what motherland do you love?" In the official patriotic appeal, emphasis thus was placed on the concord of loving the motherland and loving the party-state: Communists are the most devoted patriots and the Communist party is the best representative of the nation's interests (see *Red Flag* No. 4, p. 3, 1983); and socialism is the only road through which China can become a first-class world power (see *People's Daily* March 19, 1981; November 12, 1986; January 12, 1987). Deng Liqun put it simply: "One cannot demonstrate that one

[6]On the state as a political entity and the nation as an ethnic and emotional complex, see Benjamin Akzin (1966) for an inspiring treatment.

loves the motherland if one shows no deep love for the socialist system and the Communist party. In short, in our times, loving the Chinese Communist party is the highest expression of Chinese patriotism."[7]

To make this "communized patriotism" work, the leaders relied on the strategy of vertical comparison: They compared the level of economic-technological development, military capacity, and international status of post-1949 China with those of China from the Opium Wars (1840s) to the 1930s, when China suffered countless humiliations. (See Hsu 1975 and Chesneaux, Bastid, and Bergere 1976 for a general survey of this period.) The regime recommended that this kind of comparison is the only method that can lead young people to the correct conclusion as to which government serves the nation's interests best (*Jiaoxue yu Yanjiu* No. 4, 1983; *Zhongguo Jiaoyu Bao* August 25, 1983; *People's Daily* February 12, 1987).

The counterelite's patriotic campaign

The counterelite took the "banner of patriotism" from the regime, transformed it to suit its purposes, and turned it into an extremely effective means to delegitimize the Communist system. Those active in this counteraction were CIs and independent-minded OIs in research and educational institutions, the mass media, and think tanks, plus a small number of politically concerned TIs and MIs working for science and industry. Their counterappeal went through two phases: the "furor of cultural studies" (*wenhua re*) before the 1986 student movement, which was a mild one, and the outcry over the "national crisis" (*minzu weiji*) in 1988 and early 1989, which was more radical.

In contrast to events discussed in earlier chapters, when the counterelite encountered the ruling elite in the battle over patriotism, the various kinds of voluntary institutions described in Chapter 2, such as professional associations, discussion groups, workshops, and clubs, played a notable role.[8] Most of these

---

[7]Personal notes of Deng's speech on the "patriotic education" program in the fall of 1983.

[8]These institutions included the "Toward the Future" group led by Bao Zunxin and Jin Guantao; the Shanghai Research Center for Chinese-Western Cultural Comparison headed by Wang Yuanhua; the Cultural Studies Institute at Huadong Chemistry College; the Center for Research on the History of Chinese Thought and Culture and the Center for Research on the History of the World's Cultures at Fudan University in Shanghai; the Salon for Studies of the Cultural History of the Ming-Qing Period in Wuhan; the *Youth's Forum* group; the Yueluan Cultural Studies Institute at Hunan University; the Institute for Studies of Traditional Cultures at Shandong University; the Discussion Group on Studies of the Cultural History of the Han-Tang Period in Xian; the Institute of Chinese Cultural Studies at Fujian Normal University; the Center for Studies on Lingnan's Modern Thought and Culture at Huanan Normal University in Guangzhou; the Institute for Chinese Learning at Shenzhen University; the "Cultures: China and the World" group led by Gan Yang and Su Guoxun; the Chinese Cultural Academy chaired by Zhang Dainian and Tang Yijie; the Center for Comparative Studies of Chinese and Western Cultures at Beijing Normal Univer-

146 The decline of communism in China

voluntary institutions were attached to semiofficial and official bodies and staffed by state employees, and they relied on resources obtained through informal and formal channels (see details in Chapter 2). Together with semiofficial and official bodies headed by liberals, these voluntary organizations provided institutional space for the counterelite to oppose the Communist version of patriotism.

During the "furor of cultural studies," these institutions initiated a variety of activities. One was sponsorship of large conferences and seminars held in many major cities across the country.[9] Another was special "book series" projects (*congshu:* see Chapter 2 for the background). For example, the leading book series "Toward the Future" (Sichuan/Beijing) had a number of special titles published during 1984–86, including Alex Inkeles's and David Smith's *Becoming Modern: Individual Change in Six Developing Countries,* Michio Morishima's *Why Has Japan "Succeeded"?,* Cyril Black's *Dynamics of Modernization,* the Club of Rome's *Reports,* Sigmund Freud's works, and Joseph R. Levenson's *Liang Chi-chao and the Mind of Modern China.* In the meantime, the influential book series "Cultures: China and the World" (Beijing/Shanghai) published Samuel Huntington's *Political Order in Changing Societies,* Karl Mannheim's *Ideology and Utopia* and *Man and Society in an Age of Reconstruction,* Simone de Beauvoir's *Second Sex,* Max Weber's *Protestant Ethic and the Spirit of Capitalism* and *Religion of China,* Talcott Parsons's *Structure of Social Action,* Daniel Bell's *Cultural Contradictions of Capitalism,* and Joseph Levenson's *Confucian China and Its Modern Fate,* among other titles. These titles were recommended to the editors for translation and publication mainly by Western scholars of Chinese descent and Chinese students studying abroad.

sity; the Institute for Studies of Thought and Cultures at Qinghua University in Beijing; and the Division for Studies on Modern Cultural History at the Institute of Modern History in the CASS. (Based on Informants nos. 18, 19, and 34. See also Ge Qiyung, *Youth's Forum* No. 5, pp. 33–40, 1986; and Li Xiaobin 1987: 399–422.)

[9] Of which the major ones were: "The Causes of China's Backwardness in Science and Technology in Modern Times" at Chengdu in October 1982, about seventy people attending; "The National Coordination Conference on Studies of Chinese–Cultural History" at Shanghai in December 1982; "Studies of Modern Chinese Culture" at Zhengzhou in August and September 1984; a pair of seminars held at Beijing in March 1985 and January 1986, respectively, the "Chinese Culture Seminar" and the "Seminar on Chinese-Western Cultural Comparison," with more than a thousand participants from all over the country; the "National Coordination Conference on Eastern–Western Cultural Comparative Projects" at Shenzhen in April 1985; "Modernization and Traditional Chinese Culture" at Huangzhou in Hubei in December 1985; an international conference on Chinese cultural studies at Shanghai in January 1986; "Confucianism, Traditional Chinese Culture, and Socialism" at Qufu, Confucius's hometown, in April 1986; in the same month a meeting at Beijing on "The Causes of Cultural Conflict Between the East and the West"; "Strategies for Cultural Development in Urban Areas" at Shanghai in May 1986; and in the same month "The Second National Coordination Conference on Cultural Comparative Projects" at Hangzhou.

Other major book series projects undertaken during this period were "Phoenix Series" (Hunan), "Comparative Culture Series" (Shanghai), "Collections of Studies of Chinese Culture" (Shanghai/Beijing), and "Modern Cultural History Series" (Beijing). In addition to publishing controversial works by PRC authors, these projects reprinted pre-1949 Chinese books on China's political culture by people like Hu Shi and Liang Shuming, and works resulting from Taiwan's political-cultural debate in the 1960s, by such authors as Bo Yang and Xu Fuguan, as well as the scholarship of Chinese Americans, such as the works of Yu Ying-shih and Lin Yu-sheng, on modern and contemporary political and intellectual events in China. Because they contained facts and analyses detrimental to the Communists, these works had hitherto been banned in the PRC.

When the political climate was stormy, for instance in 1983–84, the counterelite skillfully took "tradition" ("feudalism" was the code) as its target,[10] showing how China's traditional power structure of total bureaucratic domination, traditional personnel system that prohibited horizontal mobility, traditional economic policy that stressed agriculture to the neglect of commerce, traditional social organization that suppressed individual freedom, and traditional values that respected the old had all prevented the growth of modern industrial democracy in China. Looking at what the counterelite described as "traditional" or "feudal," PRC citizens with a minimum level of political awareness could quickly see a striking resemblance to the here and now.

While the political climate was relatively mild, for instance in 1985–86 when Zhu Houze headed the PCPD, the counterelite immediately extended the critique of "tradition" or "feudalism" to include the continuation of the "tradition" (the code for this was *fengjian yidu* or "feudal legacies"), arguing that these legacies remain to harm the market-oriented economic reforms and the growth of political and intellectual freedom in today's China. Hence, in the PRC of the mid-1980s, political critique first took the form of cultural critique, then cultural critique became political critique. (See an interesting note in *Far Eastern Economic Review* April 23, 1987.) This strategy reminds us of a famous quotation from Marx: "The criticism of heaven is transformed into the criticism of earth, the *criticism of religion* into the *criticism of law*, and the *criticism of theology* into the *criticism of politics*" (Marx and Engels 1972: 12).

In the appendix, I stress the importance of decoding in studying political contention in communist systems. The dichotomy of "feudalism"[11] versus

---

[10]The following summary is based on the *Dialectics of Nature Journal* (1983), Fudan Journal Editorial Department (1986, 1987), Li Xiaobin (1987), and Informants nos. 13, 14, 18, 19, and 34.

[11]On the characterization of "feudal influence" in the writings of post-Mao China, see Edward Friedman (1983).

"capitalism" in post-Mao China serves as a perfect example. It is a highly accurate indicator whereby the observer can determine an actor's political stance. "Feudalism" has been used to denote the structural and cultural attributes characteristic of Oriental despotism and totalitarianism of the twentieth century. Hence, all those placing emphasis on "antifeudalism" were for political liberalization, radical economic restructuring, the rule of law, and greater openness to the outside. And all those stressing "anticapitalism" were for absolute power by the party-state, unlimited bureaucratic privilege, strict government control of the economy, suppression of intellectual activism, and hostility toward Western influence.

After the student movement of late 1986, as the regime's patriotic appeal surged to a new high tide, the counterelite's move entered its radical stage. This was reflected in the debate on China's "global membership" and the television documentary *River Elegy* in 1988 and early 1989.

The term "global membership" (*qiuji*) came from Mao Zedong. In August 1956 when addressing a central party gathering, he proposed that China's annual steel output would be over four million tons in 1956 and exceed 20 million tons by 1967. Urged Mao (1977: 314–15, with minor editing):

We must work hard to reach this target. There are about a hundred countries in the world, but only a few produce over twenty million tons of steel a year. Therefore, once built up, China . . . will radically transform the situation in which for over a century it was backward, despised, and wretched. Moreover, it will be able to catch up with the most powerful capitalist country in the world, the United States. . . . Sixty years ago it too produced four million tons of steel, so we are sixty years behind. Given fifty or sixty years, we certainly ought to overtake the United States. This is an obligation. You have such a big population, such a vast territory and such rich resources, and what is more, you are said to build socialism, which is assumed to be superior; if after working at it for fifty or sixty years you are still unable to overtake the United States, what a sorry figure you will cut! You should be terminated from global membership.

"Termination of global membership" thus means the enslavement of the Chinese nation by others or the extinction of Chinese civilization.

The "global membership" discussion was orchestrated by the *World Economic Herald*, whose editors chose a very special moment to start it – on the eve of the Year of the Dragon; the dragon, as generally noted, is the symbol of China. The *Herald* (February 15, 1988) put forward its special commentary under the heading "Facing the Last Year of the Dragon of this Century, the Most Pressing Question for the Chinese Nation is Still 'Global Membership.'" Topping the front page, the commentary goes:

The new year is the Year of the Dragon; the next Year of the Dragon will be the first year of the 21st century.

"Entering the 21st century, nothing but technological-economic performance will decide political rankings of the world powers," observed the *Die Welt* of West Germany two years ago. . . .

What position, then, has today's China in the world economy?

A variety of data and information our reporters have collected shows that the gap between China and the developed countries is widening. Worse still, China is even lagging behind some developing countries and regions. It is the time to sound the alarm loudly. (Ibid.)

The *Herald* made full use of statistics, which meant "hard science" in the context of Chinese political culture. As pointed out before, this statistical approach cast a magic legitimating power spell over all the accompanying arguments. The effect was truly impressive:

According to the World Bank's annual reports, China's per capita GNP has been ranked around number 108 of 128 countries accounted in the reports, close to Somalia's and Tanzania's.

China's GNP growth rate, structure of exports, and level of educational and public health investments are even lower than those of the East Asian "four little dragons."

In 1955, China's GNP shared 4.7% of the whole world's GNP; in 1980, the share went down to 2.5%.

In 1960, China's GDP was equal to Japan's; in 1980, one-quarter of Japan's; in 1985, one-fifth.

In 1960, the United States' GDP exceeded China's by $460 billion; in 1985, by $3.68 trillion. (Ibid.)

During 1966–77, the Chinese media carried many reports about the primitive economies and societies of Somalia and Tanzania and the great benefits China's aid conferred on them. In the Chinese perception, these African countries were centuries behind China; now they were told that their country was as backward and poor as them.

Based on its interpretation of the statistics, the *Herald* drew this striking conclusion:

Since the establishment of the People's Republic, though considerable progress has been made in various respects, from the point of view of national economic strength, especially per capita indexes, however, we can say that the Chinese nation is once again at her "most critical moment." The threat to her is no smaller than the life-or-death threat she faced during the time when the March of Volunteers came into the world. (Ibid.)

The phrase "most critical moment" was taken from that March; originally a song of the anti-Japanese volunteer army, it became the national anthem after the PRC was founded. When the March came into the world, China was under the heel of the Japanese invaders and to all appearances at its last gasp. Since the Communist takeover, no one has dared to describe China's situation in such language. Interestingly enough, as the correspondence to the *Herald* later showed, most of the readers joining the discussion agreed that China of the late twentieth century was once again at its "most critical moment."

The national crisis alarm was amplified by two conferences. In early April 1988 the National Congress, China's parliament, held an assembly in Beijing, at which the country's VIPs all appeared. Intellectual delegates took this chance to air China's "global membership" crisis by quoting the *Herald's* statistics and arguments, and all the major media gave their speeches significant coverage – a three-part report, for example, appeared in *People's Daily* April 6–8, 1988. The congress assembly used to be a ceremony for rubber-stamping the party's decisions and eulogizing the party leadership's "achievements." This time, however, it turned out to be an occasion for criticism and protest.[12]

Another conference, held in Beijing on August 23 and 24, 1988, was cosponsored by the *Herald,* the *Science and Technology Daily,* the Beijing Institute for Research on Social and Scientific-Technological Development, the New Knowledge Academy, and "The 21st Century Scholarship Collection" editorial committee. About three hundred people attended this meeting on "China's Global Membership Problem and Its Choices for the Next Century," and all were well-known official, cultural, and technical intellectuals. People like Ge Yang, Lin Zixin, Li Honglin, Wan Runnan, and Jin Guantao (see Chapter 2 for their backgrounds) voiced harsh criticism of the regime's patriotic appeal (*World Economic Herald* September 5, 1988).

The discussion in the *Herald* lasted about a year. For much of that period, the editors put an eye-catching slogan in large characters on the top of the page – "Rise up, all you who don't want to see the motherland lag behind!" This is a modification of the first line of the national anthem – "Rise up, all you who don't want to be slaves!" The party's patriotic action program urged people to sing the anthem; the *Herald* responded to it in an ingenious way.

During the discussion, thousands of readers sent letters to the weekly, and several other major newspapers, such as the *People's Daily* and the *Guangming Daily,* carried reports about the event. The "global membership" issue aroused strong reactions particularly in institutions of higher education, research centers, and think tanks.[13] Participants in the discussion concentrated on two issues:

First, they debunked the regime's version of patriotism as attempting to cover the pressing and profound national crisis with "national pride," which, in the

---

[12]The senior party leaders were very unhappy about this assembly and directed that things would never be allowed to go this way at future meetings (Informant no. 29).

[13]Based on my reading of all the letters published in the *Herald* during this period. See also a survey by Chen Jian in the Sociology Department at Shanghai University (*World Economic Herald* April 11, 1988), according to which the percentage expressing "a great interest in the discussion" was 78 percent among social science and humanities professors (all rankings), 68 percent among university students in the same fields; 42 percent among natural science and engineering professors, 44 percent among students in the same fields; 29 percent among white-collar workers, 7 percent among blue-collar workers.

participants' view, was unfounded and deceitful. Lin Zixin noted that the state leaders probably felt privately that the country was in a crisis but never admitted it. "In order to demonstrate the superiority of socialism, they conceal the real crisis" (*World Economic Herald* September 5, 1988; see also *People's Daily* April 6, 1988). A letter from Zhejiang described the officially bred sense of national pride as "foolish and ridiculous," and as "a combination of illusion and feudal culture" (*World Economic Herald* April 4, 1988). An article by a Sichuan civil servant pointed out that since the founding of the PRC, the people had been intoxicated by Mao's saying, "The Chinese people have finally stood up!" In fact, taking account of China's society, polity, economy, and culture, it was hard to maintain that statement.

China's relative status in the international community is declining in some respects. . . . No matter how much progress we have made in comparison with our own past, China's fate, or any backward country's, is determined by its relative state of development vis-à-vis advanced countries. As soon as there is a big gap between them, the backward country is in danger, and it cannot be said that its people have stood up. (*World Economic Herald* July 11, 1988)

The second issue dominating the discussion was the implication of the rise of industrial East Asia, in particular, the "four little dragons" (Taiwan, Hong Kong, Singapore, and South Korea). As the *Herald* was based in Shanghai, China's largest industrial center, and many well-known Shanghai industrialists fled to Hong Kong and Taiwan after the Communist takeover and made big fortunes there, Shanghai was often singled out for contrast:

Shanghai used to be the first city in the Far East, known for fusing the Oriental and the Occidental and for her great wealth. It was she that hosted the journal *New Youth* which first brought Marxism into China. She was a birthplace of the revolution as well as the industrial capital of China. . . . During the 40 years [1949–88], however, turbulent politics and changing policies have turned the city upside down and wasted great opportunities for her. (*World Economic Herald* April 17, 1989)

A result of forty years of Communist politics was the distressing downfall of Shanghai (ibid.): With a population of 10 million, Shanghai had a total output in 1988 of only 73.6 percent of Singapore's in 1985, which had a population of 2.5 million; 38.9 percent of Hong Kong's in 1985, whose population was half of Shanghai's; and Shanghai's per capita income in 1988 was 34.9 percent of Taiwan's in 1985. These statistics meant a lot to the people in southeastern China: Many were old enough to recall that in the 1940s, Shanghai women would not marry men living in Hong Kong, which was, in the eyes of Shanghainese, "too poor and rustic." Taiwan was totally out of the question: "a primitive island."

To observers in the PRC the implication of the rise of industrial East Asia was profound: Japan and the four little dragons were either parts of the greater Chinese community, or long under the influence of Chinese culture. Why had they succeeded, but not the PRC? Its failure, obviously, could not be explained away by cultural or ethnic reasons. In fact, traditional Chinese culture has helped economic growth in Japan and the four little dragons. Therefore, the PRC's failure must be explained by other factors (*World Economic Herald* October 24, 1988). By quoting a Chinese American, the weekly made the point that "where the Chinese don't do socialism, there the Chinese enjoy prosperity" clearly and appealingly:

To the course of reform and openness in mainland China, the existence of Taiwan, which created an economic miracle through decades of hard work under extremely difficult conditions, is undoubtedly a pressure and stimulus. The reason is simple: both sides are Chinese. . . . A system that produces no incentive for people to work hard and to take responsibilities can hardly attain fast economic growth (*World Economic Herald* March 14, 1988)

In exploring the cause of China's "global membership" crisis in the late twentieth century, most of the participants put their finger on the existing political and economic institutions. As a letter from Gansu commented:

China's economy is backward, its technology backward, its culture backward, its education backward, and so on. What is the root of all this? . . . It makes no sense today to attribute its backwardness to history. . . . The root is . . . the backward institutions, that is, the highly centralized political institutions and the economic institutions dominated by politics. (*World Economic Herald* March 28, 1988)

This backward institutional structure was characterized as low in competence, efficiency, moral standards, and morale, but large in size and extensive in jurisdiction. It was like a "black hole": absorbing everything but releasing nothing. Gradually, the life forces of the Chinese nation were exhausted (ibid. November 14, 1988; see also March 7 and July 4, 1988). Participants working at economics research institutes cited, apparently without preauthorization from the higher level, internal data to show that 62 percent of the 600 billion yuan in capital investments made during 1958–78 was wasted because of mistakes in decision making and management; vast quantities of energy and materials were consumed every day in China's industry but yielded no usable products (ibid. October 3, 1988). These highly sensitive data had never been published before, because, to use a senior leader Wan Li's words, "Suppose workers, peasants, and intellectuals knew these facts. I'd think it rather strange if they didn't rise to overthrow the Communist party!" (quoted from Chen Yizi 1990: 2).

The authorities were held directly responsible for the enduring educational crisis, which caused the decline in the "quality" of the Chinese population, which was believed to be part of the reason why China was facing "global membership termination." The illiteracy rate was 25 percent, but the government only used 2.5 percent of the GNP to invest in education (*World Economic*

Herald September 5, 1988). From 1965 to 1984, the high school attendance rate in China rose from 24 to 37 percent, but from 35 to 91 percent in South Korea, from 29 to 69 percent in Hong Kong, and from 45 to 71 percent in Singapore (ibid. February 15, 1988). In 1931, there was 1 college graduate per 10,000 Chinese; by 1978, the number had moved up to 7.9, and the government kept using this as a "great socialist achievement" in its patriotic propaganda. But during the same period, the number in Australia, Italy, and Japan "multiplied 10 to 30 times, in India 73.7 times. . . . In this respect, China is behind Asian countries such as the Philippines, Iran, Iraq, Malaysia, Thailand, Bangladesh, Indonesia, Turkey, Nepal, Burma, Vietnam, and Sri Lanka, and African countries such as Algeria, Egypt, Syria, Morocco, and the Sudan" (ibid. October 24, 1988).

The participants in the discussion also quoted sensitive internal data to portray how miserable the lives of Chinese intellectuals were. A sociologist used a Beijing survey to show that in the early 1980s, "mental laborers' income was 13% less than manual laborers'" (ibid. May 9, 1988). Another survey showed that because of low income, the average life-span of Chinese professionals was fifty-eight, about ten years less than the average life-span of the general population (ibid.).

The government invested little in education and gave intellectuals inadequate pay not because it lacked money. In sharp contrast with the terrible conditions in these areas, official spending in general set new records every year. Hu Jiwei revealed that from 1977 to 1986, official spending increased 343 percent. In 1980, public money spent in purchasing cars for office use was less than 400 million yuan; in 1986, 5.34 billion. In 1987, fifty-nine county or city governments invested 8.3 billion yuan in building vacation hotels and guesthouses for their own convenience. "That amount of money is enough to build classrooms nationwide for those school children who are now sitting in perilous old buildings," Hu remarked (ibid. May 30, 1988). Here he referred to the internal reports that, in 1987 alone, several hundred school children were killed by collapsing school buildings, and the construction of some local vacation hotels, guesthouses, and theaters was in fact funded with money taken from the educational budget by local party officials.

That the participants in the "global membership" discussion paid special attention to the crisis in education and intellectuals' living conditions reflected both the general mood in Chinese society at that time and, in particular, the arresting rise of "class consciousness" among intellectuals and professionals (see Link 1992: 90–122). The combination of hyperinflation in the second half of the 1980s and the almost fixed income of intellectuals and professionals put the best educated in a grievous state. During a short four-month period in early 1987, seven middle-aged scientists in the CAS – all among the best in the country – died of disease caused by long-term malnutrition and overwork. Successive obituaries in the media shocked the general public (*Guangming Daily* July 15, 1988). A wide-ranging investigation revealed that intellectuals died suddenly and at a young age because poor living and working conditions were a common phenomenon in the country (*Science and Technology Daily* August 22, 1988). The media reported that in 1986 when a joint-venture Hilton Hotel was hiring waiters and waitress in Shanghai, most applicants were junior professors, graduate students, and college students at Chinese universities. The report called this event "the Hilton's glory and China's shame," and this story made many Chinese angry about their government's policy of underpaying the better educated (*Shehui* No. 1, pp. 16–17, 1987).

In 1987–88, investigations by journalists, sociologists, and policy consultants revealed that a sizable number of teachers in local schools had to sell snacks and drinks to their students during the break in order to supplement their low incomes (*Guangming Daily* July 13, 1988); that in major cities, some female teachers took second jobs as dance-hostesses at bars, and graduate students sold cigarettes (*World Economic Herald* June 20, 1988); and that because they saw that education would not bring rewards, a large number of parents let their children quit school to work, and consequently during 1980–87, nationwide more than 40 million students dropped out of grade schools and high schools (*Zhongguo Funu* No. 12, 1988; *Shehui* No. 3, pp. 12–14, 1988).

These reports were first circulated internally and then published openly. In a nation that used to believe "All occupations are inferior to book learning" (*wanban jie xiapin, weiyou dushu gao*), and which knew that industrial East Asia's success was greatly helped by investment in human capital, such reports plus the reality of how intellectuals lived naturally produced a burning sense of national crisis. This situation largely explains not only why the regime's self-glorifying patriotic campaign failed, but also why the intellectuals, including university students, were so ready to take to the streets in the spring of 1989.

Many of the participants in the discussion concluded that the national crisis was in fact the crisis of socialism (*World Economic Herald* July 18 and 11; October 3, 1988) and that, to save the Chinese nation, all the once sacred "doctrines" or "principles" impairing the nation must be eliminated (ibid. May 16; April 25 and 11; March 28 and 21, 1988). The following two statements are typical:

The best approach [to solve China's "global membership" problem] is to separate politics from ideology. . . . We ought to study the success, and failure, of socialism as well as those of capitalism, in order to find out what is good for the development of China, taking this as the reference for decision making. (Speech by Yuan Zhiming, a faculty member at the Cadre School of the CYL Central Committee, at the Beijing conference on the "global membership" problem on August 23, 1988)

We should borrow everything potentially conducive to the advance of Chinese society and make use of it in our enterprise, no matter what class character these foreign things have, which social system they belong to, or under what historical conditions they came into the world. (A letter by a bank employee in Xinjiang, *World Economic Herald* May 9, 1988)

In the television documentary *River Elegy,* the counterelite's attack on the regime's patriotic appeal took a more emotional form. The production team was composed of young professionals in their twenties and thirties: Su Xiaokang, a faculty member at the Beijing Broadcasting College; Wang Luxiang, a junior professor at the Beijing Teachers College; Xia Jun, a reporter for the Central Television Station; Zhang Gang, a research fellow at the IRESR under the State Council; Xie Xuanjun, an instructor at the Cadre School of the CYL Central Committee; and Yuan Zhiming, the faculty member just quoted. In addition, two persons served as advisers: Jin Guantao, who was an activist in the "furor of cultural studies" and whose background was given in Chapter 2, and Li Yining, an economics professor at Beijing University and a leading advocate of the privatization of China's economy.

Within the Central Television Station, deputy director Chen Hanyuan's role was critical, as he gave his full support for the production and release of *River Elegy* when its theme caused controversy and resulted in political pressure being applied from some old leaders at the top (*Wenhui Yuekan* No. 1, pp. 9–10, 1989).

In the fall of 1987, when the team gathered to draft the screenplay, its members arrived at a consensus:[14] As the most popular form of the mass media, television should be used to promulgate those ideas generally accepted by the intellectual elite during the "furor of cultural studies," and "a political-commentary television film" (*dianshi zhenglun pian*) was in order; this prospective documentary, whose subject was to be the Yellow River, must not fall into the stereotype that the PCPD and the party's Central Secretariat's Research Center had set up for the patriotic campaign – homeland worship, history worship, and ancestor worship; and this film was to throw light on the tragic national psyche of the Chinese people and ponder the destiny of Chinese civilization under contemporary conditions.

The six-part television documentary chose three familiar symbols of China to start its journey of criticism – the dragon, the Great Wall, and the Yellow River. As 1988 was the Year of the Dragon, with the government's endorsement, great

[14]The following is based on interviews with Su Xiaokang in October 1990, Princeton, and Yuan Zhiming in August 1990, Boston. See also Su's recollection in the *Xiaofei Shibao* (Beijing) July 6, 1988.

enthusiasm for the dragon emblem was exhibited everywhere in China. The Ministry of Posts and Telecommunications issued a dragon stamp; huge dragon statues were erected in the parks and centers of major cities such as Tiananmen Square in Beijing; in television and radio broadcasting, programs centering around dragons were overwhelming. *River Elegy* unwraps what lies at the center of this dragon worship – a slave mentality of revering absolute power (see an interview with Wang Luxiang, *Yuanjian* [Taiwan] No. 12, p. 206, 1988):

Have people ever considered why the Chinese worship this fierce-looking monster? . . .

Some people say that there is a part of the Chinese culture that tolerates evil forces. Others say that the fatal flaw of the Chinese national character is its slickness and slyness, worldly wisdom, fatalism, and submissiveness. If that is the case, it did not happen accidentally. The lifeblood of this huge ancient agricultural nation was water. Yet water was controlled by the Dragon King. Thus the Chinese nation hated it even as it loved it, cursed it even as it praised it. . . .

This ancient idol [i.e., the dragon], both awesome and fearsome, embodies many of our ancestors' nightmares. How can we let it express our present sorrow and nostalgia too? (*River Elegy* Part I, in *People's Daily* June 12, 1988)[15]

Then *River Elegy* opens fire on the Great Wall, the reification of "an inward-looking culture that prizes stability."

[About B.C. 350] Alexander, a great king of the West who ruled by the Aegean Sea, led his invincible Macedonian army on an expedition taking him far from home to conquer ancient European, African, and Asian empires.

As if echoing to Alexander the Great's eastward conquering, the First Emperor of Qin embarked on a massive anti-Hun war. Yet this great Chinese ruler, unlike Alexander who wandered from place to place, built the Great Wall in accordance to his way of thinking and imagination characteristic of an Oriental emperor. Alexander could never conceive such a wall even in his dreams. . . .

The Great Wall enveloped this quiet, mature agricultural civilization closely, which, over time, lost. . . . acquisitiveness. . . .

The Great Wall is the object of unparalleled adulation. People are proud of the fact that it was the only piece of human engineering on the earth visible to the moon-landing astronauts and insist on using it as the symbol of Chinese power and vitality. Yet if somehow the Great Wall could speak, it would certainly tell the descendants of Chinese civilization bluntly that it was created by fate, and that it cannot stand for strength, acquisitiveness, and glory, but only isolation, conservatism, passive defenses, and tim-idity. Worse still, because of its massiveness and ancientness, the Great Wall also made self-glorification, arrogance, and self-deception an integral part of the national character (*River Elegy* Part II, *Wenhui Bao* June 28, 1988).

Compared with the reexamination of the dragon and the Great Wall, com-ments in *River Elegy* on the Yellow River were even more imaginative, full of metaphors. The critical effect of the text was greatly enhanced by the fact that

[15]The text of *River Elegy* was translated into English anonymously. All the quotations here are taken from this translation (with minor alterations made by me), a copy of which is in the Fairbank Center Library, Harvard University. I am indebted to both the anonymous translator and the library.

the Chinese language does not have tense; most comments, unless specific temporal words were in place, could be interpreted as referring to both the past and the present.

The Yellow River, says the text of *River Elegy*, is both the "cradle of Chinese civilization" and at the same time a tyrant over the nation. During a 2,540 year period (B.C. 602 – A.D. 1938), the river broke over its banks an average of twice every three years and changed its course once every hundred years, causing countless loss of human life and property. In order to bring this "most brutal river on the earth" under control, the Chinese had to build water conservancy works from ancient times. Here lies the secret of the long-lasting Oriental despotism, because "given the level of productive forces at that time, such works could be completed only by mobilizing tens of thousands of people under a highly centralized autocratic regime." In this hydraulic society, "myriads of insignificant individuals were organized according to one order to support the supreme ruler at the very top" (*River Elegy* Part I, in *People's Daily* June 12, 1988).

Are not the thousand-kilometer long dikes that contain the swirling Yellow River an excellent symbol of our unified social structure? . . .
This distinctive social structure made China flourish greatly. But within this marvel of great unity, and beneath the glowing exterior of this overly ripe civilization in which absolute adulation of the emperor, of sages, of the old, and of ancestral memorial tables were entwined, the core of that social structure was slowly rotting. This situation very much resembled the present situation in which the Yellow River dikes are silently being hollowed out by mole crickets, ants, and field mice. The Confucian bureaucracy had an irresistible tendency to corrode, power itself becoming a corrosive agent. Hence, once a dynasty reached its peak, collapse lay just ahead. (*River Elegy* Part V, in *Guangming Daily* July 1, 1988)

Although dynasties replaced one another, the underlying social structure was almost unchanged.

This mysterious superstable structure dominated us for 2,000 years. . . . Today, the specter of the great unity seems to linger still in the good earth of China . . . Bureaucratism, the idea that prerogative and privilege go with position, and corruption continue to damage the "four modernizations" program. These persistent ancient social disorders are somewhat like the silt that the Yellow River carries every year, which clogs the lower reaches of the watercourse, gradually building up to a crisis. (ibid.)

Disasters brought about by political crises are analogous to those brought about by the flooding Yellow River, occurring cyclically. In Chinese history, a political cataclysm

occurred every 200 or 300 years, . . . very much like the endless flooding of the Yellow River. . . . Young sprouts of new elements in Chinese civilization came to an early end again and again during cyclical cataclysms.
In fact, frightening social cataclysms are by no means either remote or strangers to the Chinese people of today, for instance, the "Cultural Revolution." . . . Have the kind-

hearted folks ever wondered why this cataclysm broke out within the short space of less than 20 years following the Liberation? Does this mean the cyclical shocks to society of ancient times are to continue? . . .

The Chinese people's hope that there will never again be cataclysms is like the hope that the Yellow River will never again flood.

But floods are unpredictable. (ibid.)

The authors of *River Elegy* made a good prediction; a cataclysm occurred less than one year after these gloomy lines were drawn.

By censoriously looking through the three symbols of China, *River Elegy* tells viewers that "Yellow River civilization" as a way of life and a method of organizing socioeconomic activity only belongs to yesterday: "This plot of yellowish brown land cannot teach us what is the true scientific spirit. The devastating Yellow River cannot teach us what is true democratic awareness" (*River Elegy* Part VI, in *Guangming Daily* July 4, 1988).

Lucian Pye (1986: 224) remarks that "the Chinese, as David Shipler has said of the Russians, have '. . . a profound aversion to the western habit of turning the darkest defects of society into the sunlight for ruthless scrutiny. Our delight in self-criticism, and our guilt when we fail to dissect ourselves with sufficient honesty, bring to [them] something close to visceral revulsion.'" Pye's judgment lost ground when critical members of Chinese society had the chance to be heard.

River Elegy advocates that China's future depends on its absorption of "new civilizing elements" – democracy and capitalism. Its authors used "sea/azure civilization" to symbolize the new civilizing dynamism, contrasting with "continental/yellow civilization."

Back in the time of ancient Greece, the ideal of democracy was rising together with sea power, and sea power brought about a democratic revolution.

The social antecedents of modern bourgeois revolution in the West were also developed by Europeans' overseas navigation routes. The ships that began to sail on the open seas starting in the 15th century both opened the curtain on world trade and colonization, and also carried the hope for science and democracy. It was azure associated with these small sailing ships that symbolizes the modern world. (*River Elegy* Part VI, in *Guangming Daily* July 4, 1988)

To meet the challenge of "sea civilization," the Chinese must first develop a rational and open psychology. China can no longer afford to stay in blind patriotism, as reflected vividly in international athletic contests: "When the flag of the PRC is hoisted, everybody jumps and cries. And when we lose? We all curse, smash things, make a scene. A people whose psychology can no longer put up with defeat" (*River Elegy* Part I, in *People's Daily* June 12, 1988).

The political use of this blind patriotism can be seen in the "Chinese learning as essence, Western learning as utility" approach typical of China's ruling elites since the 1840s. After the Opium War the Qing foreign affairs bureaucrats bought back powerful warships and set up ordnance factories one after another. . . . When the Sino-Japanese War [1894–95] broke out, China had more warships than Japan.

But none of this prevented the Qing Empire from being beaten first by France and then Japan. . . . Technology could not rescue a regime from defeat when its institutions were corrupted. . . .

Whereas the Hundred-Day Reform [1898], in which Yan Fu [the first student the Qing regime sent to England to study naval matters] had taken part, collapsed, the Japanese Meiji reforms succeeded. . . . Ito Hirobumi, Yan's classmate in the British naval college, was appointed as Japan's prime minister for several terms and led that island nation quickly to join the club of the world powers. (*River Elegy* Part VI, in *Guangming Daily* July 4, 1988)

Today, some Chinese shout themselves hoarse denouncing the Western lifestyle, values, and ideals, though they never refuse to enjoy imported luxury sedans and upscale consumer goods. (*River Elegy* Part III, in *Guangming Daily* June 21, 1988)

Chinese ruling elites' rejection of institution borrowing from the West has caused China to lose many good opportunities to catch up with the West and, as a result, it still faces the "global membership" crisis. Now a new opportunity stands before the Chinese – the rise of Japan and the four little dragons and the emergence of the Pacific region as the most dynamic economy in the world (*River Elegy* Part IV, in *Guangming Daily* June 26, 1988). China must not repeat its previous mistakes and miss this golden opportunity again.

History provides testimony that modernizing efforts undertaken under the governmental model of a continental culture cannot give a nation a great civilizing dynamism, even though they may be able to take in new scientific-technological results, put satellites in the sky, or produce atomic bombs. . . .

Ignorance and superstition [must be] wiped out.

The azure, sweet spring water of science and democracy [must be] sprinkled on the yellow soil. . . .

The Yellow River has reached the great and suffering opening into the sea. . . . It must get rid of its fear of the great ocean. (*River Elegy* Part VI, in *Guangming Daily* July 4, 1988)

The impact of the television documentary on Chinese society was astonishing. (See Wakeman 1989.) By 1988, there were 38.7 television sets per 100 Chinese in urban areas, and 6.6 sets per 100 Chinese in rural areas (*Statistical Yearbook of China's Domestic Market* 1990: 414). Given that the average family size in urban China was three persons and in rural five, the whole urban population and about 30 percent of the rural population were exposed to television broadcasting by the time the documentary was shown.

River Elegy was shown twice on Central Television, the sole national network.[16] The first broadcast was in June 1988. The first five parts were shown on prime time, from 7:30 to 9:30 P.M. After these five parts had appeared, Hu Qili,

---

[16]The following is based on interviews with Yuan Zhiming, August 1990, and Su Xiaokang, October 1990.

Politburo Standing Committee member in charge of cultural affairs, telephoned Ai Zhisheng, minister of television, to complain about the "negative influence" of *River Elegy*. Ai responded: "Five parts have been shown. If we don't release Part VI, viewers will swear at us. It's better to show the complete documentary and criticize it afterward." Hu agreed.

After the first showing, Wang Zhen, vice-president and a vigorous supporter of the regime's patriotic campaign, took the lead in attacking *River Elegy*. He called up Tan Wenrui, chief editor of the *People's Daily,* and remarked angrily: "*River Elegy* is vicious! Su Xiaokang is a bad man. . . . Li Yining pushes for privatization and wants to restore capitalism. I fought for many years for the establishment of the Communist state, but have never thought that the PRC's educational system would produce such professors and graduate students. . . . Intellectuals are very dangerous!"[17]

Wang told the *People's Daily* to denounce *River Elegy*, but the editors were unwilling to do this dirty work. At this moment, an internal journal edited by the New China News Agency for the reference of senior leaders reported that when meeting with Lee Kuan Yew, Singapore's prime minister, Zhao Ziyang gave him a videotape of *River Elegy* as a present, and said: "It is worth viewing." Having learned that the top leaders had different views about the documentary, the *People's Daily* simply refused to organize a public condemnation, despite pressure from some senior leaders.

In August 1988 the documentary was shown again, with all six parts appearing at prime time. Soon the videotape was released. Moreover, the text of the documentary was published in major newspapers, reprinted by many other journals and local newspapers, and also appeared in the form of a book in hundreds of thousands of copies.

The subject of concern, the unconventional viewpoints, the sentimental mood, the poetic and lyrical language style, and the novel visual effects made *River Elegy* unusually attractive and provocative. While a few radical intellectuals and university students blamed it for attacking "four thousand years" (i.e., Chinese history) too much and attacking "forty years" (i.e., the Communist period) too little, most viewers appeared to be greatly affected by its argument.[18] Within a week after the first showing, the Central Television Station received more than a thousand letters from viewers of various categories, including professionals, students, young workers, servicemen, police officers, officials, and young farmers, and most of them supported the documentary. Such a positive reaction from viewers was unparalleled in the thirty-year history of the

---

[17] Upon being informed by the *People's Daily* of Wang's attack, the authors of *River Elegy* passed it on to the *Mirror Monthly* in Hong Kong (No. 11, pp. 44–45, 1988).

[18] Conversation with Su Wei, a literature critic, in July 1989 and January 1991.

station (*Zhongwai Dianshi* No. 5, p. 144, 1988; *Wenhui Yuekan* No. 1, pp. 10, 28–30, 1989).

The authors of the documentary were invited to meet viewers in many parts of the country. Wang Luxiang, Yuan Zhiming, and Xie Xuanjun went to almost all universities and colleges in Beijing and the halls were always full of excited audiences. Yuan, a former army officer, was even invited by the headquarters of the PLA Armored Force and Engineer Troops and the Beijing Garrison Command to address middle-ranking officers, who were enthusiastic about the documentary.[19] Many work units organized employees to discuss questions raised by *River Elegy*. The Beijing Public Security Bureau even issued a directive to assign the municipal police to study the documentary. Some officials recommended the documentary be made standard political study material for work units (*Zhoujia Shenghuo Bao* October 5, 1988). In the summer of 1988, the local authorities in Tianjin arranged a "*River Elegy* Week," reshowing the documentary, selling the videotapes and books of the text, and holding discussions. In the meantime, in Wuhan middle-school students participated in a summer camp whose program consisted of public speech contests on the subject of *River Elegy*.[20] In the summer of 1988, Guangzhou initiated a citywide "Azure Action" program in which youth took part in debates and essay competitions on the documentary. About the same time, the city of Taiyuan held a triumphal gathering for the documentary production team when it came to meet the local viewers (*Wenhui Yuekan* No. 1, p. 10, 1988). Those activities were usually sponsored by local CYL networks or official student councils; local governments either took part in sponsorship or, at least, gave tacit consent to the organizers.[21]

In the intellectual elite's patriotic countercampaign, the pattern of institutional parasitism was displayed in various ways. The countercampaign occurred on a national level, crossing the official boundaries between work units, systems (*xitong*, e.g., the educational system, the cultural system, and the system of journalism), and regions. Activists who worked in different units, systems, and regions could come together, arrive at a consensus, and eventually initiate the countermovement mainly because there had existed a chain of personal connections and trust: If Mr. Wang was a close friend of Ms. Li, who was a relative of Mr. Chen, who was a classmate of Mrs. Ma, then they could put confidence in each other, form a group, and start a venture. Such is the case of the preparation of the "furor of cultural studies" and of *River Elegy*.

[19] Interview with Yuan in August 1990.
[20] Interview with Yuan in August 1990.
[21] Interview with Su Xiaokang in October 1990.

As soon as personal networking provided a starting point, activists could move into a much wider scene and launch their projects by using institutional and material resources supplied by voluntary, semiofficial, and official structures.

When its undertaking provoked a strong reaction from vested interests, the counterelite might be able to take advantage of differences among the top leaders to sustain its controversial effort. In such a situation, the official mechanism of political control and social mobilization could be manipulated by oppositional elements to serve their own course. What is striking in the national discussion and dissemination of *River Elegy* is that, while the work-unit and mass-organization system of communication and mobilization (i.e., political study, group meetings, "reports on current events" [*shishi baogao*], etc.; see Barnett 1967; Schurmann 1968; Walder 1986) was largely intact by the late 1980s, it was increasingly being used to do the reverse of what it was supposed to do: Much of the same official mechanism that formerly had served exclusively to buttress the party leadership and the Communist system now also served to channel information and promulgate critical thought to delegitimize and destabilize the regime. The ambiguity of the character of institutions and their functionally multipurpose nature is expressed vividly here.

Conclusion

The post-Mao ruling elite made the patriotic appeal in response to the deep resentment against the party-state's antiintellectual policy during the Maoist era, and the outcry for "all-around Westernization" in China. The target audience was urban citizens, especially educated youth.

There was evidence that, unlike the socialist-moral appeal the regime had made before, there was indeed a potential in Chinese society for patriotism to be of great attraction. According to the nationwide survey in 1987 conducted by Min Qi et al., all categories showed a strong patriotic sentiment, and the better educated the person, the stronger the sentiment was (Table 7).

Yet the ruling elite failed to utilize this great potential because of its clumsy handling of patriotism as a political appeal. In using patriotism to repair the regime's legitimacy, the ruling elite rudely stratified the objects of loyalty: Loyalty to the Communist regime was described as higher than loyalty to the motherland per se. This was simply too outrageous to the better educated who were so resentful of the regime's misconduct.

To make this "Communist patriotism" work, the ruling elite relied on the strategy of vertical comparison, in the hope of glorifying the regime and creating system-centered national pride among educated youth. This proved to be a miscalculation in the late 1980s. By that time, the educated Chinese had be-

Table 7. *Chinese citizens' loyalty to their country (Question: "Do you agree with the statement that it is reasonable to withdraw one's love for the country if it disappoints one?")*

Category	% Disagree
Workers	76.36
Businessmen in nonstate enterprises	62.56
Professionals	80.90
Civil servants	84.73
Farmers	69.19
Illiterate	61.90
Grade school graduates	69.32
Junior high school graduates	68.61
Senior high school graduates	76.91
College graduates	85.68
Total (1,712 subjects)	74.95

Source: Min Qi (1989: 23). There are several similar question and response tabulations in this book (24–28).

come very aware of the outside world and of socialist China's relative status in the international community in terms of socioeconomic development. The regime's self-glorifying effort merely stimulated the intellectual elite's countermove, in which patriotic sentiments were fully mobilized for the purpose of delegitimizing the regime.

In debates over "global membership" and *River Elegy,* we see a different kind of patriotic appeal, which is the antithesis of the regime's. While the official version of patriotism was state-centered, the counterelite's version of patriotism was nation-centered. The former used patriotism as a means to channel emotional attachment from the nation to the government; the latter defined the nation as the sole object of Chinese loyalty and duty. The former emphasized vertical comparison; the latter, horizontal comparison. The former desensitized citizens' sense of urgency and encouraged them to be satisfied with the status quo; the latter sensitized citizens to a concept of national crisis and called on them to engage in radical change. The former used Chinese Communism to combat Western capitalism; the latter told the people that China's hope lies in comprehensive assimilation of the Western and the capitalist.

The counterelite believed that its version of patriotism was a genuine one; it does not sound as comforting as the regime's "magic potion–like" patriotism (*mihuntang shi de* – Su Xiaokang's words; see *Wenhui Yuekan* No. 1, pp. 3 and 4, 1989) but serves the nation's interests better. As Su put it:

The kind of love [for China] we advocate is bitter, but far more sacred, purer, and loftier than the kind of patriotism that advocates blind worship of one's country. . . . This "patriotism" looks like love of the country, but in fact harms her. It induces the people to love her backward and ugly parts, and delights that "A son doesn't dislike his mother because of her bad looks; a dog doesn't dislike his home because it's poor." . . .

To truly love the country is to wish her be reborn and have a new life. (*Wenhui Yuekan* No. 1, p. 6, 1988. See a similar statement by Qin Benli, the chief organizer of the "global membership" debate, in *World Economic Herald* April 10, 1989)

According to this definition, to combat political and economic structures impairing the Chinese nation's interests is the essence of patriotism and the highest duty of a patriot.

This nonconformist, independent, critical, pro-change, and cosmopolitan patriotism naturally inspired violent reaction from those having vested interests in the status quo, as Wang Zhen's behavior demonstrated. After June 1989 the "global membership" discussion was cited as one of the chief sins of the *Herald* (*People's Daily* November 26, 1990).

In its manipulation of patriotism for political purposes, the post-Mao regime provides an intriguing contrast to the Stalin regime during World War II (of the latter, see Snyder 1956: 223–26). After the 1917 Communist takeover, the Bolsheviks made "class," not the "nation," the origin of political identification and solidarity, and based their legitimacy claim exclusively on the Revolution – the total break with the past. So did the Chinese Communists after 1949; during the Cultural Revolution, patriotism was even rejected as "bourgeois ideology."

The Stalin regime moved to patriotism and called on the Russians "to fight the Fascists and save mother Russia" because few people would die to rescue Bolshevism and the party. The post-Mao regime resorted to patriotism because it was confronted by a pressing legitimacy crisis and had failed to solve it by Marxist and Communist goals and symbols.

The similarity ends here, however. When the Stalin regime made its patriotic appeal, the crisis was created by enemy invasion, and the regime's task was to organize countrymen to save their fatherland. But when the post-Mao regime made its patriotic appeal, no real enemies existed; the crisis was created by the regime's own misgovernment. The Communist regime did attempt to make capitalism and Western influence into enemies, but the Chinese people by that time did not regard Western capitalist countries as harming their nation's interests. To the contrary, in the intellectual elite's patriotic countercampaign, it was *the enemy within* – the corrupt Communist system and its policies – that harmed the Chinese nation's interests.

Moreover, during the war the Stalin regime did not stratify the objects of patriotic loyalty: Mother Russia was the only one, and the Russian people were indeed willing to die in battle for this beloved object. But the post-Mao regime

rudely made love of the motherland a reason to love the discredited party. This conduct made people think more critically about the institutional roots of China's problems. As seen in the popular protest of 1989, the result was that patriotism, which saved the Communist regime in Russia during the war, drove the Chinese Communist regime into deeper crisis.

In late communism, nationalism served as a powerful anticommunist force whenever a people began to see communist sociopolitical structures as the principal cause of their country's problems. In Poland during the 1980s the government called for a "socialist renewal" in its battle against Solidarity, which sought a "national renewal," that is, decommunization, program (Keane 1988a: 370). The result, as everybody knows, was that the government failed miserably.

At first glance, the Chinese counterelite's radical patriotism – which aimed to cast aside China's bad institutions and values in order to save the nation – as embodied in the "global membership" debate and *River Elegy* only repeated what the nationalistic intellectuals of the late nineteenth century and the iconoclasts during the May Fourth Movement of 1919 had said (on these earlier trends, see Levenson 1965: 95–108, 125–33). But a closer look will reveal an important difference. In the late nineteenth and the early twentieth centuries, there was no foundation in reality to support the idea that a modern *Chinese* industrial society was possible. Therefore, while talking about "all-around Westernization," the earlier radical intellectuals meant a total cultural transformation of China (Lin 1979). By the late 1980s, however, there was plenty of evidence that the Chinese could attain modern industrial civilization without abandoning their own culture, as Taiwan, Hong Kong, and Singapore had demonstrated, a fact obviously known to many of the participants in the "global membership" debate and the authors of *River Elegy*. Thus, when talking about "all-around Westernization" or "cultural transformation," the radical intellectuals of the late 1980s meant more institutional than cultural change; their primary target was not the traditional but the Communist.

6

Admission of the "primary stage of socialism" and the counterelite's two developmental models

This chapter covers the eve of the 1989 Spring Democracy Movement. In late 1987, party chief Zhao Ziyang at the Thirteenth Party Congress announced that China was still in the "primary stage of socialism" and urged the party-state bureaucracy to be more tolerant of economic and social practices that were conventionally regarded as nonsocialist. The theory of the "primary stage of socialism" was used to justify the economic reforms that had introduced many semicapitalist methods into China's economy. In the counterelite's interpretation, Zhao's announcement was a shy admission of the impracticability of socialism in China. In the relaxed political climate following this announcement, the counterelite began openly debating the best way to end communism in China, which resulted in two competing programs: "enlightened despotism" and "liberal democracy."

Background:
the political implications of the Dengist economic reforms

As I pointed out earlier, when I discussed the dual-traffic policy of "anti-Left in economics and anti-Right in politics," the core of the Dengist reform program was economic restructuring aiming5at productivity and efficiency. In this regard, the reforms were based on a simple principle: Any economic methods were acceptable as long as "socialist public ownership" was maintained. With this base line, the Dengist leadership allowed a variety of market mechanisms and capitalist entrepreneurship to operate. Of these the major steps taken by 1988 had been the following (see Perry and Wong 1985; Zweig and Butler 1985; Harding 1987: Chs. 4–6; Vogel 1989; Byrd and Lin 1990; Davis and Vogel 1990):

1. The abolition of the "people's commune" system and the evolution of the household responsibility system starting in 1978. The former gave the ownership and management of land and the right to distribute rural income to the

collective. The latter, though still formally preserving public ownership of land, entitled individual peasant households substantial rights in land use and ultimately acquiesced in peasants engaging in land transfer.

2. The legalization of nonstate enterprises[1] in the late 1970s, ranging from family-run retail and repair shops to mid-size firms in the service and manufacturing sectors, hiring dozens or even hundreds of workers.

3. The opening of "enclaves of capitalism," that is, "special economic zones," in 1980. The government used these places as the bridge to link the economy of the PRC with those of Hong Kong, Taiwan, and the capitalist world. The SEZs served as channels to absorb foreign technology and capital and as laboratories for the testing, modification, and spread of capitalist organizations, techniques, and managerial ideology.

4. The establishment of joint ventures and foreign-owned businesses in regions other than the SEZs starting in the early 1980s. In such companies, the foreign share could be as large as 100 percent, and management could be basically capitalist.

5. The growth of managerial independence in state industries. Experimental measures included the "managerial responsibility system" (i.e., managers rather than party secretaries were in charge); the "industrial contract system" (i.e., the firm's rights and responsibilities were prescribed by the state-firm contract, as protection against arbitrary administrative interference such as extra fees); the "rental system" (i.e., individuals were allowed to rent small to medium-sized enterprises from the state and to run the business freely); the "joint-stock system"; and the bankruptcy of small state companies.

6. The narrowing of the range of administratively decided prices. By early 1988, the pricing of most agricultural products and 55 out of 120 key industrial products had been set by the market.

7. The experiment with limited labor and capital markets starting in 1986. In the former, part of the labor force was distributed and reallocated through employee–employer contracts instead of government assignments. In the latter, the government issued stocks and bonds of state industries to individuals and collectives.

---

[1] Throughout the discussion, I prefer the term "nonstate businesses" to "private businesses" because, as pointed out in Chapter 1, few such businesses in China of the 1980s can be strictly called "private." Many nonstate businesses had state or collective institutions as their supervisors (*guakao*), party-state officials as their bosses, and official institutions as their profit sharers. "Nonstate entities" range from single persons and households to formally collective or cooperative bodies such as a village, a township, or a neighborhood. Russia under reform also has many enterprises that are neither "public" nor "private" (*Economist* January 4, 1992, pp. 40–41). In her study of the Hungarian economic reforms, Anna Seleny (1991) stresses that it is misleading to use the "private economy" concept to designate the "second economy" in pre-1990 Hungary.

At each stage of these developments, the economic reforms aroused angry reactions from within the party establishment. Their criticism focused especially on the SEZs, the growth of nonstate businesses, and decollectivization. The attack on the SEZ policy had its first high tide in early 1982, about a year after the opening of Shenzhen and Zhuhai. It was led by veteran revolutionaries in the party and the army, who blamed the SEZs for "giving up sovereignty" and "allowing the return of colonial rule." They asked, "We have been devoted to the revolution for decades and taken great pains to push imperialists out of China. Why does the government today invite foreign demons back to China to exploit our workers?" (quoted from *Guangming Daily* January 1, 1986).

To appease these angry veteran revolutionaries, the party's Central Committee, at Hu Yaobang's suggestion, invited some of them to visit Shenzhen personally in the spring of 1982, in the hope that the remarkable improvement in the local economy would change their minds. After the visit, however, the veteran revolutionaries commented sadly: "Apart from the five-star red flag flying over the municipal government building, in Shenzhen there is nothing that can still be called socialist" (quoted from *China Youth News* August 13, 1987).

The attack on the SEZ policy had another high tide during the Anti–Spiritual Pollution Campaign of late 1983. Party leaders such as Chen Yun and Deng Liqun characterized the SEZs as "material up, spiritual down" (i.e., economic progress was made at the expense of socialist values) and as "conduits for spiritual pollution."[2] *Zhuhai,* a leading newspaper in the city of Zhuhai, was prohibited from circulating in Hunan and Hubei by the respective provincial party propaganda departments, because the newspaper would bring in "bourgeois ideas" typical of the SEZ.[3]

The condemnation of the nonstate economy intensified with its growth. At the outset, during the transition to household farming, the resistance came mainly from local party officials, who saw that the change would undermine the basis of their feudal lordlike dominance over peasants, and who, therefore, blamed the new system for "bringing capitalism back to the countryside." In September 1980, when the party's Central Committee held a nationwide provincial-leadership conference, only three of twenty-nine delegates agreed to allow peasants in extremely poor areas to try the responsibility system.[4] In 1981, when Anhui province, under Deng Xiaoping's close friend Wan Li, led the rural decollectivization trend, in the neighboring province of Jiangsu peasants were

---

[2] Personal notes of late 1983.
[3] Conversation with a party official in Beijing, March 1984.
[4] Communication with Chen Yizi, advisor to Hu Yaobang and Zhao Ziyang on the rural reforms, in September 1989. See also Zhao Ziyang's recollection (*People's Daily Overseas Edition* February 8, 1988).

called on by the provincial party committee to "resist the bad influence of private farming from Anhui."[5] Up to the winter of 1982, already a year after the party's Central Committee officially decided to implement the household responsibility system nationwide, in provinces like Guangxi and Heilongjiang those who dared to take the lead to dismember public land could be imprisoned by order of local authorities.[6]

The policy allowing unemployed urban youth to open single-person stores and workshops in the late 1970s did not arouse a general negative response from urban party officials. The majority of the unemployed were former Red Guards who had just returned to cities from exile in the countryside. Numbering in the tens of millions and related to almost every urban family, their unemployment was the chief cause of urban disorder. To give them a chance to make a living would alleviate a headache for many urban families as well as local governments.

But as larger nonstate firms grew out of single-person stores and workshops, and peasant businesses expanded from rural to urban areas, a strong negative reaction emerged among party bureaucrats. By early 1986, nationwide nonstate businesses numbered 23 million (Investigation and Research Division 1986: 1).[7] In 1986, according to a sample survey by the Institute for Research on Rural Development in the CASS, 7.4 percent of the nonstate businesses hired more than seven workers; the average size of such businesses was 16 employees and 50,000 yuan in capital; and about 17,000 nonstate firms hired more than 100 employees (*Jingji Cankao* November 14, 1988). In 1985, the self-reported average annual income, surely understated, for people working in the nonstate sector was 3,063 yuan, about 2.5 times that of state employees.[8]

Moreover, within nonstate firms, income differentials between employees and employers were widening rapidly. Based on the sample survey by the Institute for Research on Rural Development just quoted, in two counties of Shaanxi Province, the differential was 1:19 in 1982, 1:21 in 1984, and 1:31 in 1986. In the southeast coastal region in the mid-1980s, within nonstate firms with seven workers or less, the differential was 1:7; within firms of more than seven workers, the differential was 1:13. In Wenzhou Prefecture, Zhejiang Province, where nonstate businesses dominated state ones as early as 1985,

[5] Based on my investigation in the neighboring counties of the two provinces in the winter of 1981.
[6] Conversation with Liu Binyan in February 1989.
[7] In August 1986, the Investigation and Research Division in the General Office of the State Council published a 302-page internal research report about nonstate businesses in China, the most comprehensive one in its kind.
[8] On the nonstate employees' average income, see Investigation and Research Division (1986: 300–2 and 135–41); on the state employees' average income, 1213 yuan in 1985, see *China's Statistical Survey* 1988: 98.

employees of nonstate firms earned about 1,500 yuan a year, their employers' from 30,000 to 50,000 yuan (*Jingji Cankao* November 14, 1988). In a society dominated by Maoist egalitarian principles for decades, such developments naturally provoked strong protest from state employees in general and government officials in particular.

On this point, Alec Nove's observation is insightful. He remarks that "though in the Soviet Union ideological principles have been adapted time and again to suit the political needs of the time," some beliefs are "genuinely held" by the general population. One of these is egalitarianism. "Market-based inequalities . . . are seen as part and parcel of the capitalist mentality, the sordid chase after 'profit,' and thus a violation of the 'socialist' ethos" (Brumberg 1990: 62–63; see a similar observation of Eastern Europe by Ash 1990: 261–62). A Soviet economist's comments present people's antimarket egalitarianism in communist countries better than any reports: "Unfortunately, there are millions of people in our country who prefer not to have any early vegetables rather than see their neighbors make money by growing them" (Brumberg 1990: 61). The Chinese have a nickname for this attitude – *hongyan bing* (redeye disease).

To defend nonstate businesses in China, which contributed so much to economic growth, the Dengist leadership offered several justifications. In the earlier stages when such businesses were no more than a single person or household stores and workshops, the reformers explained that people working in these businesses were either self-employed laborers or cooperative laborers operating on a family base. Since there was no exploitation involved, these businesses were socialist rather than capitalist (*Jingjixue Dongtai* No. 1, 1981; Liu Long et al. 1986: 4–5).

As employment in nonstate businesses extended to nonfamily members, Zhao Ziyang and his colleagues, under greater pressure from within party officialdom, drew a line in July 1981: Nonfamily members employed by such a firm must not exceed seven (*Geti Laodongzhe Shouce* 1984: 5–9).

Why seven? Because after a long search for "theoretical foundations" to legitimate the nonstate economy, assistants to the reformist leaders finally found a paragraph in Marx and Engels, which contained the number "eight" that allegedly designates the boundaries between the capitalist and the noncapitalist. That paragraph reads:

On the basis of his previous examination of constant and variable capital and surplus-value, Marx draws the conclusion that "not every sum of money, or of value, is at pleasure transformable into capital. To effect this transformation, in fact, a certain minimum of money or of exchange-value must be presupposed in the hands of the individual possessor of money or commodities." He then takes as an example the case of a worker in any branch of industry, who works eight hours daily for himself – that is, in producing the value of his wages – and the following four hours for the capitalist, in producing surplus-value, which immediately flows into the capitalist's pocket. In this case, a person would have to have at his disposal a sum of value allowing him to provide two workers with raw materials, instruments of labor and wages, in order to pocket enough surplus-value every day to live as well as one of his workers. As the aim of capitalist production is not mere subsistence but the increase of wealth, our man with his two workers would still not be a capitalist. Now in order to live twice as well as an ordinary worker and turn half the surplus-value produced back into capital, he would have to be able to employ eight workers, that is, he would have to possess four times the sum of value assumed above. It is after this [that] Marx observes: "Here, as in natural science, is shown the correctness of the law discovered by Hegel (in his *Logic*), that merely quantitative differences beyond a certain point pass into qualitative changes." (Engels 1976: 158–59; see Marx 1967: 291–92 for the quotations)

Citing this paragraph, the economic reformers argued that a nonstate firm with less than eight workers will not cause a "qualitative change" that brings about capitalism. So the compromise on seven workers as the maximum was reached.[9]

In all these respects regarding the legitimation of nonstate business, communist reformers resorted to the same strategies. In Kadar's Hungary eight employees were the maximum;[10] in Gorbachev's Soviet Union legally no one was allowed to employ anyone outside of the narrowly defined family. If someone wanted to set up a nonstate business, it must be done in a "cooperative" way, namely, a minimum of three persons were required in forming such a body (Brumberg 1990: 60). In a politicoeconomic culture that equates private economic activity with exploitation, one has to put a "collective" mask on anything that is nonstate.

Yet in practice, many nonstate firms in China soon exceeded the maximum of seven employees. The Fool's Water Melon Seeds Company in Wuhu, Anhui, exemplified this controversial breakthrough: During 1980–82, its founder, Nian Guangjiu, expanded his single-family workshop into a chain business with more than 180 employees and several million yuan of capital. By the summer of 1983, his business had even broken the state monopoly of international trade and established trade relations with Southeast Asian companies.[11]

Meanwhile, in places like Wenzhou, Guangdong, and Fujian, nonstate firms grew larger and larger and took over much business from state companies. More provocatively, about 15 percent of owners of nonstate businesses nationwide were Communist party members, and many nonmembers among the new rich tried hard to get party membership, calculating that "having a red hat"

[9]Several fellows in the CASS played a part in this legitimation process and I was told about it by them in late 1982; see also Liu Long et al. (1986: 4–5).

[10]Communication with Anna Seleny, a Hungary scholar, in the fall of 1990.

[11]Based on my interviews with r)sidents of Wuhu in the fall of 1983. Nian himself was not available for an interview because at that time he was under investigation by the local police for alleged tax evasion and bribery. See also *World Economic Herald* February 15, 1988.

would protect their business from arbitrary governmental interference (*Jingji Cankao* November 14, 1988).

Admission of the "primary stage of socialism"

From the mid-1980s on, attacks by party bureaucrats on the development of nonstate businesses intensified. They charged that exploitation did exist in such businesses and that these businesses had grown too fast and too large in the Southeast and were taking over the state economy's position as the dominant economic force there. They demanded that party members who owned such businesses should be expelled from the party and the new rich should not be allowed to obtain party membership (Investigation and Research Division 1986: 1–9; *Xueshu Jiaoliu* No. 1, pp. 50–53, 1987; Hu Guohua, Liu Jinghuai, and Chen Min 1988: 149–210).

Confronted by these criticisms, which were absolutely legitimate from the Communist point of view, the reformers could hardly find anything in the existing Marxist literature usable for their defense. As Richard Lowenthal (1984: 111–13) notes, by citing Marxist ideals, reformers in communist countries were able to speak for democratic change in their systems, but not for privatization. Marxism definitely leaves no room for private property. In all communist countries, economic reforms were doomed to encounter the toughest challenge when coming to address the question of property rights, for it was not an economic issue but a political one of fundamental importance (Schroeder 1988).

To meet the objections against the growth of nonstate businesses still using socialist language and to obtain more leeway for pragmatic economic policies to be implemented over the long run, Zhao Ziyang, backed by Deng Xiaoping and assisted by his think tanks, put forward a formula called "the theory of the primary stage of socialism" at the Thirteenth Party Congress in October 1987. According to this theory, after forty years of Communist rule, socialism in China

is still in its primary stage. We must proceed from this reality and not jump over this stage. . . .

During this primary stage we must . . . put the expansion of the productive forces at the center of all our work. Helping to expand the productive forces should become the point of departure in our consideration of all problems, and the basic criterion for judging our work should be whether it serves that end. (Zhao 1987: 14)

Following this theory, "the development of different types of ownership" is both necessary and desirable, as is the opening of labor and capital markets, for they are good for "the expansion of the productive forces [read: economic growth]" (ibid.: 31). As China will remain at "the primary stage of socialism" for one hundred years or more, any evaluations of economic policy that are not grounded on economic growth, but instead on ideological criteria, are "utopian," and doom one to commit to "Left mistakes" (ibid.: 10).

On the one hand, Zhao's formula spoke to the critics of the economic reform in the language of historical determinism: China's objective conditions determine that it has not entered the socialist stage as defined by Marx and Lenin; it is, at most, socialist in a marginal sense. One must not apply strictly socialist standards to judge things. For many decades to come, socialism in China will be mixed with capitalism.

On the other hand, Zhao's formula was designed to send a message to those eager to follow the nonsocialist road of doing business: "Go ahead, folks! The limits have been removed, and now there is plenty of leeway for you to get around." The Chinese people picked up this message instantly; a popular saying goes: "The theory of the primary stage of socialism is like a big basket: everything can be put in" (*Chuji jieduan shi ge kuang, sheme dou keyi wang li zhuang*).

To the counterelite, the publication of the "primary stage of socialism" formula as the framework of reform symbolized the regime's formal retreat from its commitment to a communist destiny. Until then, though the regime allowed many nonsocialist economic experiments to take place, it never forgot to remind the people that all this was expedient and that, as a Communist party, its ultimate goal was to put communism into reality. The outline "Communism as Practical Activity and as Ideological Education" of 1983, discussed in Chapter 4, was but one in a series of such announcements. Such reminders, of course, meant a lot to the people who had witnessed so many dramatic changes in policy.[12] The publication of the "primary stage" formula as the party's general framework was indeed intended to relieve their anxiety.[13]

This formula was especially meaningful in the light of the fate of its predecessor. As described in Chapter 3, during the 1979 Theory Forum, Su Shaozhi and Feng Lanrui proposed an essentially identical theory in order to open sufficient space for introducing nonsocialist policies. Yet for many years their proposal had been listed as one of the major examples of "bourgeois liberalism" by leaders such as Wang Zhen, Hu Qiaomu, and Deng Liqun (see,

---

[12] In communist politics, reperiodization of societal development always preludes major policy changes. For instance, after Lenin's death, the New Economic Policy (NEP) was defined by the Stalin regime "as a 'transitional' phase from capitalism to communism, whose negative characteristics were merely capitalist survivals, to be erased as quickly as possible so as to make way for the reign (*tsarstvo*) of full socialism, itself the first step toward communism. Consequently the basic economic principles and methods of NEP were unacceptable" (Brumberg 1990: 171; see also 98). Officially declared reperiodization has tremendous impact on the behavior of citizens of socialist systems, who by personal experience know their rulers too well.

[13] Conversation with Wu Guoguang in October 1990, who was on the drafting group for Zhao's report to the thirteenth Congress.

e.g., *People's Daily* October 25, 1983). Now a slightly modified version of that proposal became the party's general framework of reform, indicating that the ruling elite not only realized at heart that socialism is unfeasible in China, but also admitted this fact to the general public, albeit implicitly.

The consequences

In the political climate relaxed by the regime's implicit announcement that "socialism is dead in China," the counterelite quickly launched a campaign to seek alternatives to the existing system. The national debate on "new authoritarianism versus democratic liberalism" in 1988 and early 1989 constituted the core of that campaign.

The debate can be traced back to 1987,[14] immediately after the late 1986 student movement that led to Hu Yaobang stepping down as party chief. First in Shanghai and then in Beijing, young professionals deeply concerned with strategic choices for the endangered reform program began internally discussing political instability in changing societies. In Shanghai the discussion took place within three circles, whose memberships overlapped:

1. The Special Research Fellows Discussion Group of the Shanghai Party Propaganda Department was a forum made possible by Pan Weiming, a former CYL official who became head of the department in 1985, largely as a result of his connection to Hu Yaobang. In 1986, Pan initiated the Discussion Group by inviting fifty to sixty intellectuals to meet from time to time to talk over political, economic, and cultural issues in the reform process and offer concrete suggestions. Most of those invited had M.A. and Ph.D. degrees, having graduated in the 1980s and then taught or done research in universities and research institutes in Shanghai. When Jiang Zemin became the municipal party chief, he also asked for advice occasionally from these "special research fellows."[15]

2. The Shanghai Young Theoretical Workers Association, founded in early 1986, had nearly two hundred members, mainly employees of the Shanghai Academy of Social Sciences.

---

[14]The following is based on Informants nos. 17 and 18, conversations with Yuan Zhiming, and on recollections by Wu Jiaxiang (*World Economic Herald* January 16, 1989), Lu Tong (*New Observer* No. 21, pp. 2–3, 1988), Li Yuan (*China Spring* No. 1, pp. 7–9, 1990), Shao Jun (ibid., pp. 10–13), and Qiu Shaoqi (ibid., No. 2, pp. 44–47). Wu was among the most active participants in the debate. Lu's journal, the *New Observer*, was one of the organizing forces behind the debate. Li and Shao are pseudonyms of the same person also involved in the debate. Qiu's data largely came from a person who was doing field research in China during the controversy.

[15]After June 1989, when Pan lost his position and some members got in political trouble, the Discussion Group was no longer in operation. Jiang, as new party General Secretary, once tried to transfer a few members of the group to Beijing to work for him but did not succeed. The reason is unclear. In 1992 Pan was imprisoned for alleged "sexual misconduct" (based on Informant no. 42).

3. The Fudan University Young Theoretical Workers Association, also founded in early 1986, had about three hundred members, including junior professors, graduate students, and upper-class undergraduate students.

In Beijing the discussion was conducted first in an informal symposium called "The Salon Speeches," organized by junior members on the faculties of Beijing University and the Central Party School. In 1987, when such internal meetings were under way, dozens or even as many as a hundred people attended each one, mostly young intellectuals and professionals working in universities, research institutes, and think tanks.

This situation showed a great resemblance to Hungary in 1955–56 (Brzezinski 1967: 210–29) and the whole of Eastern Europe in the late 1980s (Ash 1990): Politically active intellectuals gathered informally, in the Petofi Clubs, discussion groups, and so forth, to exchange views about the current political development. Such discussions eventually prepared the intellectual climate for the revolutions in 1956 and 1989.

After the Thirteenth Party Congress approved the theory of the "primary stage of socialism" and the political climate thawed, the previously closed discussions quickly came to the surface. Many more people became involved, and many speeches that were delivered earlier to small circles were published in national newspapers and journals.

In Shanghai, the three circles stirring up the debate expanded: People from Huadong Normal University, Shanghai University, Shanghai Teachers College, and the local CYL took part. New outlets for publication included the *World Economic Herald,* the *Wenhui Bao,* and the *Jiefang Daily.* In Beijing, the debate was carried out on an even larger scale than in Shanghai.[16]

---

[16]The debate unfolded mainly on the following occasions: a conference to commemorate the tenth anniversary of "The Debate on the Criterion of Truth" in May 1988, organized by the Institute of Marxism, Leninism, and Mao Zedong Thought; "A Middle-aged and Young Theoretical Workers Symposium" in June 1988, held at the Research Division of the PCPD; a meeting to commemorate the ninetieth anniversary of the Hundred Day Reform of 1898 in September cosponsored by the *New Observer* magazine, the *Zhongguo Bing* (China's malady) editorial board, and the Capital Institute for Research on Legal Systems and Social Development; "The First National Symposium on Problems Concerning Intellectuals" co-initiated by the *China Youth News,* the *World Economic Herald,* the *Guangming Daily,* and the New Knowledge Academy in the same month; a conference to commemorate the May Fourth Movement of 1919 in July 1988 hosted by the magazine *Huaren Shijie* (Chinese world), belonging to the party's United Front Work Department; "The First National Conference on Theories of Modernization" in November cosponsored by the Beijing Institute for Research on Social and Scientific-Technological Development, the *Guangming Daily,* and the PLA General Logistic Department; a meeting on the problem of intellectual liberalization in December hosted by the *Science and Technology Daily;* a gathering on "New Authoritarianism in the Current Political-Ideological Trends" in January 1989 coorganized by the Beijing Institute for Research on Social and Scientific-Technological Development and the *Theoretical Information Press;* a symposium on "Democratic Progress and China's Conditions" in February initiated by the *People's Daily* and the *Guangming Daily;* two gatherings in April, one on political reform organized by the IRESR, the

Because a sizable portion of the most influential statements made in the national debate has been translated into English,[17] I shall not present the whole discussion in detail here. Instead, I shall emphasize the major spokesmen on each side, highlight the unique points in their arguments, and provide brief contextual analyses.

All the participants in the debate agreed that the problems China faced in the late 1980s were attributable to the existing power structure and that China must move to a constitutional democracy. But they debated passionately over when and how that goal should be reached. The major arguments can be summarized as two opposing programs: "enlightened despotism plus market" and "immediate democratization plus market." The former maintained that democratic reform in China was both unrealistic and undesirable in the present period. China must first develop a free-market economy whose operation is guaranteed by property rights. This fundamental economic change can be achieved only under a centralized leadership headed by an enlightened strongman or a tiny elite. Without such an "enlightened despotism plus market" phase, it is impossible to establish a democratic system in China.

Here the use of the term "centralized" (*jiquande*, as well as "semicentralized" and "decentralized") is confusing. In some cases it referred to "centralized" systems, in some cases it referred to "totalitarian" ones, and sometimes it referred to both.[18] In the China of the late 1980s, to use "totalitarian" to describe the PRC government could still invite political trouble. To reduce the probability of state interference and sustain the public debate, most participants avoided employing the term "totalitarian" (*jiquande*: It sounds exactly the same as "centralized" in Chinese but the written forms are different). Such terminological manipulation creates difficulties for outsiders who try to interpret the argument.

The opponents of the "enlightened despotism plus market" program argued that China's reform has been impaired by the centralized political structure. To expect a centralized, powerful government, which could only be Communist under the present conditions, to bring about a free-market economy is to go south by driving the car north. Without fundamental change in the existing political system, which necessarily involves democratic reform, meaningful progress in either the economy or the polity is out of the question.

Science and Technology Daily, the *New Observer,* and the *Economics Weekly;* and another on "Democracy, Science, and Modernization" organized by the *World Economic Herald.*

[17] See Rosen and Zou (1990–91, 1991a, 1991b); Oksenberg, Sullivan, and Lambert (1990: 123–50); and *FBIS China Daily Reports* during the debate period.

[18] Rosen and Zou translated *jiquande* and *ban jiquande* into "authoritarian" and "semi-authoritarian" (1990–91: 14 and passim). This is misleading, because some Chinese authors, e.g., Zhang Bingjiu, used *jiquande* to refer to totalitarian regimes and *ban jiquande* to refer to authoritarian regimes.

Of course, not all those involved in the debate expressed themselves so clearly, and a minority even identified themselves as a third party. But the two programs characterize the most influential statements and the third party's views could be largely assigned to one side or the other.

In the debate, the individuals favoring the "despotism plus market" recipe as an alternative to the Communist system tended to be relatively young, in their thirties and forties; they had received degrees from colleges and graduate schools after the Cultural Revolution; they had studied economics or political science; and they served as consultants to decision makers rather than as social and cultural critics.

On the other hand, noted OIs, people majoring in the humanities, and frequent targets of the regime's persecution gravitated to the side that believed in the "democracy and market" solution. This background helps to understand differences in opinion.

One of the first to propose the "despotism and market" program was Zhang Bingjiu, a junior professor at Beijing University and director of its Research Center for Contemporary Chinese Social Development.[19] To justify it, he presented a three-stage developmental scheme: "The various forms of historical and existing political systems can be classified into three models: the centralized, the semicentralized, and the decentralized." Each of these has a compatible economic structure: the traditional economy, the developing market economy, and the mature market economy.

In Zhang's classification, planned socialist economies are a "modern subtype of the traditional economy," for they conform to its three qualifications: (1) internal relations of the economic structure are maintained by noneconomic coercive forces or naturally bred inertia; (2) agriculture is dominant; and (3) the growth rate is slow. Such an economic life inevitably gives rise to a "centralized" political system, which is headed by a tightly disciplined party and relies on orders and propaganda to manage every aspect of society.

The marriage between "a semicentralized political system and a developing market economy" is transitional. In this stage, a crucial process takes place: the separation of enterprise and government, which makes possible the establishment of property rights and the growth of markets. From the political point of view, the separation "will transform the government's erstwhile function of directly managing the economy into a government that indirectly 'manages' the economy, and thus actually serves the economy."

Such a "service-oriented government" should be called "semicentralized" because somehow

---

[19]See the English translations in Rosen and Zou (1990–91: 8–35; 1991a: 7–15). I made many alterations.

service-oriented governments continue to use the old structures and adopt the institutions, methods, and norms of the centralized political system. Nevertheless, . . . a decisive transformation has taken place. The centralized political system that in the past encompassed and swallowed up all spheres of social life now has a reduced area in which it exerts a direct influence, and the government under this new system is different from the old in function, duty, mode of behavior, and so on. Moreover, it is moving toward a new system – the decentralized model.

Lastly, at the stage of "a decentralized political system and a mature market economy," there exist a completely separated economy and government, a strong civil society, a constitutionally bounded government, popular participation, the separation of powers, a well-balanced central–local and civilian–military governmental structure.

In Zhang's analysis, China was still at the first stage and should not ask for democracy because (1) at the outset, the progressive forces in society should and could only concentrate on developing the market economy – lacking the power to fight a war in the political domain, they had to tolerate an authoritarian government; (2) the marriage between Western-born democracy and China's special conditions takes time; (3) a pluralist polity must have a pluralist economy as its premise; and (4) in China in the late 1980s, to demand democracy would be to invite strong reactions from many vested interests. Zhang concluded: "The proponents of new authoritarianism can be called moderate democrats because they concentrate their efforts on nurturing and creating the bases, conditions, and means of democracy by cultivating the market."

Wu Jiaxiang is the best known among the proponents of the "despotism and market" program. A fellow in the Investigation and Research Division of the General Office of the Party Central Committee, Wu built his reputation within political circles by publishing a volume in 1987 on Deng Xiaoping's strategy of reform. His justification for the new authoritarianism proposal was also grounded on a general, three-stage theory of history, similar to Zhang's.[20] It is interesting that in the debate, many participants were selling an anticommunist political program, but their reasoning was somewhat Marxist: a belief in a general law of history and the primacy of the economy in social change.

Wu's starting point was that, without fully developed markets, neither violent revolutions (e.g., the Soviet Union under Stalin) nor popular elections (e.g., Germany under Hitler) can give birth to a genuine democracy.

But democratic reform cannot help China build a market economy, asserts Wu. Expanding political participation can only increase the opportunities of many greedy people to carve up public property and power, and political leaders coming to power through general elections have to make concessions to their constituents and interest groups. They are unable to exercise powerful leader-

---

[20] See the translations in Rosen and Zou (1990–91: 36–45; 1991a: 7–23), and Oksenberg et al. (1990: 130–34; 144–49). I made a few alterations.

ship to root out widespread corruption, privilege, and administrative obstacles set up by local bureaucrats to stop the circulation of raw materials and technology, which are so harmful to the growth of a national market. To cope with these problems, Wu believed, a charismatic dictatorship is more effective: "At this time, there is a need for a suddenly born authority that can strengthen the internal unity of the government before it finds a way to obtain legitimacy, and thereby overcome crises in society in accordance with the demands of modernity. This sudden authority is what we call the new authority."

Why "new"? Because it promotes and guarantees individual freedoms in the economic sphere by autocratic methods and thereby prepares the preconditions for a liberal democracy.

Wu's discussion shows that when people like him called for a strongman government, what bothered them was the socioeconomic disorder in the reform process mainly caused by arbitrary party-state bureaucrats. Taking advantage of the abstract "public ownership" system, those bureaucrats did whatever they could to transform public assets into their own. For example, they bought goods with public funds at state-set low prices and then sold them at high market prices, thereby making huge profits for themselves; they asked for bribes for services they performed, though as civil servants their duty was to do such day-to-day work; or they used their official power to block the flow of raw materials, energy, goods, services, and personnel from their jurisdiction to others, if doing this could enhance their personal interests.

The environment that made all this possible was the introduction of market mechanisms into a predominantly "public ownership" economy and the administrative reform of decentralization: These greatly increased the opportunities for officeholders to violate both administrative discipline and the rules of the market. Citing these widely hated irregularities, Wu argued that China has only two choices: a phony democracy under which tens of thousands of "local emperors" put the country in a "neither ordered nor free situation," or an enlightened dictator who is independent of all entrenched interests and who therefore can push China out of the mess rooted in the existing socialist system.

Compared with Zhang and Wu, Xiao Gongqin's proposal was less clear.[21] An associate professor at Shanghai Teachers College, Xiao opposed democratization in China not by citing any general theory of history but by contrasting the quality of the Chinese to that of people in the West. Since the Communist takeover, Xiao remarked, the Chinese people have lived in an "omnipotent" structure for forty years, in which "the state is in charge of everything – the social, the political, the economic, the cultural, and the ideological. . . . Within

---

[21] See Xiao's statement in Liu Jun and Li Lin (1989: 54–60, 61–85). Only the first piece was translated into English by Rosen and Zou (1990–91: 69–76). The quotations were all translated by myself.

such a structure, there almost exist no self-governing social units that are independent of state control." The consequence is that the Chinese have lost their "autonomous personality" and the ability to "form contractual interpersonal relationships." The only quality they possess is "the instinctive impulse driven by personal interests and desires" as expressed, at the macro level, in the pattern that "once the state tightens control, things are dead; once it relaxes control, things are chaotic."

In contrast, in the West, there are "highly autonomous social individuals (including their associations) and highly developed contractual interpersonal relationships." These are the very preconditions of democratic politics.

Xiao recommended that to ensure a successful transition from the "omnipotent structure," China needs a "transitional authority" that would use the authoritarian methods that fit the Chinese people's quality best to combat disorder in public life. At the same time it would separate the economic and cultural systems from the political one, creating a favorable environment for further modernizing fforts. More specifically, this "transitional authority" should meet the following needs:

Administratively, it must reinforce public authority and rely on coercive means to run the state, severely punishing crimes and corruption, especially corruption and laxity in officialdom. . . . Economically, it should separate the economy from the government and transform the omnipotent government into a limited one. Culturally, it should encourage ideological diversity. . . . It must understand that in the PRC that lacks a middle class and modernizing forces, intellectuals' modern consciousness and values are a priceless source of the modern spirit. To protect their enthusiasm for modernization is to protect the life forces of China's modernization.

Equally important, Xiao warned, is that the intellectuals must realize that the "four cardinal principles" remain the basis of legitimacy for the "transitional authority" and therefore must not be challenged. As to how this "transitional authority" can fulfill its mission with the four principles in place, he gave no clear explanation.

Wang Huning, a young professor of world politics at Fudan University, was among the champions of new authoritarianism who were little known to the outside world.[22] He made his point principally in an article published in the *Fudan Journal* No. 2 of 1988, which was based on his talks in late 1987 at "The Special Research Fellows Discussion Group of the Shanghai Party Propaganda Department." It was widely reported in the municipal political circles that Wang's paper had been praised by Zhao Ziyang and recommended by Zhao to the Politburo.

---

[22]The following discussion is based on communication with Informant no. 18, Wang's paper "Xiandaihua Jincheng Zhongde Zhengzhi Lingdao fangshi Fenxi" (*Fudan Journal* No. 2, 1988), and his interview in the *People's Daily* (October 8, 1987).

Wang centered on the "comparative effectiveness" of regimes. "Since World War II, a group of countries and regions have made admirable achievements in modernization," such as Japan, the four little dragons, and Brazil. They had one thing in common: "Their regimes put effectiveness above democracy. . . . Their successes are the result of the centralized political leadership model."

In contrast, "countries under the decentralized leadership model have performed very poorly." (India is the typical case.) The reasons are:

(1) A centralized leadership can avoid unnecessary conflicts between different ideas and opinions. . . . (2) A centralized administration can provide a sound, perfect civil-service system to implement policies. . . . (3) A centralized government is highly sensitive to circumstances, quickly reacts to urgent issues emerging in modernization processes, and can provide effective solutions. . . . (4) A centralized leadership can concentrate its forces on critical areas, put disturbances under control, and make efficient allocations of resources.

In recommending "the centralized leadership model," Wang made clear that it must not be confused with the socialist model, which refuses to give relative autonomy to economic and social actors and puts the state in charge of every detail, resulting in economic inefficiency.

Wang concluded that his favored model neglects democracy, but this does not devalue the model, because "a political structure is not window dressing. It should be judged by its effectiveness with regard to its social functions."

Another well-known advocate of the "enlightened despotism" strategy was Dai Qing, a senior staff member of the *Guangming Daily*.[23] Her personal background as the adopted daughter of the late Marshal Ye Jianying gave her a tremendous advantage in promulgating her ideas.

While designing a practical program to end dictatorship in the PRC, Dai called attention to two types of rulers of modern China: One is "enlightened but not autocratic enough," such as the Kuang-hsu Emperor (1875–1908) and Dr. Sun Yat-sen, who intended to bring modern political institutions into China but failed because they were unable to accumulate enough power to crush conservative resistance. Another type is "autocratic but unprogressive," such as Chiang Kai-shek and Mao, who "did not use their authority to protect freedom and social stability and develop democratic institutions and the economy. They were overly obstinate in destruction of their opponents, and blinded by the fighting and slaughtering to which they were committed . . . Hence, there was only one possible outcome – killing, turmoil, stagnation."

In Dai's view, there has been only one successful reform in modern China: Chiang Ching-kuo's in Taiwan during the mid-1980s. A truly enlightened dicta-

---

[23]See Lu Tong's report (*New Observer* No. 21, 1988) and the translation of Dai's speech in Rosen and Zou (1991a: 61–66).

tor, the junior Chiang symbolized the end of traditional Chinese politics, because "he arranged for the end of the Chiang Dynasty and for the repeal of the banishment of political parties and a free press. 'It is true,' he said, 'I am an autocrat, but I shall be the last; I will ensure, with autocracy, the beginning of democracy.'"

In contrast to the smooth democratic reform and economic growth in Taiwan, mainland China has witnessed many massive democratic movements. The result is neither freedom nor prosperity, but "the incessant cycle of autocracy, corruption, and turmoil." Dai was convinced that, "given China's national conditions, autocracy can be ended only at the hands of an enlightened dictator." The "Chiang Ching-kuo model" is the hope for the PRC.

Among the promoters of new authoritarianism, Wang Juntao was unique because, as mentioned before, he was an activist in the 1978–79 Democracy Movement and had long been on the police's blacklist. Nevertheless, he displayed a rather realistic perspective on China's political evolution.[24] He pushed for "strengthening administrative authority for the present period" and opposed any attempts at weakening it by democratization. He gave three reasons. First, China was not ready for the replacement of administrative control of society by a legal order: The existing legal institutions were far from systematic; the quantity and quality of the lawyer corps were insufficient; and the population's general education was low. Without these preconditions for the rule of law, Chinese society under a weakened government would become disorderly and people's lives and property would be threatened.

Second, as a latecomer in modernization, China needs a "clean, centralized, and powerful" government to mobilize human and material resources to catch up with advanced nations. But a democratic and decentralized system would slow down development.

Third, China's population is too large and society's self-organizing ability too weak; without a strong administration, much of the functioning of society would stop. But, Wang remarked, the Communist party must "withdraw from the administrative sphere." Of several possible ways of withdrawal, Wang was inclined to this one:

As the representative of a constitutional order, the ruling party first withdraws from day-to-day management, then from policy-making processes, and then from institution-building activity. Eventually, it serves as the guardian of the constitution, like the Turkish army led by Kemal Ataturk, which played such a role only when a constitutional crisis emerged . . . The cabinet should be composed of technocrats and responsible to the congress.

---

[24]The following is based on Wang's talk, entitled *"Zhongguo Dangqian Xuyao Xingzheng Quanwei"* (*Guoqing Yanjiu* No. 3, 1989).

Yang Baikui, a division chief at the Institute of Political Science in the CASS, was another enthusiastic champion of new authoritarianism.[25] Yang used Sun Yat-sen's theory of three-stage government to support his political program. According to Sun (1986: 7–19), a successful democratic revolution in China has to go through three stages: (1) a military government, which employs force to overcome the old regime's resistance and meantime raises the people's political consciousness to the modern level by propaganda; (2) a tutelary government, which is composed of nonelected civilian officials and whose duty it is to guide social reforms, build a modern economy, and train the people to familiarize themselves with ways of democratic life through local self-government; and (3) a constitutional government, formed by general elections and subject to checks and balances.

Yang found that the whole of modern history backs Sun's theory: Countries that adopted a constitutional government at their early stage of modernization were bound to fail; on the other hand, "economic developments in Britain, France, Germany, Brazil, Chile, and the four little dragons were all very rapid during their military or tutelary governments." China must follow the rule:

In this stage, there must be a modernization-oriented social group that will, with a certain coercive force, guide and push the whole society from tradition into modernity. . . . The group may make up only a minority of the population throughout the entire transition; and this would be particularly true in the early stage of the transition. The coercive "guidance" or "propulsion" by this minority is what is commonly called "enlightened despotism," "elite democracy," or "new authority."

In a public debate at the People's University in Beijing in early April 1989, Yang stressed that only two kinds of individuals are qualified to be members of the group: elite intellectuals and political leaders who favor free enterprise. Among the Chinese intellectuals, the self-consciousness of being an elite that fought for a new system vis-à-vis the Communist one had never been stronger than in the late 1980s.

The most influential among those pushing for a new authoritarian government were perhaps members of the IRESR, including its director Chen Yizi, deputy directors Wang Xiaoqiang and Li Jun, and division chiefs Cao Yuanzheng, He Weiling, and Gao Liang, who had long assisted Zhao Ziyang on economic reform. They claimed that "social turmoil is more likely to occur in . . . developing countries with per capita GNP ranging from $400 to $1,000." China just falls into this category (*People's Daily Overseas Edition* October 8, 1987).

[25]The following discussion is based on conversation with Informant no. 35, and Yang's paper, whose translation is in Rosen and Zou (1991a: 67–80). I made alterations.

Social turmoil directly threatens "efficiency," the issue of most concern to the IRESR. "To overemphasize democracy or to prematurely erect democratic structures can only impair the country's development" (Chen Yizi, *World Economic Herald* May 9, 1988). Centering on "efficiency," Chen and his associates divided the latecomers in modernization into four categories:

"Hard [read: autocratic] government and hard [read: planned] economy." For instance, the Stalin model of a centralized government and a command economy. This model is somewhat effective under the conditions of war mobilization and wartime economy. However, it becomes ineffective once technology goes beyond a certain level. . . . In the contest for modernization, this model is more and more falling behind.

"Soft [read: democratic] government and hard economy." . . . India has adopted this model with very unsuccessful results. The consequence of parliamentary politics is great exhaustion of energy and indecision, resulting in a serious waste of national strength.

"Hard government and soft [read: free enterprise] economy." Relatively successful countries and regions, such as the four little dragons, Brazil, and Turkey, have generally adopted this model in the "take-off" stage. . . . Essential to this model is that political power be relatively centralized, conducive to effective coordination and control, and that economic power be decentralized, conducive to dynamism and efficiency . . .

"Soft government and soft economy." Before World War II, some countries adopted this model with success. After the war, however, many latecomers have adopted this model but are unsuccessful. The reason is that the whole international environment has changed.[26]

China, of course, should shift from model 1 to model 3, and in doing so, the new regime has to handle three crucial issues properly:

The first is the relation between the quality of the masses and their participation in politics. It must be realized that, because of their financial and educational level, the vast majority of the masses, for a long period of time, will be unable to take part directly in the management of the state. During this period, what is feasible is "elite politics," i.e., a small elite holds the leadership and sets, in representing the people's interests, the direction of national development.

The second is the relation between the "power elite" and the "intellectual elite." If the former is self-enclosed and frozen, in time it will become a special interest group. If, on the other hand, it consistently integrates elite intellectuals possessing modern ideas, competence, and knowledge, the power elite will be able to keep representing the people's interests and increase the pace of modernization.

The third issue concerns the establishment of a set of institutions and procedures within the power centers involved in the decision making related to major national and state affairs; such institutions and procedures ensure elite democracy prior to decision making and efficiency afterward.[27]

[26] Quoted from a paper by Chen Yizi et al., whose translation is in Rosen and Zou (1991a: 39–60). I made alterations. See a similar classification in Cao Yuanzheng's two-part article published in *Zhongguo: Fazhan yu Gaige* No. 10, pp. 55–60, 1987 (translation in Rosen and Zou 1991a: 24–38), and his speech printed in *Guoqing Yanjiu* No. 3, pp. 11–13, 1989.

[27] Chen Yizi et al., in Rosen and Zou (1991a: 39–60). Their proposal in fact had been expressed by the institute's overseas delegate He Weiling two years before; see He's interview, under the pseudonym Shao Ding, in *The Contending* No. 8, 1986.

It should be noted here that the belief in a powerful government and a strongman to push forward reform is not unique to the Chinese political tradition, as some observers suggest (Chirot 1991: 134). This belief has been widely held by political and social elites in noncommunist developing countries[28] and reformers in communist countries as well. For instance, a number of reformist Soviet intellectuals in the late 1980s argued that "a direct transition from totalitarianism to democracy in the Soviet Union is likely to prove impossible, and a transitional phrase of enlightened authoritarianism may be necessary" (Rigby 1992: 13). The purpose is to hold things together and to create a capitalist economic base for future democracy (Brumberg 1990: 181–83). Hungarian reformers in the late 1980s were inclined to the same idea. "Ideally, we should have had the economic reforms [of privatization] first, then move toward democracy," a leading economist remarked. He and his fellows believed that the pattern of institutional transition in Spain, South Korea, and Japan was more suitable to conditions in Hungary (*Boston Sunday Globe* April 2, 1989).

The propensity to enlightened authoritarianism in these countries cannot be explained by their political tradition alone; the preference for "effectiveness" is another, equally important, reason. Elites and reformers in developing and communist countries strive to change their systems mainly because of their awareness of the relative backwardness of their own country. This sense of crisis and urgency naturally leads them to place government effectiveness, regardless of what concrete form it may take, above anything else. Driven by such political rationality, many reformers start as liberals but end as authoritarians paradoxically.

Now I turn to those against the "enlightened despotism plus market" solution and for the "immediate democratization plus market" alternative in China. Many of them are familiar to us and we have learned a great deal about them: Yu Haocheng, Hu Jiwei, Su Shaozhi, Li Honglin, Xu Liangying, and others.

Yu[29] found that "those who uphold new authoritarianism share a common mistake in perception with some of our leaders: They confuse democracy and freedom with anarchism and disorder, and centralization and authority with autocracy and total control." Some people do so, suggested Yu, because of ignorance of political science, but some are making an excuse to suppress popular demands for democratic reform. In fact, democracy necessitates law and discipline. Despotism, on the other hand, often breeds social turmoil: "In our own history, it is the extreme tyranny of the Qin and Sui dynasties that made them such short-lived regimes. In South Korea today, the people's struggle

---

[28] Both Latin America (Collier 1979; Malloy 1977) and Africa (Gibbon, Bangura, and Ofstad 1992) are good examples.

[29] See the translation of Yu's paper in Rosen and Zou (1991b: 44–55). I made alterations.

against dictatorship and for democracy and freedom is being carried out in an intense and violent way."

Hu, Su, and Li all[30] challenged the claim that the "hard government and soft economy" plan is realistic and fits China's conditions best. On the contrary, they argued, the plan is out of touch with China's reality. The PRC, unlike the four little dragons, does not have an institutional framework protecting property rights, an autonomous economic sphere, and an independent middle class of entrepreneurs and professionals. China's national conditions, Li underlined, are that "it is a socialist country, whose government uses administrative order to command, from the political center, the operation of the economy." In such circumstances, expecting a "reinforced administrative authority" to liberate the economy from its own hands, in Hu's words, "is similar to using gasoline to extinguish a fire." A hard government could help economic takeoff in capitalist Taiwan or South Korea, but is doomed to stifle the economy in the socialist PRC. Xu[31] went further to protest that the Chinese have suffered enough from Mao's strongman politics; following the new authoritarianism recipe, China would subject itself to Nazism.

To solve the entrenched problems in their country, Su and Hu believed that the Chinese should learn from the East European and Soviet experiences and do the following: (1) appeal to the people with a "democratization and modernization" reform program instead of Marxism; (2) attempt "political openness," for example, telling the truth, allowing different interest groups to speak out, and exposing official corruption to the public; and (3) set up a legal framework to encourage privatization, allowing single person or household businesses to grow and become China's "Ford" or "Exxon."

Reading these senior intellectuals' criticism of "new authoritarianism," one cannot help recalling that in the late 1970s they were committed party intellectuals and worked hard to design programs to make the socialist system work. Ten years later, these same individuals stood up against young intellectuals' attempts to preserve authoritarian elements of the established political structure, and called for a total restructuring. This is really a remarkable intellectual transformation!

But on a deeper level, one still finds a continuity in these senior intellectuals – their commitment to the ideal of a "Great Society," in which liberty, justice, and prosperity are granted to all. They joined the Communist party in the KMT era

[30] See the translation of Hu's paper in Oksenberg et al. (1990: 138–42) and his conference presentation in the *New Observer* No. 8, pp. 11–13, 1989; Su's paper in the *Science and Technology Daily* December 22, 1988, and interview in the *World Economic Herald* December 5, 1988; Li's paper in the *New Enlightenment* No. 2, pp. 37–57, 1988, and speech in the *New Observer* No. 8, pp. 19–20, 1989.

[31] See Xu's conference presentation in *Guoqing Yanjiu* No. 3, pp. 8–9, 1989.

with the trust that the CCP would build such a Great Society as it promised. They became a counterelite criticizing the Communist regime after they painfully witnessed the CCP's total betrayal of the ideal.[32]

In repudiating the "new authoritarianism" model, young critics provided more sophisticated arguments. Rong Jian[33] and Sun Hui, graduate students at the Chinese People's University in Beijing, questioned their opponents:

> You propose to establish a new authoritarian polity through forceful, iron-hand methods. How can you guarantee that this new authority will not degenerate into the kind of despotic authority that we have had? You insist on rule of a political-military strongman or an elite. What is your criterion of strongman and elite? What kind of political elite will enter into the authority system? By what procedure? All these questions are unanswered in the "new authoritarianism" proposals. (*Guangming Daily* March 31, 1989)

Rong and two staff members of the *People's Daily*, Huang Shiqing and Zhang Dehua, pointed out[34] that much of the chaos in the reform process has been caused by the PRC's power structure, which intensifies the tension between the central and the local. During the ten-year reform, a fight has persisted between the central and local governments over the redistribution of power. But the leadership never thinks of changing the power structure through constitutional reform to define clearly the powers and limits of government at each level. Disturbed by the present chaos, the "new authoritarianism" group urges that powers allocated to local governments should be taken back. This approach can only make things worse. Huang and Zhang recommended that, to get out of the vicious circle of "centralization–decentralization–recentralization," China should move in the direction of federalism.

Huang Wansheng, a junior professor at Huadong Normal University and an organizer of the Shanghai Young Theoretical Workers Association, asserted that the democratic reform program advertised by people like him is realistic, because

> we do not insist on a high standard for democracy; we do not expect it to ensure the best results. We merely require that it ensure reasonable procedures. . . . Democracy posits, as a premise, that power is evil and that the free exercise of power is bound to lead to terrible results. The basic function of democracy . . . is to prevent power from wreaking evil. . . . The new authoritarians ask for "good" despotic authority but have failed to prove that it would work. They assume a despot could be "good" or "enlightened" and use this hypothetical premise as a basis to discuss political change in China. I would like to ask how can they be so romantic and even naive? (Rosen's and Zou's translation, 1990–91: 82, with my alterations)

---

[32] Based on my communications with these senior intellectuals after the spring of 1989. Link's book (1992) contains rich material on this topic. I am thankful to anonymous reader "A" for suggesting that I bring this point out.

[33] Elizabeth Perry (1991: 144) mistook Rong as a spokesman for new authoritarianism.

[34] See the translation of Rong's article in Rosen and Zou (1990–91: 46–68); Huang's and Zhang's paper in Liu Jun and Li Lin (1989: 294–302).

In the opinion of Wang Yizhou, a research fellow at the Institute of Marxism, China does not have to chose between democratic reform and economic development. China could have both, as Hungary is aiming to do.

Practice has shown that the relationships between economic effectiveness and political freedom, between marketization and democratization, and between economic-institutional reform and political-institutional reform can be complementary and of mutual assistance. . . . In comparison with most neighbors in the socialist bloc, Hungary, as a "trail blazer" of reform, has led the way in the liberalization of banking, the transformation of state enterprises into a stock and shares system, the liberalization of prices, and the introduction of a real-estate market. It was also the first to recognize the value of political pluralism and the multiparty system. . . . Everyone who has been to Hungary knows that although it still has many problems, its people have a relatively good livelihood, its economy is dynamic, and it is much better than most "Eastern countries" in terms of political democratization, freedom of expression, and tolerance of political criticism. (Rosen's and Zou's translation, 1991b: 63–64; with my alterations)

According to two activists of voluntary association making, Cao Siyuan, director of the Stone Institute for Social Development, and Zhang Zhonghou, deputy director of the Capital Institute for Research on Legal Systems and Social Development, the "crisis of authority" China faced in the late 1980s was the crisis of the old revolutionary authority.[35] To rebuild an authority system, China needs the rule of law, not the rule of a strongman. A legal authority in China is out of the question if the party acts in accordance with its own will. Therefore, the transformation of rule by the party to rule by the Constitution is crucial. These suggestions were echoed strongly by influential OIs such as Yan Jiaqi, who regarded the growth of the authority of law as the precondition of a market economy and a democratic polity (*New Observer* No. 8, pp. 14–15, 1989).

Cao proposed in particular a program to breed "parliamentary democracy" in China. He believed that, in the face of a deepening political crisis, the Chinese need democratic training more than ever. The existing "people's congress system" at various levels is a much better place for the people to gain experience in democratic politics than is Tiananmen Square (meaning street protests). The party should stop running the congress as it runs the army, and restore rights to the people's delegates. Debates in the congress should be open to the public. The Constitution should be revised so that citizens' rights, such as private property and lobbying, are actualized step by step.

A 23-article program prepared in early 1989 by Wen Yuankai, the noted chemist deeply involved in politics, and Wang Kang, director of the Chinese Association for Studies of Talented People, was perhaps the most comprehensive document to summarize the major points made by the "immediate democratization and market" wing. The program (*World Economic Herald*

---

[35] See a two-part article by Cao in the *World Economic Herald* November 21 and 28, 1988; Zhang's paper in Liu and Li (1989: 172–87).

April 10, 1989) blames the party leadership's dual-traffic policy for the "structural, pervasive, and total" social crisis facing China in the late 1980s. A wise strategy to lead China out of that crisis is to "learn humbly from the reform experience of the Soviet Union and East European countries," and implement comprehensive political reform to clean corruption jointly generated by a bureaucratic polity and a partial market economy. Central to this strategy are the following steps: (1) The Communist party undergoes a radical remodeling (e.g., the party withdraws from the government and the economy, stops using the state treasury to support party activity, and allows other political parties to compete), (2) the People's Congress replaces the Communist party as the sovereign power, and (3) the Constitution grants equal rights to state, collective, and private enterprises.

When engaged in the debate on new authoritarianism, both sides sensed that the country was sitting on a political volcano.[36] Many of the fruits that the economic reforms had yielded were being eaten away by official corruption and hyperinflation. The angry urbanites were on the edge of an uprising. Many old leaders such as Chen Yun, Li Xiannian, and Peng Zhen blamed the reform program executed by Zhao Ziyang with the endorsement of Deng Xiaoping for widespread corruption and popular grievances. An ambitious faction in the leadership, led by premier Li Peng and his deputy Yao Yilin, was ready to take advantage of the crisis and push Zhao and his men out of the leadership. Worst of all, most top leaders, including Deng, Yang Shangkun, and Wang Zhen, agreed to strengthen the armed police to suppress any protest. In a word, in late 1988 and early 1989, China had a perfect environment for a revolution: Both the rulers and the ruled were disgruntled at the current situation and wanted to do something about it.[37]

A publicized dialogue between Yan Jiaqi and Wen Yuankai well expressed the fear of a great setback in the reforms:

Wen: "There is a great danger at the present time: the ruin of the fruits of the reforms and the return of the old forces. . . ."
Yan: "I feel the existence of a crisis. Those who have resisted reform love to see China getting into trouble. They view China's difficulty as their opportunity in the power struggle, are prepared to 'clean the mess caused by reform,' and want to put China in a state of long-time stagnation or even to move backward. . . ."
Wen: "They want to launch a vindictive counterattack against the reforms."
Yan: "We must watch out for such figures. They are trying to stop reforms by taking advantage of the chaotic situation in China." (*Economics Weekly* December 11, 1988)

---

[36] Based on communications with Chen Yizi in July 1989 and September 1990, with Zhu Jiaming in the fall of 1990, with Jin Yanshi in the winter of 1988–89, and with Ge Yang and Informant no. 8 in April 1989.
[37] See Lenin (1966: 358) for a discussion on revolutionary situations.

Cao Siyuan was even more disturbed. He warned both the ruling elite and the general public that grievances in Chinese society had accumulated to a critical level. Without a legitimate channel for the people to express themselves, violence would break out – "the people will rebel and the government will use force to suppress the unarmed masses" (*World Economic Herald* November 21 and 28, 1988).

Their warnings proved prescient only too soon. On April 15, 1989, on the death of the former party chief Hu Yaobang, who had lost his position because of refusing to suppress the student movement of late 1986, university students immediately took the opportunity to go to the streets, pouring out what they had discussed within small circles for years. This sudden student movement ended the "enlightened despotism versus immediate democratization" controversy. Both sides of the debate were deeply involved in the movement. To the "immediate democratization" wing, the movement provided a great forum for them to speak out for radical democratic change. To the "enlightened despotism" wing, the movement offered them a chance to press the leadership to transform itself from a Communist regime into a new authoritarian one.

When the Communist regime prepared to use the army to subdue the students, most participants in the debate rose up to protest against the action. After the crackdown in June 1989, almost all leading members of the two sides were severely punished by the regime.[38]

Conclusion

The target audience of the reformist leadership's "primary stage of socialism" theory was party-state bureaucrats whose political and socioeconomic privileges had been undermined by the economic reforms. Deng Xiaoping, Zhao Ziyang, and their allies intended to use this schema to blur the lines of demarcation between socialism and economic capitalism and provide a justification for market mechanisms and entrepreneurship under a Leninist political structure.

Seeing the leadership's appeal as an implicit acknowledgment of the total failure of socialism in China, the counterelite publicized its efforts to search for alternatives to the dying socialist system. This resulted in the public debate on the two political programs, "enlightened despotism plus market" and "immediate democratization plus market." Whereas the former mainly took China's

[38] On the "immediate democratization" side, Hu Jiwei, Li Honglin, Yu Haocheng, Qin Benli, Yan Jiaqi, Wen Yuankai, Xu Liangying, Su Shaozhi, Ge Yang, Cao Siyuan, Bao Zunxin, Wang Ruoshui, Wang Yizhou, and others were imprisoned, detained, condemned, or forced into exile. On the "enlightened despotism" side, those punished in a similar way included Wang Juntao, Wu Jiaxiang, Chen Yizi, Dai Qing, He Weiling, Yang Baikui, Zhang Bingjiu, Wang Xiaoqiang, and others.

noncommunist East Asian neighbors, Taiwan and South Korea in the 1960s and 1970s, as its reference group, the latter took China's communist neighbors in the north, the Soviet bloc under Gorbachev, as its reference group.

Reactions to the two programs were very different. "New authoritarianism" received particular attention from Zhao Ziyang (Informant no. 17). In January 1989, he asked his chief assistant Bao Tong to prepare a detailed report on the debate. Although the report actually did not come to Zhao's desk because of delay and the incidents in April, he might have been informed of the debate by other channels such as the IRESR. An unconfirmed story spread widely in Beijing and Shanghai even mentioned Deng Xiaoping's personal inclination to the "new authoritarianism" schema (Oksenberg, Sullivan, and Lambert 1990: 125–26).

To the majority living in urban China, however, any programs postponing democratic reform were unpopular. In the late 1980s, outraged by the naked official corruption, most intellectuals and urban dwellers and even many ordinary office workers were eager for the democratization of China's government. For them, the image of democracy was, to borrow from Louis Hartz (Sills 1968: Vol. 4, p. 116), "basically the negation of what they wanted to destroy." We can sense this popular sentiment from an earlier national survey conducted in July 1987. To the question "Do you think it is necessary to start reforming the political system right now?" those who said "necessary" numbered 79.5 percent among college graduates, 70.8 percent among senior high school graduates, and 56.2 percent among junior high school graduates. By location, those who said "necessary" were about 72 percent among the urban and suburban population (Min Qi 1989: 83–84). In responding to the question "Does China need democracy now?" about 80 percent of the urban and suburban residents said yes (ibid.: 179–80). Official corruption was getting worse every day, and the demands for democratic reform became even stronger in 1988–89, when the debate on new authoritarianism was under way.

There was another significant variable that increased urban Chinese readiness to take action for political change. During 1988–89, information about democratic reforms in Taiwan and the Soviet Union flooded into China. In late 1987, the KMT government in Taiwan passed a new law permitting residents on the island to visit their relatives in the mainland. By the end of 1988, the visits totaled about 750,000 (*People's Daily* December 27, 1988). These visitors brought in the latest news about the legalization of independent newspapers and the birth of opposition parties on the island.[39] Some Taiwanese journalists

---

[39] Based on communications with colleagues and friends in the PRC, and conversations with PRC visitors to the United States during 1988–90. I was often surprised by their knowledge of political events in Taiwan.

took the opportunity to visit major intellectual circles and campuses in the mainland, and discussed the possibility of similar developments in the PRC's political system.[40]

Meantime, in the PRC press, such as *World Economic Herald,* the *New Observer, China Youth News,* and *Economics Weekly,* and in Chinese language programs by foreign broadcasting stations, such as Radio Freedom and Progress of Moscow, the Voice of America, and the BBC, reports on Gorbachev's *glasnost* and *perestroika* attracted great attention.

As mentioned earlier, to the PRC residents, political developments in Taiwan and the Soviet Union carry a special meaning that no other places can possess (see Wen Yuankai's speeches in New York, August 1988, *Global Views Monthly* No. 10, pp. 81–84, 1988). Taiwan is under the rule of another Chinese regime, which has been in bitter rivalry with the CCP for almost seven decades. And in the PRC-USSR comparison, the ideological, institutional, and size variables were all under control. Both sides not only justified their polity in Marxist-Leninist language and were ruled by a single Communist party, but also both had an extensive territory and a large population.[41] In the PRC regime's self-justification of one-party dictatorship, the issue of size has always played a notable role: A small country might be able to afford democratic politics, but a large country like China cannot – democracy is doomed to cause *luan* (disorder). But when the Soviet Union began to move in a pluralist direction, Chinese intellectuals could not restrain themselves from emulating Soviet democrats.[42] Radical democratic reforms in Taiwan and the Soviet Union put the CCP in a situation very much like being attacked by a pincer drive, and its political conservatism and gerontocracy became ugly and unbearable in the eyes of many urban Chinese.[43]

Within the particularly restless section of the population, university students, the "new authoritarianism" strategy was generally detested. They were the most

---

[40]Communications with journalists of major Taiwanese newspapers and magazines in December 1989 in Taiwan. See also *Global Views Monthly [Yuanjian]* No. 7, pp. 71–82, 1988.

[41]In contrast, in the comparison between the PRC and Eastern Europe, the size variable was not "controlled"; therefore the impact of democratization in Eastern Europe on China was limited.

[42]The economic difficulties and ethnic conflicts in the former Soviet republics since the collapse of communism were welcome news to the PRC ruling elite, who made the best use of these negative developments in their efforts to defame democratization. To many of the Chinese counterelite who remain in China after June 1989 and who continue to think about strategies to change China, Russia seems to have lost attraction (based on communications with members of both the ruling elite and the counterelite).

[43]On the Soviet influence on China, see Bernard Gwertzman and Michael T. Kaufman (1991: 49–56). On Taiwan's impact, see *Zhongguo Minyun Yuan Zhiliao Jingxuan,* edited by *October Review* [Hong Kong] (1989, Vol. 2, pp. 30, 48, 175–77, 190); in these materials of the Spring 1989 Movement, Taiwanese political terms such as *kai dang jing* and *kai bao jing* (lifting bans on political parties and the press) were borrowed for protest by PRC residents.

radical in the "immediate democratization" camp.[44] During 1988 and early 1989, in universities in Beijing, Shanghai, Nanjing, Wuhan, Xian, and elsewhere, public debates over China's political future went on passionately in voluntary student groups such as "movie clubs," "fitness associations," and "salons for music lovers," whose apolitical appearance was a mask that had helped them survive,[45] a technique some East European student groups also used in the 1980s.[46]

In some universities in Zhejiang, Wuhan, and Beijing, students voluntarily formed "research groups on Taiwan," with the open intention of learning about the Taiwanese political and economic experience.[47] In leading schools such as Beijing University, the Chinese People's University, and the Graduate School of the CASS, students discussed concrete strategies for uncoupling pseudosocial organizations from the party. They proposed that the party and CYL organizations withdraw from campuses; that party committees withdraw from cultural associations; and that the PCPD stop interfering in the Ministry of Culture's affairs.[48] The first demand was inspired particularly by radical students in Taiwan, who had demanded the KMT cells withdraw from campuses.

In summarizing revolutions in modern history, Jack Goldstone (1982: 189–90) notes: "Prior to a great revolution, the bulk of the 'intellectuals' – journalists, poets, playwrights, essayists, teachers, members of the clergy, lawyers, and trained members of the bureaucracy – cease to support the regime, writing condemnations and demanding major reforms." On the eve of the Spring 1989 Democratic Movement, China was indeed in such a state. In the debate over new authoritarianism, intellectuals of all categories, the cultural, the technical, the official, the marginal, and university students, took part, attacking the existing Communist system and clamoring for a political and economic transformation.

These intellectuals worked in a variety of organizations, which were directly or indirectly linked to the state machinery, and some even worked in key party and government organs. Their involvement in dissent against communism indicated that the party-state system was increasingly disintegrating and that a counterelite was growing larger and larger within the matrix of formal institutions. These facts support the theoretical argument in Chapter 1 that, in order

[44]Communications with student leaders Xiang Xiaoji in October 1990, Sheng Tong in July 1989, and Informant no. 18.
[45]Interviews with Xing Ku in July 1989, Li Lu and Cai Congguo in September 1989, all student leaders; conversations with Yuan Zhiming in October 1990, Informants nos. 18 and 35.
[46]Conversation with Miklos Sukosd, a Hungarian sociologist studying at Harvard University, in winter 1990.
[47]Personal letters from China in late 1988.
[48]Interview with Wang Chaohua, a student leader at the Graduate School of the CASS, in October 1990.

to explain decommunization in those countries where Solidaritylike movements were absent, one should look inside to search for the cause of the transition – the process of how the organizational structure of communist systems was eroded by those working within.

The discussions on how to solve the breakdown of the socialist system were organized in both Shanghai and Beijing, by different kinds of voluntary associations and semiofficial and official institutions acting cooperatively, providing vital resources for the public debate. Involved official institutions included not only civilian ones but also military ones. All this demonstrated vividly the peculiar pattern of institutional parasitism in nonconformity and opposition in late communism: the "abuse" of official resources by citizens, the partial conversion of state structures from the means of party control into the instrument for opposition, the amphibious nature of institutions, and the ambiguous line between what is conventionally called "state" and what is called "societal."

Concluding remarks

The collapse of communism in Eastern Europe and the Soviet Union has raised a most serious challenge to the recent mainstream theories of revolution in the social sciences, which neither prepared researchers to catch key signs presaging the revolutions of 1989 nor provided a satisfactory explanation afterward (Brumberg 1990: 3–16; EEPS 1990; Chirot 1991). In the light of the historic events in the communist world in the late 1980s and early 1990s, theoretical revisions and conceptual innovations in the social sciences are necessary.

In a review of existing theories of transition from communism, Thomas F. Remington (1990: 177, 184) notes that these theories are either regime-centered or society-centered and that "each adopts a partial view of the relationship" between regime and society, in which concentration is placed on "the political or the social domain to the neglect of the other." "A theory of transition from communism," Remington suggests, "should instead be based upon an understanding of how the regime and the society influence and penetrate each other, and how that relationship changes during the transition itself."

Having correctly pointed out the inadequacy of these theories, Remington nevertheless fails to see that the root of that inadequacy is in the dichotomous conceptualization of civil society versus the state, which underlies both the regime-centered and society-centered theories. Such a cognitive scheme inevitably prevents researchers from seeing the transitional process in its true colors.

In contrast, the concept of institutional parasitism allows us to go beyond the antithesis of "state" versus "civil society." As a cognitive scheme it will make the researcher more sensitive to the existence and operation of amphibious structures that could be said to be both "state" and "societal"; to the interpenetration of official, semiofficial, and unofficial institutions; and to the complex interplay of political and social forces in late communism.

In studying a communist system, researchers are better prepared to see the state's penetration into the society than to see the simultaneous penetration of the state by the society. To see the latter requires, among other things, the researcher to have access to the immediate circles of nonconformity. He thereby can watch closely how people in communist societies ingeniously manipulate the system in which they themselves are manipulated every day, and how opposition-minded elements erode and riddle state structures by seemingly working for them. Without knowledge of this "mutual infiltration" between the party-state and society (see Nathan 1990: 5–6), one can hardly understand why so many communist regimes, once appearing so well organized, omnipotent, and stable, collapsed so quickly (with the exception of Poland – the only communist country that witnessed long-lasting and overt opposition) and peacefully (except Romania).

To illustrate the interpenetration and interplay between the party-state and society in contemporary China, this study selects the intellectual and professional counterelite as its focus of analysis, on the grounds that this group was particularly vital in undermining the Communist party's claim to rule. In proposing a research agenda for researchers studying the end of communism in Eastern Europe, Juan J. Linz (EEPS 1990: 203–4) suggests:

> We need to understand the enormously powerful role of the intelligentsia. A good sociology of the intelligentsia in each of these countries is very much in order. . . . We want to know, from country to country, what is on the minds of the intelligentsia, what defines the value system of intellectuals and their tensions, alignments, conflicts, linkages with parties, movements, and so on. I think this is absolutely central.

This study was done on the basis of the same understanding.

The rise of intellectual and professional strata as counterelites in communist systems was a clear indication of the increased differentiation of the communist social structure, because, as is widely acknowledged, whether a social structure is monolithic or pluralist is manifested in its elite structure (Sills 1968: Vol. 5, pp. 26–27; Parry 1969: 73–74; Bachrach 1971: 10). In communist systems, the development of institutional parasitism would have been impossible if the elite structure were not more diversified than in the Stalinist or Maoist era. In post-Mao China, official and semiofficial institutions could be manipulated for opposition, and unofficial structures could be created under the shadow of official structures and play an antisystem role. This is due to the existence of a socially upgraded and politically more ambitious intellectual and professional stratum, whose members did not command much political power but did have great "cultural capital" and enormous influence.

In this regard, post-Mao China showed great resemblances to the post-Stalin Soviet Union, in which "abutting the bureaucratic upper layers are networks of social elites that have ascended by force of their own achievement: the upper tiers of scholars, artists, technicians, social thinkers, and some administrators and bureaucrats whose prestige was acquired by merit, not rank" (Lewin 1988: 148). Under the circumstances of reform, they "frequently become political counter-elites in a period of broad societal confrontation with the communist authorities" (Remington 1990: 179).

Therefore, to underestimate the role of intellectuals would be a great mistake when studying political transition in late communism. For this reason, this work strongly criticizes the recent mainstream theories of revolution, which, when discussing regime change, focus attention on only top political leaders and traditional power centers and attach little weight to groups outside that power circle.[1]

Since the revolutions of 1989, students of communism have emphatically admitted the erroneousness of neglecting the problem of legitimacy in studies of revolution. In accounting for political change, the mainstream theorists of revolution emphasize "hard" tangible factors and underplay intangible and subjective factors. To use Daniel Chirot's (1991: 31) words, they have not taken the observation of legitimation crisis in communist systems "as anything more than a symptom of deeper class and structural conflicts, and none seem to have believed it could be the prime cause of revolution." Largely because of this intellectual orientation, most observers of communism have overlooked the subtle processes of relegitimation by communist ruling elites and counterlegitimation by critical forces. Such long and less dramatic struggles eventually prepared the conditions for the later dramatic breakthroughs.

Having realized the power of the soft factors, I devote a large portion of this work to discussing the problem of legitimation in post-Mao China, an interaction process primarily carried on between the Communist rulers and the intellectual and professional counterelite. The intellectual and professional stratum exerted the prime force on which the official modernization program relied. This population, however, was at the same time the one most susceptible to outside ideals and practices, and the most prone to make new political demands and challenges. Looking back on the Deng era, we see that, of the regime's major political appeals, the socialist-moral and the patriotic ones, in which the regime invested most efforts, were directed to the better-educated social groups. The Communist regime desperately wanted their consent and support.

---

[1]As a matter of fact, although intellectuals' role has been neglected by the mainstream social scientific theories of regime change for the sake of emphasizing political leaders, in area studies – at least in Chinese studies – intellectuals have received a good deal of attention, as shown by many works cited in this study. But such area study scholarship seems to bear little on the mainstream social scientific theories. I believe both sides were responsible for this "sad" relationship (see Fleron 1969: 1–3, 27): While most area specialists failed to treat the subject on a general theoretical level (see Perry 1989: 579), the mainstream theorists were unwilling to look at the empirical cases that did not fit their models.

Regime legitimation in a reformist communist system like China's is not limited to the small circle of top political leaders and traditional power centers as some political sociologists and political scientists have assumed.

This study points especially to horizontal comparison as a key to understanding the mechanism of regime delegitimation in late communism. China has been rich in illuminating examples. The Great Leap Forward of 1958–60 began with the promise to "sprint into the communist stage and enjoy a happy life of 'from each according to his ability, to each according to his needs.'" It ended with a general economic disaster and more than twenty million deaths from starvation. (See MacFarquhar 1983.) The bankruptcy of the promise led many people to discredit the Great Leap Forward policy and certain types of local bureaucrats. It also led a few senior officials to question Mao's role in forming the policy. But it did not lead to a general crisis of legitimacy for the political and economic system, because of the regime's tight control on information, which gave Chinese no chance to make horizontal comparisons about what kind of lives people in capitalist societies were living. Within a few years, by promising to build a perfect socialist society in China, Mao could again inspire tens of millions of people to carry out the Cultural Revolution.

During the Cultural Revolution, incompetence, misconduct, and corruption throughout officialdom were exposed, and all the major social groups were hurt by continual purges and factional fights. Economic production was gravely interrupted, and living standards declined. Political, economic, and human tragedies led to widespread hatred of cultural-revolutionary policies, Mao's radical assistants, and Mao himself. Yet, if one had the chance to witness the popular support for Deng Xiaoping's rehabilitation in 1976–77, to hear street and campus discussions in many Chinese cities in 1977–78, and to read carefully the wide range of unofficial publications of the 1978–79 Democracy Movement, one would see that the popular criticisms at that time focused more on the "bad emperor and empress" (Mao and his wife, Jiang Qing) and their inner court than on the Communist system. The majority of the prodemocracy activists had not totally lost hope of reforming the system under Deng's leadership.

In contrast, Deng's open-door policy and reform program introduced two qualitatively new factors into Chinese political life. First, the opening to the outside gave all levels and types of China's elite, as well as most ordinary citizens, the opportunity to compare the performance of communist systems with that of noncommunist systems. They saw that, in terms of advancement in technology and productivity, enhancement of quality of life, improvement in social justice and political participation, and diversity and creativity in intellectual enterprises, the West and Japan had achieved what the PRC could only dream of. Comparisons of Taiwan and Hong Kong with the Chinese mainland, of South Korea with North Korea, and of West Germany with East Germany led to a simple conclusion that nobody could deny: Socialism does not work.

Knowledge about the capitalist world produced the same effect in other communist nations. Finding out that in the new revolution in information technology the Soviet Union failed to keep up not only with Western Europe and the United States but also with East Asia, the Soviets were simply astonished (Chirot 1991: 12). The prime minister of Communist Poland, M. F. Rakowski, admitted in 1987 in a private memorandum that "due to the development of the mass media, the societies of our [communist] countries can 'peer into' the everyday life of the masses under capitalism." Since the people were "increasingly enlightened," the further history of communist systems "will be marked by shocks and revolutionary explosions" (Ash 1990: 280).

In the post-Mao era, another new factor contributing greatly to the delegitimation of the Communist regime was the Dengist economic reform. It was intended to be a blood transfusion for the half-dead socialist economy by introducing markets and semiprivate and private businesses. These practices have been described as the defining features of capitalism and the reason why "decadent and moribund capitalism will be replaced by superior socialism" according to everyday Communist propaganda. Chinese from kindergarten on have been relentlessly indoctrinated with this Communist ABC. Hence, if the open-door policy contributed to the general public's awareness of the failure of communism, then the economic reform unmistakably told the people that their leaders had themselves lost confidence in the system. Elizabeth Perry (1991: 142–43) puts it well: "Reforms are admissions by the regime of its own inadequacies. As a result, they encourage widespread disbelief. This is especially unsettling in communist systems, where claims to ideological truth have been so central." To make matters worse, the same CCP leadership was still trying to induce intellectuals and the general public to perpetuate the basic structure of the Leninist system. That doomed the official efforts of self-legitimation to failure. As Ferrero (1972: 140) observed long ago: "No government can hope to educate its subjects to respect something that it does not respect itself."

While China's Communist regime was caught in this predicament, news about radical political reforms in the Soviet Union arrived. If the comparison of the PRC with Taiwan and Hong Kong revealed to mainland Chinese that Chinese can enjoy economic prosperity when they have a working economic system, then the PRC-USSR comparison conveyed another message: Citizens of a communist country can enjoy political freedom as soon as they strive to take their rights. Sandwiched between Taiwan and Hong Kong, which had demonstrated "modernization miracles," and the USSR, which was demonstrating

"democratization miracles," the CCP regime lost every cultural, ethnic, historical, institutional, or ideological basis for arguing against the popular outcry for
radical reforms in both the political and the economic structure. Encouraged by
developments in Taiwan and the Soviet Union, Chinese from all walks of life
dared to march in large numbers in the spring of 1989 demanding civil liberties
and democracy, with full confidence in their cause. My study of political
destabilization in Dengist China is in line with previous findings about the
critical role of the "demonstration effect" in intensifying the sense of crisis,
splitting elites, provoking opposition, delegitimizing the political order, and
accelerating regime transformation in less developed societies. (See Huntington 1968: 32–49; Cohen and Shapiro 1974: 509–11; Rigby and Feher 1982: 45–
47; Janos 1986: 84–88, 120–25; O'Donnell, Schmitter, and Whitehead 1986:
Vol. 1, pp. 51–52, Vol. 3, pp. 8–9; Chirot 1987; Brzezinski 1990.)

In post-Mao China, the Dengist leadership's dual-traffic policy concurrently
benefited some and hurt others at every level of the party-state machinery and
general population. In order to sustain party-state officialdom's solidarity and
loyalty (for both keeping power and implementing policies) and to secure key
social groups' conformity and cooperation (for both preventing rebellion and
getting tasks done), the Dengist leadership had to appeal to different political
groups and social strata. The leadership tried to convince them that the current
policy was the best possible one for the state and the people in general and for
their own group or stratum in particular. The paradox of this legitimation device
was that the Dengist leadership had to justify simultaneously institutions and
policies that were obviously contradictory. To keep the Leninist one-party dictatorship intact and to institutionalize economic pluralism demand contrary
legitimizing principles.[2] The practice of a single regime's mobilizing and conflicting norms to defend antagonistic institutions and policies has led to a consequence completely contrary to the Dengists' anticipation: The appeals they
made to please specific power groups did not satisfy these groups and at the
same time angered other, less powerful but still important groups. This contributed greatly to the growing political alienation and antagonism of the
Chinese intellectuals, and to the gradual functional and organizational decay of
the massive party-state machinery. This explains to a significant degree why so
many party-state functionaries and office workers joined the student-led popular protest in the spring of 1989; why some important party-state organs, such as
newspapers, television and radio stations, and news agencies, became

[2]See Ferrero (1972: 235–36), Habermas (1975), Offe (1984), and Arato (Thompson and Held
1982: 196–218), for discussions on the problem that to use contradictory legitimizing principles to
justify various aspects of the single system will generate profound legitimacy crises.

mouthpieces of the antigovernment movement; and why the party-state's conventional political-control instruments, the grass-roots organizations, turned into the organizers of protest.

Other groups and the politics of legitimation

This study of regime legitimation highlights the interaction between the most powerful and the best educated in contemporary China. Although the best educated were, among various social categories, particularly active and influential in the politics of legitimation, a work on their reaction to the regime cannot tell the whole story about political legitimacy in post-Mao China. Comparable studies of the role of other social classes and political groups in the legitimation process would significantly advance our understanding of the problem.[3] For example, what was the role of peasants vis-à-vis that of urbanites? What was the political attitude of ordinary urbanites vis-à-vis that of the intellectual and professional stratum? How about the vast middle stratum of government officials – the civilian bureaucracy? And how about middle- and low-ranking army officers – the military bureaucracy?

All these questions are worth asking and should be included in comprehensive studies of political legitimation in post-Mao China. The chief reason for not being able to answer them is, needless to say, the unavailability of reliable empirical data collected by means of sophisticated social-scientific methods. But it is possible to find substitutes for data on important segments of urban China.

One substitute is opinion polls and social surveys done by PRC academic and government institutions at various levels (national, municipal, district, county, etc.) and in different localities during the second half of the 1980s.[4] Not conducted in the strict social scientific manner, these polls and surveys nevertheless cover a wide range of socioeconomic and political issues (excluding highly sensitive ones). A few research reports have been published, but most have not, because the contents are too critical.[5] If the raw records of these polls and surveys can be collected from those individual Chinese involved in the original projects, the material will throw light on China's legitimacy crisis.

Another substitute is records of political meetings. Every cell of the party and of the unit system in China was required by the higher authorities to hold regular meetings to discuss current policy issues and study party-government

---

[3] I appreciate Reader B's suggestion that I spell out this need.
[4] The better educated and the urban were usually overrepresented in these surveys (personal communications with some of the researchers).
[5] Personal communications with some researchers involved in these projects.

documents.[6] Although brief records of proceedings were expected by the higher authorities, in most cases only when major events took place (e.g., policy changes, the release of important official documents, or nominations and elections) would a person take minutes during the meeting. Generally speaking, political meetings (including their recording) in party cells (e.g., *dang xiaozu* and *dang zhibu*) were conducted more seriously than in cells of the work-unit system; and in party-state organs, military units, schools and universities, and cultural and communicative institutions such meetings and their recording were conducted more seriously than in factories and street committees.

During the proceedings, participants rarely concentrated on the officially assigned topics, but instead they used the meeting to exchange unofficial information (*xiaodao xiaoxi*) and pour out grievances. Corruption and special privileges, household economic difficulties, mismanagement and misgovernment, and dramatic political developments (e.g., student demonstrations in the streets or personnel changes in the national or local government leadership) were the most frequent topics.

To be sure, not everything said was recorded on paper, and the most critical and cynical statements were usually modified (similar to the "question and answer" material; see the appendix for details). But an experienced reader can gather valuable information from the records. Since such records were made and kept best in party cells and government organs, careful reading of the records can open new windows for research on the legitimacy problem within China's civil service.

Institutional parasitism:
the explanation of the contemporary transition and beyond

In this study we see that the criticism, dissent, and opposition that culminated in China's Spring 1989 Democracy Movement had grown under the circumstances of institutional parasitism. In other studies (as cited in this book) we see that many developments leading to the radical change in the Soviet Union and Eastern Europe took place under the similar institutional circumstances.

A question of great interest is, Why has institutional parasitism led to different outcomes in China and the European communist countries?[7] Is this because these countries had different degrees of institutional parasitism? As a result, the organizational structures of the sociopolitical systems were corroded to different levels, which made the revolutions of 1989 the final stroke to some

[6]After Mao's death political meetings were held less frequently, sometimes (e.g., in the late 1980s) even less than twice a month. (Once a week was the normal frequency required by the authorities during the Dengist era.)

[7]I am thankful to Stephen Hanson and Margaret Levi for their comments on this question.

communist regimes but not to the Chinese regime. Or the different outcomes may be attributable to different types of institutional parasitism in these countries. If so, then we need to know the variables that distinguish one type from another, such as regulations on formation and operation of semiofficial and unofficial structures, personnel and financial resources of these structures; regime-imposed limits on the differentiation between unofficial institutions and official or semiofficial ones to which the former had to attach at the beginning, or relations between reformers in key party-state organs and oppositional forces in unofficial and semiofficial organizations. These matters deserve systematic exploration in comparative studies of decommunization.

The purpose of devoting so much space to arguing the analytic advantage of the notion of institutional parasitism goes beyond seeking a better characterization or explanation of decommunization, albeit it has the broadest applicability in late communist societies. As an analytic concept, institutional parasitism applies to a class of social and political phenomena that crosses temporal and national boundaries. It can be used, for example, to analyze the welfare-state system in contemporary Western society, in which the public and private sectors have become increasingly interpenetrated.

As a comparative sociologist, I am particularly concerned with a pattern of state–society relations existing in historical as well as existing non-Western societies (what the transition from communism has displayed is but a specific case of that pattern). Its character differs noticeably from that of the modern Western pattern and does not simply disappear after these societies have attained industrialization or democratization. In many historical and existing non-Western civilizations, the states are organizationally pervasive or have vague institutional boundaries. They are functionally diffuse and lack respect for due process. Consequently, the lines between public and private, between political and personal, between formal and informal, between official and nonofficial, between government and market, between legal and customary, between procedural and substantial are all blurred. (See Bill and Hardgrave 1981: 50–57; C. Johnson 1982; Migdal 1985; Anderson 1986: 270–79; Deyo 1987; Hosking 1990: 21–30; van Wolferen 1990: 44–45, 109–10, 164–66; Wade 1990.) To this high degree of institutional ambiguity and indifferentiability, dichotomous models and ideal-typical concepts based exclusively on Western experience[8] have proved highly insensitive. They often produce misconception, misplaced emphasis, and distorted comparison. For instance, government–business relations in industrial East Asia (i.e., Japan, South Korea, Taiwan, and Singapore) are so different from these relations in North America that standard analytic schemes,

---

[8]The influential Parsonian "pattern-variables" (Parsons 1951: 58–67) are a perfect example of conceptualization of this type.

such as the state versus the market or the public versus the private, have given us little help in understanding the workings of the East Asian institutions. The use of popular terms, such as "the Japan Inc.," in the social science literature signifies our dissatisfaction with the existing analytic tools' inability to capture the substantial differences between the institutions of industrial, capitalist East Asia and those of industrial, capitalist North America.

To achieve a better description and understanding of state–society relations in non-Western civilizations, we must escape from Western ethnocentrism deeply couched in the problematics and conceptual systems of the social sciences. And we have to formulate, accordingly, a set of descriptive and analytic concepts that are more appropriate and sensitive to non-Western institutional environments.[9] I hope that the discussion here on the notion of institutional parasitism is a step in that direction.

[9]This need has been long felt by comparative sociologists, as some put it: "Redrawing the boundaries between private and public, between state and society, need not entail making them more distinct and clearly defined but may mean widening the boundary zones and blurring the distinctions" (Nee and Stark 1989: 25).

Appendix:
Notes on methods and methodology

In this work I examine the interaction between the PRC ruling elite and the counterelite by focusing on a series of events that occurred during the post-Mao era. The standard for the selection of events is that they constituted the major issues in the conflict between the two elite groups concerning the direction of reform; they both received great attention from and exerted a major impact on the politically concerned Chinese population, thereby exercising a noticeable influence on the courses of political development.

Some of the subject matter of this study is highly publicized and some is politically sensitive. Because of this, some needed material was easily obtainable (e.g., material about the regime's political appeals) while other material was not (e.g., material about the reaction to the appeals from social segments that had less access to means of expression). The material used in this study is of varying quality and can be classified as follows.

1. Information I accumulated when in China. Sociological literature usually divides information of this sort into two categories, "background knowledge," which the participant obtained as the result of living a long time in the society, and "formal knowledge," which he collected as the result of his purposeful research. With regard to the former, my life experience in China provides the background.

I was born and grew up in a rural township in South Anhui. I took part in the Cultural Revolution as an active Red Guard. From early 1969 to mid-1975, I first worked as a *zhishi qingnian* (sent-down youth) in the countryside, then as a functionary in a county government, then a blue-collar worker in a machine-building plant, and then a low-ranking manager in the same plant, all in Anhui. Afterward I spent three years in Hefei Polytechnic University as one of *gong-nong-bing xueyuan* (students of worker-peasant-soldier backgrounds, who were the subject of the Maoist educational revolutionary experiment). In college I had the chance to be in the army as a trainee for several months, and was embroiled in political trouble in 1976 for attacking the radical Maoist educational policy.

With a college degree I went back to the machine-building plant to introduce wage-bonus reforms. From 1979 to 1982 I was enrolled in a graduate program at Fudan University, Shanghai, in which I witnessed the de-Maoization campaign on campus. During the following two years I did research in the Institute of Marxism, Leninism, and Mao Zedong Thought under the CASS in Beijing. I participated in the debate on humanism and socialist alienation, and was criticized in the Anti–Spiritual Pollution Campaign of 1983–84. These varied experiences gave me an opportunity to familiarize myself with many different social strata and to experience firsthand the major political events in China till the mid-1980s. This background knowledge serves as a useful reference.

With regard to formal knowledge, what I collected includes material from contact with participants in the major events in question (they are labeled as "Informants" in this book for their protection); records from my observations; notes of proceedings of meetings at which I was present; and data from surveys and research projects in which I was involved.

In this respect, my situation resembles the early Chicago School fieldworkers: They were members first and researchers second (Hughes 1971: 543–49). This pattern, which combines the roles of member and observer, has its advantages, clearly. One observes people acting in the natural courses of their business; data obtained in this way are more credible, for "they come to the observer as a 'volunteered statement' rather than in response to a question put by the observer" (Emerson 1983: 101; see also Becker 1970: 30). As an insider you have "more access to the backstage of the movement" than do nonmembers (Emerson 1983: 232). And more "levels of insight are gained from actually doing an activity rather than simply watching it being done" (ibid.: 183).

As many researchers have pointed out, the double role of participant and observer also has its disadvantages. First, total involvement and strong commitment lead to biased observation and conception. Second, intimacy with some informants may constrain access to others in the same community. And third, identifying with the local people makes it difficult for the researcher to ask certain types of questions (S. Miller 1952; Vidich 1955; R. Gold 1958; Becker et al. 1968; S. Johnson 1975; Douglas 1976; Fahim and Helmer 1980).

In my case, the third difficulty was irrelevant as my research did not involve culturally "inconvenient" questions. I did experience the second one. Because of my close connections with some well-established intellectuals, in 1982–83 I was not treated by the Beijing democracy activists of 1978–79 as fit to know all their secrets. My knowledge of their activities was mostly gained afterward. The first problem also affected me. Fortunately, my potential biases were effectively counterbalanced by my later experience as a sociologist in the United States. Many years lie between the time when I participated in events in China and my present research in an American university. This temporal and spatial separation helped me achieve my goal of creating "sufficient distance and detachment to begin to look at these matters sociologically" (Emerson 1983: 13).

2. *Interviews I conducted with Chinese in the West.* There have been an abundance of critical comments on the peculiar weaknesses of émigré interviewing as a research technique. These criticisms center, as summarized (Whyte and Parish 1984: 383), on the "selectivity issue" (i.e., émigrés are not representative of individuals who remain in their home country, and often come from nonrepresentative places and organizations), and the "bias issue" (i.e., émigrés are particularly anticommunist and are unlikely to give objective information about the society in which they lived). Keeping these cautions in mind, however, a number of researchers have developed special methods for émigré interviewing to avoid pitfalls and bring its potential value into full play (see Inkeles and Bauer 1959: 41–64; Thurston and Pasternak 1983; Nathan 1985: 235–56; Walder 1986: 255–69).

The interviews I conducted were dissimilar in several respects from "ordinary" émigré interviews of the sort described. The chief purpose of their interviewing was to determine certain structural or institutional patterns in the émigrés' home society. My purpose primarily was to elicit factual background and details of important recent events. Therefore, my interviewees had to be participants in or around the center of the drama or close observers of these participants. A frequently encountered problem in my interviewing was that some interviewees exaggerated the importance of the processes in which they themselves took part, and meanwhile played down other processes of which they were not a part. The interrelation between these processes was thus distorted.

In order to cull fact from exaggeration, (1) I used the background knowledge I accumulated in China as common sense in evaluating information I was given; (2) I asked the same interviewees for as many concrete details as possible, especially the names and addresses of those participating in the same activity with them. This inquiry was particularly useful, as the interviewee knew that the interviewer was Chinese too and could meet his fellow participants sooner or later to cross-check information; and (3) I inquired of as many individuals as possible about the same matter and checked conflicting reports with previously established data. Some researchers call this the "triangulation method" (Walder 1986: 256–57).

One more issue needs to be mentioned here about my interviews: They all were intellectuals and professionals working in research and educational institutions or think tanks, and came predominantly from the capital of Beijing, with a few from other major Chinese cities. This is understandable to a certain extent: The Chinese government system has been unusually centralized, institutions of national importance being all located in the capital. In the meantime, the best-educated population was highly concentrated in the major cities. Based on the 1982 10 percent sampling population census in China, Chinese sociologists found that, while college graduates, college dropouts, and enrolled college students together made up 0.6 percent of the Chinese population, this category made up 4.9 percent of Beijing's, 3.4 percent of Shanghai's, and 2.4 percent of Tianjin's (*Baike Zhishi* No. 5, pp. 2–6, 1984). Despite this, however, if I had more interviewees from other lesser cities, the picture this work depicts would be widened. Constrained by financial difficulty, I could not reach wider Chinese visitor communities in the West to conduct more interviews. The following is a summary of my interviewees: Of a total 42, 29 were from Beijing, 4 from Shanghai, 3 from Tianjin, 2 from Nanjing, 2 from Xian, 1 from Wuhan, and 1 from Kaifong.

3. *Surveys done by the PRC academic and administrative bodies.* As to the political and technical limitations in survey research practiced in communist countries, social researchers in the West have fairly good knowledge (Rosen and Chu 1987; *New York Times* May 27, 1988; Otava 1988). Stanley Rosen and David Chu (1987: iv–v) have made a sound judgment on the methodological problems in the data collecting and analyzing that affect the quality of Chinese surveys. These include

traditional Chinese political culture, which inhibits honest responses to questions; surveys designed to support a political agenda or to affirm a predetermined conclusion, as showing broad support for the "open policy" or the four modernizations; infrequent use of scientific probability sampling to choose representative samples, more often resorting to personal relationships (*guanxi*), because the sensitivity of much survey research and the nature of Chinese society make it difficult for researchers to gain access to respondents; overgeneralizations and sweeping conclusions drawn from very limited or unrepresentative samples; overaggregation of responses into large, all-encompassing categories which disregard important sociological variations; and the failure to build an academic literature on any of the social issues being investigated or to draw together and summarize findings.

Despite all these limitations, Rosen and Chu (ibid.) still recommended that "Chinese surveys have already imparted a great deal of information about Chinese society, including information on . . . trends in PRC society (such as decline in interest in politics, and the state's inability to control social change), on distinctions and differing attitudes among social groups and subgroups, as well as information on a wide variety of sensitive topics."

From 1987 to the spring of 1989, with relaxation in party-state control, more

introduction of Western survey research methods into China, and more technical advice from Western social researchers and Western-trained Chinese students, survey research in China saw remarkable improvements. Questionnaires
were designed to contain issues more sensitive and controversial in nature;
linguistic sophistication was employed to reduce ambiguity and confusion
among the interviewed; better techniques were put into practice, such as stratified sampling, more accurate codification, multiregression, and computer analysis; and published research reports contained more raw data, methodological
explanations, and concrete accounts of the research process that allow the
reader to judge the quality of the data. One of the surveys quoted in this work,
the 1987 "Survey research on Chinese citizens' political minds" conducted by
Min Qi et al. and sponsored by Chen Ziming's and Wang Juntao's Beijing
Institute for Research on Social and Scientific-Technological Development,
represents the sort of improved work Chinese social scientists produced during
this period.

In addition to conventional survey data gathered by the Chinese, I also made
use of "question and answer" material, which could be called quasi opinion
surveys. This sort of material was derived in the following way: Officials in
charge of politicoideological issues in each institution in China had to collect
their subordinates' questions, doubts, grumbles, and complaints, presented in
informal or formal gatherings, about current policy or social problems. Then
low-ranking officials had periodically to report these popular opinions and re-
sentments to the higher authorities. When the department for political and
ideological work in the responsible party organization received many such reports and felt that "problematic sentiments" among the masses had spread wide
enough to jeopardize the implementation of official policies or work performance, then a task force composed of party officials and political doctrine
teachers would be called upon to form answers, in the light of current party
documents, to the typical "problematic sentiments." The "question and answer"
material was the result of this process. Such material came out more frequently
during periods of major policy turning points.

In the published "question and answer" material, the most critical and cynical
parts of the "problematic sentiments" were often smoothed over and the daring,
nonconformist statements of the public were presented as milder questions. In
a society where large-scale surveys on the most sensitive political issues could
not be directly carried out as they were done in the West, the "questions" part of
the "question and answer" material, if interpreted correctly, can be taken as a
meaningful indicator of the public opinion on important social and political
issues. As each major profession or social category, such as industrial workers,
the army, university students, and urban youth, had its own "question and

answer" material, the researcher can discern interesting similarities and differences between them.

4. *Lawful publications in the PRC.* These include party documents, statistics, and a wide variety of open (*gongkai*) and internal (*xianguonei faxing* and *neibu faxing*) publications. Western readers have long been troubled by the obscurity of publications in communist states in general and communist official material in particular (Moore 1951: 414–15; Ludz 1972: 19–20; Schurmann 1968: 62–68; Barnett 1969: 577–606; Leys 1990). While the official pronouncements "have crystallized into that esoteric jargon which to the outsider appears either meaningless or unrealistic, delusory, and self-deceptive" (Meyer 1966: 276), the counterelites normally "play the game of taking the rulers 'at their own word'"(Tismaneanu 1990: 2) – that is, opposing the rulers by seeming to accept them. The outsider is often led to underestimate the significance and influence of the counterelites' expression in their own society. In view of the peculiar grammar and vocabulary employed in political discourse in the communist system, interpretative translation is imperative.

5. *Secret PRC official material disclosed in overseas journals.* While the past records have shown that the disclosed official documents are highly reliable, the PRC leaders' "speeches" exposed this way are much less accountable. Considering this, I only used those disclosures which have been verified by either my own experience in the PRC or other reliable sources.

As many Western students of Communist China have experienced, "perhaps the most difficult problems the foreign researchers will face . . . are dilemmas of scholarly ethics." Of these ethics, "protection of the rights of subjects is a fundamental tenet . . . , and the guarantee of respondents' anonymity is fundamental to that protection" (Thurston and Pasternak 1983: 28–29). As a PRC citizen I am more sensitive to individual Chinese's political safety. I maintained throughout this study the principle that all Chinese informants will not be mentioned by name or by home institution, irrespective of where they live now.

As the purpose of this study is to examine the CCP regime's struggle to repair and maintain its political authority in the era of reform, the countermovements its struggle encountered, and the eventual failure of its efforts, my approach is essentially descriptive and interpretive. Chapters 3 to 6 are arranged roughly chronologically. I gave detailed representation of the original material concerning each event under investigation, unless there is already English translation of the material available to the public. I have chosen to take the interpretative or, to use a heuristic term, "thick description" (Geertz 1973: 6–7), approach, because under communist rule not only written material is puzzling, but men's social actions can be cryptic as well (see Thompson 1984: 174). Without proper decoding, what was couched in a social action could be widely mistaken by the outside observer. Let me cite two well-known examples.

On April 22, 1989, tens of thousands of university students in Beijing rallied at Tiananmen Square in defiance of the government's ban. They demanded an official explanation of the ouster of Hu Yaobang, the late party chief who died just a few days before, and a formal "dialogue" (meaning "discussions between equals" in the Chinese political terminology) meeting with the hard-liner premier, Li Peng. Three representatives were elected by the demonstrators to present the petition to Li Peng, who was inside the People's Great Hall at that time attending an official memorial ceremony for Hu Yaobang. Yet the guards did not allow them to enter the Great Hall. Then a dramatic scene appeared: The three representatives knelt on the steps of the Great Hall and refused to stand up unless officials came out to take their petition and pass it to Li Peng.

Western observers have made numerous comments on this act of the students. The following by Elizabeth Perry (1991: 132) is a typical one:

A striking feature of the April 22 counter-ceremony was its adherence to traditionally sanctioned modes of behavior. Three student representatives attempted – in the aged-old manner of Chinese scholarly remonstrance – to present a petition. . . . Denied entrance to the Great Hall of the People, the young emissaries suddenly fell to their knees and began to kowtow. . . . The obsequious demeanor of the petitioners was a stark reminder of the degree to which contemporary intellectuals remain bound to traditional styles of protest.

"Traditional?" Yes. "Obsequious?" Disputable. To achieve a correct interpretation of the "thick" implications of the representatives' act, one must fathom two highly symbolic contextual factors – the meaning of the rallying place in contemporary Chinese politics and the meaning of petitioners kneeling before an official in traditional Chinese political culture.

The place the students rallied and tried to present their petition was the *People's* Great Hall, where China's parliament, the *People's* Congress, holds meetings. Both were named as such because, according to the Communist propaganda, in the new, *People's* Republic of China the common people are the masters of their country. Yet, the students were denied entrance to the People's Great Hall to meet the self-claimed "*people's* servant" Li Peng by guards who were soldiers of the *People's* Liberation Army! Is that not ironic enough?

To make this even more ironic, the three representatives fell to their knees before the doors of the Great Hall. In traditional China when powerless subjects sought justice, they normally went to an imperial official with a piece of petition or complaint and knelt before him, asking, *Fu-mu guan wei xiaomin zuozhu* – "You parentlike official, please make a just decision for we little folks."

The official, according to the imperial code of civil service, must accept the petition or complaint, though he might make a decision not in favor of the petitioner or plaintiff. In Chinese historical writings, especially the popular ones, only the most tyrannical, totally corrupted officials would throw a petition or complaint away.

Now we are able to read the three representatives' act. By kneeling with a petition before the doors of the People's Great Hall in which government officials hid while carefully watching the rallying students, the representatives accused the Communist regime as well as spoke to the Chinese people: "You, the Communist party, always claim to be the servant of the people and a government system that embodies the highest political and moral values in human history. Yet you even refuse to take a petition from the people. So we kneel to you to let the people see what kind of government you really are!"

Hence, the students' act is not "obsequious" as it appeared to be; it is a powerful protest aimed to satirize the Communist regime by mobilizing abundant historical and contemporary symbols that were familiar to most Chinese, well educated or not. This is a Chinese version of the famous "As If" strategy used by opposition-minded people in the Soviet bloc (cf. Rothberg 1972: 237–38; Havel et al. 1985: 23–96; Ash 1990: 115–16).

The student representatives' act was correctly interpreted by the government officials who hid in the People's Great Hall. They were "embarrassed." (It would be hard not to be.) Eventually the doors were opened, and several officials came out and took in the students' petition, although their demands received no response from the officials.

Here is another example of misinterpretation. During the Spring 1989 Movement, many demonstrators carried banners with large English letters and small Chinese characters. This action was sometimes interpreted as showing that educated Chinese demonstrators were interested in addressing the foreign audience rather than the average Chinese. This interpretation is superficial. The demonstrators knew that there was sufficient sympathy for their course of action among the average Chinese. But they also knew that support only from their fellow countrymen did not grant them safety or success. Experience taught the demonstrators that the Communist leaders were more concerned with international reaction to their behavior than with domestic reaction. The better publicized a matter on the outside, the less the regime would be arbitrary in its acts. Hence, in order to put sufficient pressure on the regime to prevent it from taking immediate violent measures – this was vital to the sustenance and further growth of the movement's momentum – the demonstrators put their slogans and statements in English. It looked as though they were speaking to the outside, but actually they were targeting the inside: They intended to increase their bargaining power in dealing with their rulers. There is a name in Chinese for strategies of this sort: *chukou zhuan neixiao* (exports returning to the domestic market).

To conclude, to bring out the "stratified hierarchy of meaningful structures" (Geertz 1973: 7) hidden in words and deeds of members of a communist society, the researcher must rely on complex descriptive and interpretative methods.

Selected bibliography

Akzin, Benjamin. 1966. *States and Nations*. Garden City, NY: Doubleday.

Althusser, Louis. 1971. *Lenin and Philosophy and Other Essays*. New York: Monthly Review Press.

Anderson, Lisa. 1986. *The State and Social Transformation in Tunisia and Libya, 1830–1980*. Princeton, NJ: Princeton University Press.

Arato, Andrew. 1981. "Civil Society Against the State: Poland 1980–81." *Telos* 47:23–47.

    1982. "Critical Sociology and Authoritarian State Socialism." Pp. 196–218 in *Habermas: Critical Debates*, edited by J. B. Thompson and D. Held. Cambridge, MA: MIT Press.

Ash, Timothy Garton. 1989. "The Revolution of the Magic Lantern." *New York Review of Books* 36:21.

    1990. *The Uses of Adversity: Essays on the Fate of Central Europe*. New York: Vintage.

Bachrach, Peter, ed. 1971. *Political Elites in a Democracy*. New York: Atherton Press.

Bai Hua. 1981. *Unrequited Love*. Taipei: Institute of Current China Studies.

Baloyra, Enrique A., ed. 1987. *Comparing New Democracies*. Boulder, CO: Westview.

Barker, Ernest. 1951. *Principles of Social and Political Theory*. London: Oxford University Press.

Barnett, A. Doak, 1967. *Cadres, Bureaucracy, and Political Power in Communist China*. New York: Columbia University Press.

    ed. 1969. *Chinese Communist Politics in Action*. Seattle: University of Washington Press.

Barnett, A. Doak, and Ralph N. Clough, eds. 1986. *Modernizing China: Post-Mao Reform and Development*. Boulder, CO: Westview.

Becker, Howard S. 1970. *Sociological Work: Method and Substance*. Chicago: Aldine.

Becker, Howard S., Blanche Greer, David Riesman, and Robert S. Weiss, eds. 1968. *Institutions and the Person*. Chicago: Aldine.

Bell, Daniel. 1978. *The Cultural Contradictions of Capitalism*. New York: Basic Books.

    1988. *The End of Ideology: On the Exhaustion of Political Ideas in the Fifties*. Cambridge, MA: Harvard University Press. (Originally published in 1962.)

Benda, Vaclav, Milan Simecka, Ivan M. Jirous, Jiri Dienstbier, Vaclav Havel, Landislav Heidanek, and Jan Simsa. 1988. "Parallel Polis; or, An Independent Society in Central and Eastern Europe: An Inquiry." *Social Research* 55:1–2:211–46.

Bendix, Reinhard, John Bendix, and Norman Furniss. 1987. "Reflections on Modern Western States and Civil Societies." *Research in Political Sociology* 3:1–38.

Bialer, Seweryn. 1980. *Stalin's Successors: Leadership, Stability, and Change in the Soviet Union*. Cambridge: Cambridge University Press.

    ed. 1989. *Politics, Society, and Nationality Inside Gorbachev's Russia*. Boulder, CO: Westview.

Bill, James A., and Robert L. Hardgrave, Jr. 1981. *Comparative Politics: The Quest for Theory.* Lanham, MD: University Press of America.

Black, Antony. 1984. *Guilds and Civil Society in European Political Thought from the Twelfth Century to the Present.* London: Methuen.

Bonnin, Michel, and Yves Chevrier. 1991. "The Intellectual and the State: Social Dynamics of Intellectual Autonomy During the Post-Mao Era." *China Quarterly* 127:569–93.

Bottomore, Tom. 1966. *Elites and Society.* Harmondsworth: Penguin.

Brovkin, Vladimir. 1990. "Revolution from Below: Informal Political Associations in Russia 1988–1989." *Soviet Studies* 42:2:233–57.

Brumberg, Abraham, ed. 1990. *Chronicle of a Revolution: A Western-Soviet Inquiry into Perestroika.* New York: Pantheon.

Brzezinski, Zbigniew. 1967. *The Soviet Bloc: Unity and Conflict.* Cambridge, MA: Harvard University Press.

    1990. *The Grand Failure: The Birth and Death of Communism in the Twentieth Century.* New York: Macmillan.

Buckley, Christopher. 1991. "Science as Politics and Politics as Science: Fang Lizhi and Chinese Intellectuals' Uncertain Road to Dissent." *Australian Journal of Chinese Affairs* 25:1–36.

Burke, Edmund. 1904. *The Works of the Right Honorable Edmund Burke.* Boston: Little, Brown.

Burns, John P., and Stanley Rosen, eds. 1986. *Policy Conflicts in Post-Mao China.* Armonk, NY: Sharpe.

Butterfield, Fox. 1982. *China: Alive in the Bitter Sea.* New York: Bantam.

Byrd, William, and Lin Qingsong, ed. 1990. *China's Rural Industry: Structure, Development and Reform.* New York: Oxford University Press.

Carnoy, Martin. 1984. *The State and Political Theory.* Princeton, NJ: Princeton University Press.

Chen Yizi. 1990. *Zhongguo: Shinian Gaige yu Bajiu minyun (China: the ten-year reform and the People's Movement of 1989).* Taipei: Linking Publishing.

Chen Yun. 1986. *Chen Yun Wenxuan* (Selected works of Chen Yun). Beijing: People's Publishing House.

Chesneaux, Jean, Marianne Bastid, and Marie-Claire Bergere. 1976. *China from the Opium Wars to the 1911 Revolution.* New York: Pantheon.

Chirot, Daniel. 1987. "Ideology and Legitimacy in Eastern Europe." *States and Social Structures Newsletter* 4:1–4.

    ed. 1991. *The Crisis of Leninism and the Decline of the Left: The Revolutions of 1989.* Seattle: University of Washington Press.

Cohen, Leonard J., and Jane P. Shapiro, eds. 1974. *Communist Systems in Comparative Perspective.* Garden City, NY: Anchor.

Collier, David, ed. 1979. *The New Authoritarianism in Latin America.* Princeton, NJ: Princeton University Press.

Current Soviet Policies VIII. 1981. Columbus, OH: Current Digest of the Soviet Press.

Dahl, Robert A. 1984. *Modern Political Analysis.* 4th ed. Englewood Cliffs, NJ: Prentice-Hall.

Dai Qing. 1988. *"Lishi jishi: Zouchu xiandai mixin"* (Historical records: leaving modern superstition behind). *Zhongshan* (Nanjing) No. 3, pp. 4–44.

Davis, Deborah, and Ezra F. Vogel, eds. 1990. *Chinese Society on the Eve of Tiananmen.* Cambridge, MA: Council on East Asian Studies Publications, Harvard University.

Deng Xiaoping. 1984. *Selected Works (1975–1982).* Beijing: Foreign Languages Press.

    1987. *Fundamental Issues in Present-Day China.* Beijing: Foreign Languages Press.

d'Entreves, Alexander P. 1967. *The Notion of the State.* Oxford: Clarendon.

Deyo, Frederic C., ed. 1987. *The Political Economy of the New Asian Industrialism.* Ithaca, NY: Cornell University Press.

Dialectics of Nature Journal, ed. 1983. *Kexue Chuantong yu Wenhua* (The tradition of science and culture). Xian: Shaanxi Science and Technology Press.

Ding, Xueliang. 1988. "The Disparity Between Idealistic and Instrumental Chinese Reformers." *Asian Survey* 28:1117–39.

Domes, Jurgen. 1985. *The Government and Politics of the PRC: A Time of Transition.* Boulder, CO: Westview.

Douglas, Jack D. 1976. *Investigative Social Research: Individual and Team Field Research.* Beverly Hills, CA: Sage.

Duus, Peter. 1976. *The Rise of Modern Japan.* Boston: Houghton Mifflin.

Editorial Board of *Who's Who in China*, ed. 1989. *Who's Who in China: Current Leaders.* Beijing: Foreign Languages Press.

EEPS. 1990. "A Survey of Opinion on the East European Revolution." *East European Politics and Societies* 4:2:153–207.

Eisenstadt, S. N., and Louis Roniger. 1980. "Patron–Client Relations as a Model of Structuring Social Exchange." *Comparative Studies in Society and History* 22:1:42–77.

Ekiert, G. 1990. "Transitions from State-Socialism in East Central Europe." *States and Social Structures Newsletter* 12:1–7.

Emerson, Robert M., ed. 1983. *Contemporary Field Research.* Prospect Heights, IL: Waveland.

Engels, Frederick. 1976. *Anti-Duhring.* Beijing: Foreign Languages Press. (Originally published in 1878.)

Fahim, Hussein, and Katherine Helmer. 1980. "Indigenous Anthropology in Non-Western Countries: A Further Elaboration." *Current Anthropology* 21:644–63.

Fairbank, John King. 1983. *The United States and China.* 4th ed. Cambridge, MA: Harvard University Press.

Fang Lizhi. 1989. *My Selected Speeches and Writings.* Rev. Ed. Taipei: Commonwealth Publishing Company.

　　1991. *Bringing Down the Great Wall: Writings on Science, Culture, and Democracy in China.* New York: Knopf.

Ferguson, Adam. 1980. *An Essay on the History of Civil Society.* New Brunswick, NJ: Transaction. (Originally published in 1767.)

Ferrero, Guglielmo. 1972. *The Principles of Power.* New York: Arno. (Originally published in 1942.)

Finkle, Jason L., and Richard W. Gable, eds. 1966. *Political Development and Social Change.* New York: John Wiley.

Fleron, Frederic J., Jr., ed. 1969. *Communist Studies and the Social Sciences.* Chicago: Rand McNally.

Frentzel-Zagorska, Janina. 1990. "Civil Society in Poland and Hungary." *Soviet Studies* 42:4:759–77.

Friedman, Edward. 1983. "The Societal Obstacle to China's Socialist Transition: State Capitalism or Feudal Fascism." Pp. 148–74 in *State and Society in Contemporary China*, edited by V. Nee and D. Mozingo. Ithaca, NY: Cornell University Press.

Fudan Journal Editorial Department, ed. 1986. *Wenhua de Chongtu yu Jueze* (Cultural conflict and choice). Beijing: People's Publishing House.

　　ed. 1987. *Duanli yu Jicheng* (Break and inheritance). Shanghai: Shanghai People's Publishing House.

Geertz, Clifford. 1973. *The Interpretation of Cultures.* New York: Basic Books.

Gibbon, Peter, Yusuf Bangura, and Arve Ofstad, eds. 1992. *Authoritarianism,*

Democracy, and Adjustment: The Politics of Economic Reform in Africa. Stockholm: Nordiska Afrikainstitutet.

Giddens, Anthony, and David Held, eds. 1982. *Classes, Power, and Conflict.* Berkeley and Los Angeles: University of California Press.

Gilbert, Jess, and Carolyn Howe. 1991. "Beyond 'State vs. Society': Theories of the State and New Deal Agricultural Policies." *American Sociological Review* 56:204–20.

Ginsberg, Norton, ed. 1984. *China, the 80s Era.* Boulder, CO: Westview.

Gold, Raymond L. 1958. "Roles in Sociological Field Observations." *Social Forces* 36:217–23.

Gold, Thomas B. 1985. "After Comradeship: Personal Relations in China Since the Cultural Revolution." *China Quarterly* 104:657–75.

Goldman, Merle. 1991. "Hu Yaobang's Intellectual Network and the Theory Conference of 1979." *China Quarterly* 126:219–42.

Goldman, Merle, Timothy Cheek, and Carol Lee Hamrin, eds. 1987. *China's Intellectuals and the State: In Search of a New Relationship.* Cambridge, MA: Council on East Asian Studies Publications, Harvard University.

Goldstone, Jack A. 1982. "The Comparative and Historical Study of Revolutions." *Annual Review of Sociology.*

Goodman, David S. G. 1981. *Beijing Street Voices: The Poetry and Politics of China's Democracy Movement.* London: Marion Boyars.

Gorbachev, Mikhail. 1988. *Perestroika.* New York: Harper and Row.

Gramsci, Antonio. 1971. *Selections from the Prison Notebooks.* New York: International Publishers.

Grimm, Dieter. 1986. "The Modern State: Continental Traditions." Pp.89–110 in *Guidance, Control, and Evaluation in the Public Sector,* edited by F. Kaufman, G. Majone, and V. Ostrom. Berlin: de Gruyter.

Gruliow, Leo, ed. 1960. "The Documentary Record of the Extraordinary 21st Congress of the CPSU." *Current Soviet Politics* 3:1–199.

Gwertzman, Bernard, and Michael T. Kaufman, eds. 1991. *The Collapse of Communism.* New York: Times Books.

Habermas, Jürgen. 1975. *Legitimation Crisis.* Boston: Beacon.

1979. *Communication and the Evolution of Society.* Boston: Beacon.

Hankiss, Elemer. 1988. "The 'Second Society': Is There an Alternative Social Model Emerging in Contemporary Hungary?" *Social Research* 55:1–2:13–42.

Hann, C. M., ed. 1990. *Market Economy and Civil Society in Hungary.* London: Frank Cass.

Hao Mengbi and Duan Haoran, eds. 1984. *Zhongguo Gongchandang Liushilian* (Sixty years of the Chinese communist party). Beijing: Liberation Army Publishing House.

Harding, Harry. 1987. *China's Second Revolution: Reform After Mao.* Washington, DC: Brookings Institute.

Havel, Vaclav, et al. 1985. *The Power of the Powerless.* Armonk, NY: Sharpe.

Hayward, Jack, and R. N. Berki, eds. 1979. *State and Society in Contemporary Europe.* New York: St. Martin's.

Hegel, G. W. F. 1942. *Philosophy of Right.* Oxford: Oxford University Press. (Originally published in 1821.)

Hobbes, Thomas. 1962. *Leviathan.* New York: Collier. (Originally published in 1651.)

Hodnett, Grey, ed. 1974. *Resolutions and Decisions of the Communist Party of the Soviet Union.* Vol. 4. Toronto: University of Toronto Press.

Hosking, Geoffrey. 1990. *The Awakening of the Soviet Union.* Cambridge, MA: Harvard University Press.

Hough, Jerry F. 1972. "The Soviet System: Petrification or Pluralism?" *Problems of Communism* 3–4:25–45.

Hsu, C. Y. 1975. *The Rise of Modern China.* 2nd ed. New York: Oxford University Press.

Hu Guohua, Liu Jinghuai, and Chen Min. 1988. *Duosediao de Zhongguo Geti Jingyingzhe* (Colorful Individual Businessmen in China). Beijing: Beijing Economics Institute Press.

Hu Yaobang. 1982. *The Twelfth National Congress of the CPC.* Beijing: Foreign Languages Press.

Hughes, Everett C. 1971. *The Sociological Eye: Selected Papers.* Chicago: Aldine.

Huntington, Samuel P. 1968. *Political Order in Changing Societies.* New Haven, CT: Yale University Press.

   1991. *The Third Wave: Democratization in the Late Twentieth Century.* Norman: University of Oklahoma Press.

Hyman, Herbert H. 1942. "The Psychology of Status." *Archives of Psychology.* Vol. 38, No. 269.

Inkeles, Alex. 1971. *Social Change in the Soviet Russia.* New York: Simon and Schuster.

Inkeles, Alex, and Raymond A. Bauer. 1959. *The Soviet Citizen: Daily Life in a Totalitarian Society.* Cambridge, MA: Harvard University Press.

Inkeles, Alex, and Kent Geiger, eds. 1961. *Soviet Society: A Book of Readings.* Boston: Houghton Mifflin.

Institute for the Study of Chinese Communist Problems, ed. 1980–85. *Collection of the Mainland Underground Publications.* Vols. 1–20. Taipei.

Investigation and Research Division, General Office of the State Council, ed. 1986. *Geti Jingji Diaocha yu Yanjiu* (Investigation and studies of the individual economy). Beijing: Economic Science Press.

Jakobson, Linda. 1990. "'Lies in Ink, Truth in Blood': The Role and Impact of the Chinese Media During the Beijing Spring of '89." Discussion Paper D-6, JFK School of Government. Cambridge, MA: Harvard University.

Janos, Andrew C. 1986. *Politics and Paradigms: Changing Theories of Change in Social Science.* Stanford, CA: Stanford University Press.

Johnson, Chalmers, ed. 1970. *Change in Communist Systems.* Stanford, CA: Stanford University Press.

   1982. *MITI and the Japanese Miracle: The Growth of Industrial Policy, 1925–75.* Stanford, CA: Stanford University Press.

Johnson, John M. 1975. *Doing Field Research.* New York: Free Press.

Joseph, William A. 1984. *The Critique of Ultra-Leftism in China, 1958–1981.* Stanford, CA: Stanford University Press.

Jowitt, Kenneth. 1971. "The Concepts of Liberalization, Integration, and Rationalization in the Context of East European Development." *Studies in Comparative Communism* 4:79–91.

Judt, Tony. 1988. "The Dilemmas of Dissidence: The Politics of Opposition in East-Central Europe." *Eastern European Politics and Societies* 2:2:185–240.

Kant, Immanuel. 1887. *The Philosophy of Law.* Edinburgh: T. and T. Clark. (Originally published in 1797.)

Kaufman, Robert R. 1974. "The Patron–Client Concept and Macro-Politics: Prospects and Problems." *Comparative Studies in Society and History* 16:3:284–308.

Keane, John, ed. 1988a. *Civil Society and the State: New European Perspectives.* London: Verso.

   1988b. *Democracy and Civil Society.* London: Verso.

Keller, Suzanne. 1963. *Beyond the Ruling Class: Strategic Elites in Modern Society.* New York: Random House.

1968. "Elites." Pp. 26–29 in *International Encyclopedia of the Social Sciences*, Vol. 5, edited by D. L. Sills. New York: Macmillan and Free Press.

Kelly, David, and He Baogang, 1992. "Emergent Civil Society and the Intellectuals in China." Pp. 24–39 in *The Developments of Civil Society in Communist Systems*, edited by R. F. Miller. North Sydney: Allen and Unwin.

Kennedy, Paul. 1987. *The Rise and Fall of the Great Powers*. New York: Random House.

Kleinman, Arthur. 1986. *Social Origins of Distress and Disease*. New Haven, CT: Yale University Press.

Kligman, Gail. 1990. "Reclaiming the Public: a Reflection on Creating Civil Society in Romania." *East European Politics and Societies* 4:3:393–427.

Konrad, George, and Ivan Szelenyi. 1979. *The Intellectuals on the Road to Class Power*. New York: Harcourt Brace Jovanovich.

Lasswell, Harold D. 1966. "Introduction: The Study of Political Elites." Pp. 3–28 in *World Revolutionary Elites: Studies in Coercive Ideological Movements*, edited by H. D. Lasswell and D. Lerner. Cambridge, MA: MIT Press.

Lee, Hong Yung. 1978. *The Politics of the Chinese Cultural Revolution: A Case Study*. Berkeley and Los Angeles: University of California Press.

1991. *From Revolutionary Cadres to Party Technocrats in Socialist China*. Berkeley and Los Angeles: University of California Press.

Lefort, Claude. 1986. *The Political Forms of Modern Society: Bureaucracy, Democracy, Totalitarianism*, edited and introduced by J. B. Thompson. Cambridge, MA: MIT Press.

Lehman, Edward W. 1987. "The Crisis of Political Legitimacy: What Is It; Who's Got It; Who Needs It?" *Research in Political Sociology* 3:203–21.

Lenin, V. I. 1966. *The Lenin Reader*, edited by S. T. Possony. Chicago: Henry Regnery.

Levenson, Joseph R. 1965. *Confucian China and Its Modern Fate: A Trilogy*. Berkeley and Los Angeles: University of California Press.

Lewin, Moshe. 1988. *The Gorbachev Phenomenon: A Historical Interpretation*. Berkeley and Los Angeles: University of California Press.

Lewis, Bernard. 1968. *The Emergence of Modern Turkey*. New York: Oxford University Press.

Lewis, Paul G., ed. 1984. *Eastern Europe: Political Crisis and Legitimation*. New York: St. Martin's.

Leys, Simon. 1990. "The Art of Interpreting Nonexistent Inscriptions Written in Invisible Ink on a Blank Page." *New York Review of Books* October 11, pp. 8–13.

Li Cheng and Lynn T. White III. 1991. "China's Technocratic Movement and the *World Economic Herald*." *Modern China* 17:3:342–88.

Li Xiaobin, ed. 1987. *Bashiniandai Zhongxi Wenhua Taolun Ji* (A collection of discussions on the Chinese and Western cultures in the 1980s). Beijing: Party Central School Scientific Research Office.

Li Yongchun, Shi Yuanqin, and Guo Xiuzhi. 1987. *Shiyi Jie Sanzhong Quanhui Yilai Zhengzhi Tizhi Gaige Dashiji* (Major Events in the Political System Reform Since the Third Plenary Session of the Eleventh Central Committee of the CCP). Beijing: Chunqiu Publishing House.

Li Zehou and Vera Schwarcz. 1983–84. "Six Generations of Modern Chinese Intellectuals." *Chinese Studies in History* 17:2:42–56.

Lin Yu-sheng. 1979. *The Crisis of Chinese Consciousness*. Madison: University of Wisconsin Press.

Lindblom, Charles E. 1977. *Politics and Markets: The World's Political-Economic Systems*. New York: Basic Books.

Link, Perry. 1992. *Evening Chats in Beijing: Probing China's Predicament*. New York: Norton.

Linz, Juan J. 1975. "Totalitarian and Authoritarian Regimes." Pp. 175–412 in *Handbook of Political Science*. Vol. 3, *Macropolitical Theory*, edited by F. I. Greenstein and N. W. Polsby. Reading, MA: Addison-Wesley.

Lipset, Seymour Martin. 1981. *Political Man: The Social Bases of Politics*. Baltimore: Johns Hopkins University Press. (Originally published in 1960.)

Liu Binyan. 1990. *A Higher Kind of Loyalty*. New York: Random House.

Liu Jun and Li Lin, eds. 1989. *Xin Quanwei Zhuyi: Dui Gaige Lilun Gangling de Lunzhen* (New authoritarianism: debate on the theoretical framework of reform). Beijing: Beijing Institute of Economics Press.

Liu Long, Du Yi, Lin Wei, Mei Zhiguang, and Yu Dexin, eds. 1986. *Zhongguo Xianjieduan Getijingji Yanjiu* (Studies of the individual economy in today's China). Beijing: People's Publishing House.

Locke, John. 1960. *Two Treatises of Government*. Cambridge: Cambridge University Press. (Originally published in 1690.)

Lowenthal, Richard. 1984. *Social Change and Cultural Crisis*. New York: Columbia University Press.

Lu Yi, ed. 1989. *Qiuji: Yige Shijixing de Xuanze* (Global membership: a choice of the century). Shanghai: Baijia Publishing House.

Ludz, Peter C. 1972. *The Changing Party Elite in East Germany*. Cambridge, MA: MIT Press.

Lukes, Steven. 1974. *Power: A Radical View*. London: Macmillan.

Luo Bin. 1981. "Deng Xiaoping shouchongji he fanchongji." *Contending* (Hong Kong) 4:7–10.

MacFarquhar, Roderick. 1983. *The Origins of the Cultural Revolution*. Vol. 2, *The Great Leap Forward 1958–1960*. Oxford: Oxford University Press.

Macridis, Roy C., and Bernard E. Brown, eds. 1977. *Comparative Politics: Notes and Readings*. 5th ed. Homewood, IL: Dorsey Press.

Madsen, Richard. 1984. *Morality and Power in a Chinese Village*. Berkeley and Los Angeles: University of California Press.

Malloy, James M., ed. 1977. *Authoritarianism and Corporatism in Latin America*. Pittsburgh: University of Pittsburgh Press.

Malloy, James M., and Mitchell A. Seligson, eds. 1987. *Authoritarians and Democrats: Regime Transition in Latin America*. Pittsburgh: University of Pittsburgh Press.

Mao Zedong. 1977. *Selected Works of Mao Tsetung [Zedong]*. Vol. 5. Beijing: Foreign Languages Press.

Marx, Karl. 1967. *Capital*. Vol. 1. New York: International Publishers. (Originally published in 1867.)

    1972. *Critique of Hegel's "Philosophy of Right."* Cambridge: Cambridge University Press. (Originally published in 1927.)

Marx, Karl, and Friedrich Engels. 1972. *The Marx-Engels Reader*, edited by R. C. Tucker. New York: Norton.

Merquior, J. G. 1980. *Rousseau and Weber: Two Studies in the Theory of Legitimacy*. London: Routledge and Kegan Paul.

Merton, Robert K. 1957. *Social Theory and Social Structure*. London: Free Press.

Meyer, Alfred G. 1966. "The Functions of Ideology in the Soviet Political System." *Soviet Studies* 1:273–85.

Michael, Franz, Carl Linden, Jan Prybyla, and Jurgen Domes. 1990. *China and the Crisis of Marxism-Leninism*. Boulder, CO: Westview.

Migdal, Joel S. 1985. "A Model of State–Society Relations." Pp. 41–55 in *New Directions in Comparative Politics*, edited by H. Wiarda. Boulder, CO: Westview.

Miller, Robert F., ed. 1992. *The Developments of Civil Society in Communist Systems*. North Sydney: Allen and Unwin.

Miller, S. M. 1952. "The Participant Observer and 'Over-Rapport.'" *American Sociological Review* 17:97–99.

Miller, William Green, ed. 1989. *Toward a More Civil Society? The USSR under Mikhail Sergeevich Gorbachev.* New York: Harper and Row.

Min Qi. 1989. *Zhongguo Zhengzhi Wenhua* (China's political culture). Kunming: Yunnan People's Publishing House.

Moore, Barrington, Jr. 1951. *Soviet Politics: The Dilemma of Power.*5Cambridge, MA: Harvard University Press.

1969. "Revolution in America?" *New York Review of Books* January 30:6–12.

Mosca, Gaetano. 1939. *The Ruling Class.* New York: McGraw-Hill. (Originally published in 1896.)

Moulakis, Athanasios, ed. 1985. *Legitimacy: Proceedings of the Conference Held in Florence, June 3 and 4, 1982.* Berlin: de Gruyter.

Nadel, S. F. 1956. "The Concept of Social Elites." *International Social Science Bulletin* 8:413–24.

Nathan, Andrew J. 1985. *Chinese Democracy.* New York: Knopf.

1990. *China's Crisis: Dilemmas of Reform and Prospects for Democracy.* New York: Columbia University Press.

Nee, Victor, and David Stark, eds. 1989. *Remaking the Economic Institutions of Socialism: China and Eastern Europe.* Stanford, CA: Stanford University Press.

Nisbet, Robert A. 1966. *The Sociological Tradition.* New York: Basic Books.

O'Donnell, Guillermo, Philippe C. Schmitter, and Laurence Whitehead, eds. 1986. *Transitions From Authoritarian Rule: Prospects for Democracy.* Vol. 1, *Southern Europe;* Vol. 2, *Latin America;* Vol. 3, *Comparative Perspectives;* Vol. 4, *Tentative Conclusions.* Baltimore: Johns Hopkins University Press.

Offe, Claus. 1984. *Contradictions of the Welfare State.* Cambridge, MA: MIT Press.

Oi, Jean C. 1989. *State and Peasant in Contemporary China: The Political Economy of Village Government.* Berkeley and Los Angeles: University of California Press.

Oksenberg, Michel, and Steven Goldstein. 1974. "The Chinese Political Spectrum." *Problems of Communism* 3–4:1–13.

Oksenberg, Michel, Lawrence R. Sullivan, and Marc Lambert, eds. 1990. *Beijing Spring, 1989: Confrontation and Conflict. The Basic Documents.* Armonk, NY: Sharpe.

Oppenheim, Felix E. 1975. "The Language of Political Inquiry: Problems of Clarification." Pp. 283–336 in *Handbook of Political Science,* Vol. 1, edited by F. I. Greenstein and N. W. Polsby. Reading, MA: Addison-Wesley.

Otava, Jiri. 1988. "Public Opinion Research in Czechoslovakia." Introduction by H. G. Skilling. *Social Research* 55:1–2:247–60.

Ownby, David, ed. 1985. "Changing Attitudes Among Chinese Youths: Letters to *Zhongguo qingnian.*" *Chinese Sociology and Anthropology* 17:4:1–113.

Pareto, Vilfredo. 1980. *Compendium of General Sociology.* Minneapolis: University of Minnesota Press. (Originally published in 1920.)

Parry, Geraint. 1969. *Political Elites.* London: Allen and Unwin.

Parsons, Talcott. 1951. *The Social System.* New York: Free Press.

1968. *The Structure of Social Action.* New York: Free Press.

Party Literature Research Center, the Central Committee of the CCP, ed. 1982. *Sanzhong Quanhui Yilai* (Since the third plenary session: a selection of important literature). Beijing: People's Publishing House.

ed. 1985. *Guanyu Jianguoyilai Dang de Ruogan Lishiwenti de Jueyi: Zhushiben (Xiuding)* (The resolution on certain questions in the party's history since the founding of the PRC). Beijing: People's Publishing House.

ed. 1986. *Shierda Yilai* (Since the twelfth party congress: a selection of important documents). Beijing: People's Publishing House.

Pelczynski, Z. A., ed. 1984. *The State and Civil Society: Studies in Hegel's Political Philosophy*. Cambridge: Cambridge University Press.

1988. "Solidarity and 'The Rebirth of Civil Society.'" Pp. 361–80 in *Civil Society and the State: New European Perspectives*, edited by J. Keane. London: Verso.

People's Daily History Editorial Group, ed. 1988. *Renmin Ribao Huiyilu 1948–1988* (Recollections about the *People's Daily* 1948–1988). Beijing: People's Daily Publishing House.

Perkins, Dwight H. 1986. "The Prospects for China's Economic Reforms." Pp. 39–62 in *Modernizing China. Post-Mao Reform and Development*, edited by A. D. Barnett and R. N. Clough. Boulder, CO: Westview.

Perlmutter, Amos. 1981. *Modern Authoritarianism*. New Haven, CT: Yale University Press.

Perry, Elizabeth J. 1989. "State and Society in Contemporary China." *World Politics* 7:579–91.

1991. "Intellectuals and Tiananmen: Historical Perspective on an Aborted Revolution." Pp. 129–46 in *The Crisis of Leninism and the Decline of the Left: The Revolutions of 1989*, edited by D. Chirot. Seattle: University of Washington Press.

Perry, Elizabeth J., and Christine Wong, eds. 1985. *The Political Economy of Reform in Post-Mao China*. Cambridge, MA: Council on East Asian Studies Publications, Harvard University.

PLA Publishing House Q & A Editorial Group. 1984. *Wenti Baida* (Answers to a hundred questions). Beijing: Liberation Army Publishing House.

Portes, Alejandro, and A. Douglas Kincaid. 1985. "The Crisis of Authoritarianism: State and Civil Society in Argentina, Chile and Uruguay." *Research in Political Sociology* 1:49–77.

Poulantzas, Nicos. 1974. *Political Power and Social Classes*. London: New Left Books.

1980. *State, Power, Socialism*. London: Verso.

Putnam, Robert D. 1976. *The Comparative Study of Political Elites*. Englewood Cliffs, NJ: Prentice-Hall.

Pye, Lucian W. 1986. "On Chinese Pragmatism in the 1980s." *China Quarterly* 106:207–34.

Rau, Zbigniew. 1987. "Some Thoughts on Civil Society in Eastern Europe and the Lockean Contractarian Approach." *Political Studies* 35:573–92.

Remington, Thomas F. 1990. "Regime Transition in Communist Systems: The Soviet Case." *Soviet Economy* 6:2:160–90.

Rigby, T. H., 1991. "The USSR: End of a Long, Dark Night?" Pp. 11–23 in *The Developments of Civil Society in Communist Systems*, edited by R. F. Miller. North Sydney: Allen and Unwin.

Rigby, T. H., and Ferenc Feher, eds. 1982. *Political Legitimation in Communist States*. New York: St. Martin's.

Rosen, Stanley, ed. 1990. "Selections on Education from the *World Economic Herald*." *Chinese Education* 23:2:5–92.

Rosen, Stanley, and David Chu. 1987. *Survey Research in the People's Republic of China*. A report funded by the U.S. Information Agency, Office of Research. Washington, DC.

Rosen, Stanley, and Gary Zou, eds. 1990–91. "The Chinese Debate on the New Authoritarianism (I)." *Chinese Sociology and Anthropology* 23:2:3–93.

ed. 1991a. "The Chinese Debate on the New Authoritarianism (II)." *Chinese Sociology and Anthropology* 23:3:3–92.

ed. 1991b. "The Chinese Debate on the New Authoritarianism (III)." *Chinese Sociology and Anthropology* 23:4:3–93.

Rothberg, Abraham. 1972. *The Heirs of Stalin. Dissidence and the Soviet Regime 1953–1970*. Ithaca, NY: Cornell University Press.

Rousseau, Jean-Jacques. 1967. *The Social Contract and Discourse on the Origin of Inequality.* New York: Simon and Schuster. (Originally published in 1762.)

Rozman, Gilbert. 1987. *The Chinese Debate About Soviet Socialism 1978–1985.* Princeton, NJ: Princeton University Press.

Ruan Ming. 1991. *Hu Yaobang at the Historic Turning Point.* River Edge, NJ: Global Publishing.

Rubenstein, Joshua. 1985. *Soviet Dissidents: Their Struggle for Human Rights.* 2nd ed. Boston: Beacon.

Rupnik, Jacques. 1979. "Dissent in Poland, 1968–78: The End of Revisionism and the Rebirth of the Civil Society." Pp. 60–112 in *Opposition in Eastern Europe*, edited by R. L. Tokes. Baltimore: Johns Hopkins University Press.

Saich, Tony, ed. 1990. *The Chinese People's Movement: Perspectives on Spring 1989.* Armonk, NY: Sharpe.

Saikowski, Charlotte, and Leo Gruliow, eds. 1962. FICurrent Soviet Policies IV. New York: Columbia University Press.

Scanlan, James P. 1988. "Reforms and Civil Society in the USSR." *Problems of Communism* 2:41–46.

Schaar, John H. 1981. *Legitimacy in the Modern State.* New Brunswick, NJ: Transaction.

Schabert, Tilo. 1985. "Power, Legitimacy and Truth: Reflections on the Impossibility to Legitimise Legitimations of Political Order." Pp. 96–104 in *Legitimacy: Proceedings of the Conference Held in Florence, June 3 and 4, 1982*, edited by A. Moulakis. Berlin: de Gruyter.

Schapiro, Leonard. 1969. "The Concept of Totalitarianism." *Survey* 73:93–115.

Schell, Orville. 1989. *Discos and Democracy.* New York: Anchor.

Schoenhals, Michael. 1985. "Elite Information in China." *Problems of Communism* 9–10:65–71.

———. 1991. "The 1978 Truth Criterion Controversy." *China Quarterly* 126:243–68.

Schopflin, George. 1979. "Opposition and Para-Opposition: Critical Currents in Hungary, 1968–78." Pp. 142–86 in *Opposition in Eastern Europe*, edited by R. L. Tokes. Baltimore: Johns Hopkins University Press.

Schram, Stuart R. 1984. "'Economics in Command?' Ideology and Policy Since the Third Plenum, 1978–84." *China Quarterly* 99:417–61.

Schroeder, Gertrude E. 1988. "Property Rights Issues in Economic Reforms in Socialist Countries." *Studies in Comparative Communism* 21:2:175–88.

Schurmann, Franz. 1968. *Ideology and Organization in Communist China.* Berkeley and Los Angeles: University of California Press.

Schwartz, Benjamin. 1964. *In Search of Wealth and Power. Yan Fu's Encounter with the West.* Cambridge, MA: Harvard University Press.

Seleny, Anna. 1991. "Hidden Enterprise, Property Rights Reform and Political Transformation in Socialist Hungary." *Law and Policy* 3:2:149–69.

Seligman, Adam. 1992. *The Idea of Civil Society.* New York: Free Press.

Seybolt, Peter J., ed. 1981. "'What Is the Meaning of Life?' Selections from *Zhongguo Qingnian.*" *Chinese Education* 14:1:3–73.

Seymour, James D, ed. 1980. *The Fifth Modernization: China's Human Rights Movement, 1978–1979.* Standfordvill, NY: Human Rights Publishing Group.

Shanghai Municipal Commission for Education and Public Health. 1987. *Da Daxuesheng Wen* (Answering university students' questions). Shanghai: Shanghai People's Publishing House.

Shue, Vivienne. 1988. *The Reach of the State: Sketches of the Chinese Body Politic.* Stanford, CA: Stanford University Press.

Sills, David L., ed. 1968. *International Encyclopedia of the Social Sciences.* New York: Macmillan and Free Press.

Simon, Denis Fred, and Merle Goldman, ed. 1989. *Science and Technology in Post-Mao*

China. Cambridge, MA: Council on East Asian Studies Publications, Harvard University.

Sinanian, Sylvia, Istvan Deak, and Peter Ludz, eds. 1972. *Eastern Europe in the 1970s.* New York: Praeger.

Siu, Helen F., and Zelda Stern, eds. 1983. *Mao's Harvest: Voices from China's New Generation.* New York: Oxford University Press.

Skilling, H. Gordon, ed. 1989. *Samizdat and an Independent Society in Central and Eastern Europe.* Houndmills, UK: Macmillan.

Skocpol, Theda. 1979. *States and Social Revolutions: A Comparative Analysis of France, Russia and China.* Cambridge: Cambridge University Press.

Snyder, Louis L., ed. 1956. *The Dynamics of Nationalism.* New York: Oxford University Press.

Solomon, Richard H. 1971. *Mao's Revolution and the Chinese Political Culture.* Berkeley and Los Angeles: University of California Press.

Stanworth, Philip, and Anthony Giddens, ed. 1974. *Elites and Power in British Society.* Cambridge: Cambridge University Press.

Starr, S. Frederick. 1988. "Soviet Union: A Civil Society." *Foreign Policy* 70:26–41.

Sternberger, Dolf. 1968. "Legitimacy." Pp. 244–48 in *International Encyclopedia of the Social Sciences,* Vol. 9, edited by D. L. Sills. New York: Macmillan and Free Press.

Stinchcombe, Arthur L. 1968. *Constructing Social Theories.* Chicago: University of Chicago Press.

Stouffer, Samuel A., Edward A. Suchman, Leland C. DeVinney, Shirley A. Star, and Robin M. Williams, Jr. 1949. *The American Soldier.* Princeton, NJ: Princeton University Press.

Strand, David. 1990. "Protest in Beijing: Civil Society and Public Sphere in China." *Problems of Communism* 5–6:1–19.

Sun Yat-sen. 1986. *Jianguo Dagang* (A program of state-building). Taipei: Zhongyang Wenwu Gongyingshe.

Szelenyi, Ivan. 1979. "Socialist Opposition in Eastern Europe: Dilemmas and Prospects." Pp. 187–208 in *Opposition in Eastern Europe,* edited by R. L. Tokes. Baltimore: Johns Hopkins University Press.

——— 1989. "Eastern Europe in an Epoch of Transition: Toward a Socialist Mixed Economy?" Pp. 208–32 in *Remaking the Economic Institutions of Socialism: China and Eastern Europe,* edited by V. Nee and D. Stark. Stanford, CA: Stanford University Press.

Tao Kai, Zhang Yide, and Dai Qing. 1989. *Zouchu Xiandai Mixin* (Leaving modern superstition behind). Hong Kong: Sanlian Shudian.

Taras, R. ed., 1991. *From Critical Marxism to Post-Communism.* Armonk, NY: Sharpe.

Teiwes, Frederick C. 1984. *Leadership, Legitimacy, and Conflict in China.* Armonk, NY: Sharpe.

Teng, Ssu-Yu, and John K. Fairbank. 1979. *China's Response to the West.* Cambridge, MA: Harvard University Press.

Therborn, Goran. 1980. *What Does the Ruling Class Do When It Rules?* London: Verso.

Thompson, John B. 1984. *Studies in the Theory of Ideology.* Cambridge: Polity.

Thompson, John B., and David Held, eds. 1982. *Habermas: Critical Debates.* Cambridge, MA: MIT Press.

Thurston, Anne F. 1987. *Enemies of the People.* New York: Knopf.

Thurston, Anne F., and Burton Pasternak, eds. 1983. *The Social Sciences and Fieldwork in China.* Boulder, CO: Westview.

Tilly, Charles. 1977. "Does Modernization Breed Revolution?" Pp. 453–66 in *Compara-*

tive Politics: Notes and Readings, 5th ed., edited by R. C. Macridis and B. E. Brown. Homewood, Il: Dorsey Press.

1978. *From Mobilization to Revolution.* Reading, MA: Addison-Wesley.

Tismaneanu, Vladimir, ed. 1990. *In Search of Civil Society: Independent Peace Movements in the Soviet Bloc.* New York: Routledge.

Tocqueville, Alexis de. 1955. *The Old Regime and the French Revolution.* Garden City, NY: Doubleday. (Originally published in 1856.)

Tokes, Rudolf L., ed. 1979. *Opposition in Eastern Europe.* Baltimore: Johns Hopkins University Press.

Tong, James, ed. 1980, 1981. "Underground Journals in China, Part I" and "Part II." *Chinese Law and Government* 13:3–4 and 14:3.

Turner, Ralph H. 1955. "Reference Groups of Future Oriented Men." *Social Forces* 34:130–36.

Unger, Jonathan. 1982. *Education Under Mao.* New York: Columbia University Press.

Urban, G. R., ed. 1986. *Stalinism: Its Impact on Russia and the World.* Cambridge, MA: Harvard University Press.

Urry, John. 1973. *Reference Groups and the Theory of Revolution.* London: Routledge and Kegan Paul.

van Wolferen, Karel. 1990. *The Enigma of Japanese Power.* New York: Vintage.

Vidich, Arthur J. 1955. "Participant Observation and the Collection and Interpretation of Data." *American Sociological Review* 60:354–60.

Vidich, Arthur J., and Ronald M. Glassman, eds. 1979. *Conflict and Control: Challenge to Legitimacy of Modern Governments.* Beverly Hills, CA: Sage.

Vogel, Ezra F. 1965. "From Friendship to Comradeship: The Changes in Personal Relations in Communist China." *China Quarterly* 21:1–3.

1989. *One Step Ahead: Guangdong Under Reform.* Cambridge, MA: Harvard University Press.

Wade, Robert. 1990. *Governing the Market: Economic Theory and the Role of Government in East Asian Industrialization.* Princeton, NJ: Princeton University Press.

Wakeman, Frederic. 1989. "All the Rage in China." *New York Review of Books* March 2, pp. 19–21.

Walder, Andrew G. 1986. *Communist Neo-Traditionalism: Work and Authority in Chinese Industry.* Berkeley and Los Angeles: University of California Press.

1989. "The Political Sociology of the Beijing Upheaval of 1989." *Problems of Communism* 38:9–10:30–40.

Wang Ruoshui. 1989. *Zhihui de Tongku* (Pains of the wisdom). Hong Kong: Sanlian Shudian.

Wank, David L. 1992. "The Expansion of the Private Economy in China. Explaining Its Social Organization and Political Consequences." Working Paper. Department of Sociology, Harvard University.

Weber, Max. 1946. *From Max Weber: Essays in Sociology,* edited by H. H. Gerth and C. W. Mills. New York: Oxford University Press.

1978. *Economy and Society,* edited by G. Roth and C. Wittich. Berkeley and Los Angeles: University of California Press. (Originally published in 1922.)

Weigle, Marcia A., and Jim Butterfield. 1992. "Civil Society in Reforming Communist Regimes: The Logic of Emergence." *Comparative Politics* 4:1–23.

Westoby, Adam. 1983. "Conceptions of Communist States." Pp. 219–42 in *States and Societies,* edited by D. Held et al. New York: New York University Press.

Whyte, Martin King, and William Parish. 1984. *Urban Life in Contemporary China.* Chicago: University of Chicago Press.

Widor, Claude, ed. 1981–84. *Documents on the Chinese Democratic Movement 1978–*

80: Unofficial Magazines and Wall Posters. 2 vols. Paris: Editions de L'Ecole des Hautes en Sciences Sociales-Hong Kong: Observer Publishers.

Wiener, Philip P., ed. 1973. *Dictionary of the History of Ideas.* New York: Charles Scribner's Sons.

Williams, James H. 1990. "Fang Lizhi's Expanding Universe." *China Quarterly* 123:458–80.

Womack, Brantly. 1979. "Politics and Epistemology in China Since Mao." *China Quarterly* 80:768–92.

Yu Guangyuan and Hu Jiwei, eds. 1989. *Mengxing de Shike* (A Sudden Awakening). Beijing: Zhongwei Wenhua Publishing.

Zhang Yi. 1989. *Zhongguo Shehui Redian Nandian Yidian Wenti Fenxi* (An analysis of the common, difficult, and confusing questions in Chinese society). Beijing: Liberation Army Publishing House.

Zhang Yongjie and Cheng Yuanzhong. 1988. *Di Si Dai Ren* (People of the fourth generation). Beijing: Dongfang Publishing House.

Zhao Ziyang. 1987. *Documents of the Thirteenth National Congress of the Communist Party of China.* Beijing: Foreign Languages Press.

Zweig, David, and Steven Butler. 1985. *China's Agriculture Reform: Background and Prospects.* New York: China Council of the Asia Society.

Index

"all-around Westernization," 142–44, 162, 165
Anti-Spiritual Pollution Campaign of 1983–84, 40–41, 60, 72, 92, 117–18, 132, 168, 206
"April 5 Incident" of 1976, 84–85, 90, 102

Bai Hua, 99, 140–41
Bao Zunxin, 65, 68–69, 145, 190
Beijing Institute for Research on Social and Scientific-Technological Development, 74–76, 150, 175, 209
Bo Yibo, 41, 60, 143–44
book series (congshu), 65–69, 141–47
bureaucratic recruitment, 49, 79, 128

campus magazine, 70–71. See also unofficial publication
Cao Siyuan, 59, 188, 190
Capital Institute for Research on Legal Systems and Social Development, 64, 175, 188
Central Party School, 53, 60, 75, 89, 92, 175
Chen Yizi, 69, 168, 183–84, 190
Chen Yun, 61, 111–12, 130, 168, 189
Chen Ziming, 51, 74–76, 209
China's Youth, 64, 99, 103–9
Chinese Academy of Sciences (CAS), 47, 69, 75, 153
Chinese Academy of Social Sciences (CASS), 47, 52–53, 57–61, 64, 68, 74–75, 91–92, 118, 126, 130, 146, 169, 171, 183, 193, 206
civil society versus the state, concept of, 5, 10, 22–26, 28–30, 32–35, 132, 195
Communist Youth League (CYL), 47, 53,

64, 71, 74, 92, 99, 105, 108–9, 122–23, 131, 133, 154–55, 161, 174–75, 193
comparison, vertical and horizontal, 21–22, 115, 136, 145, 151, 162–63, 198
corruption, 42, 70, 73, 102, 109, 141, 143, 153, 157, 159, 164, 179–80, 182, 186, 189, 191, 198, 202, 212
counterelite, 4–5, 9, 11–12, 15, 18–19, 22, 27–28, 36–45, 77, 79–80, 83, 100, 113–14, 130–36, 140, 144–48, 155, 162, 165–66, 173–74, 187, 190, 192–93, 196–97, 205, 210. See also cultural intellectual; elite; intellectual and professional; marginal intellectual; official intellectual; technical intellectual; university students
"crisis of three (belief, trust, and confidence)" xin, 110–12, 114–15, 122
cultural intellectual (CI), 44, 46–49, 51, 65–66, 131, 133, 144, 150, 193. See also counterelite; intellectual and professional
Cultural Revolution of 1966–76, 4, 45, 53, 71–72, 77–78, 83–86, 88–89, 93–94, 98, 103, 105, 108, 110, 115, 123–24, 133, 141, 157, 164, 177, 198, 205

de-Maoization, 101, 110, 206
Democracy Movement of 1978–79, 43, 45, 54–55, 59, 74, 76, 99–103, 182, 198, 206
Deng Liqun, 40, 57–58, 60, 65, 69, 90, 97–98, 118, 124, 134, 144, 168, 173
Deng Xiaopeng, 1, 3–4, 40, 42–43, 54, 75, 77, 83–90, 97, 110, 113, 123, 127–30, 134, 141, 143–44, 168, 172, 178, 189–91, 198

227

Party Central Propaganda Department (PCPD), 47–48, 53, 56–58, 60, 69, 92, 122, 124, 130, 133, 143, 147, 155, 175, 193
patriotism, official versus critical, 140, 142–46, 148, 150, 153–55, 158, 160–65, 197
Pen Zhen, 54, 135, 189
People's Daily, 52, 71, 85–86, 88, 130, 150, 160, 175, 187
People's Liberation Army (PLA), 1, 3–4, 42, 124, 126, 128–29, 132, 135, 141–42, 161, 168, 175, 190, 194, 201–2, 205, 209
People's Publishing House in Beijing, 53, 56–57, 67
Petofi Club, 65, 175
political climate, micro versus macro, 57
"primary stage of socialism," 5, 166, 172–73, 175, 190

Qin Benli, 53, 61–62, 164, 190
"question and answer" material, 121–22, 126–27, 142–43, 202, 209–10

reference group, 101, 120, 136–37, 191
Reference News (*Cankao xiaoxi*), 115
revolutions of 1989, 5, 17, 20, 34, 37–38, 77, 175, 195, 197, 202
River Elegy, 148, 155–65
ruling elite, 2, 4–6, 9, 11–12, 18–19, 36, 38–43, 53, 56, 59, 63, 77, 83, 90–91, 93, 98, 101, 108, 110–11, 113, 122–23, 125–26, 135, 140, 142, 144–45, 158–59, 162, 174, 190, 192, 197, 205. *See also* elite

Science and Technology Daily, 51, 53, 61, 150, 175–76
sense of national crisis, 111, 145, 149–51, 154–55, 163, 185, 189, 200
"small treasury" (*xiao jinku*), 72–73
Soviet-bloc influence on Chinese, 6, 18, 21–22, 28–37, 39, 41, 43–44, 46, 49–52, 54–55, 63, 65, 90, 93–94, 98, 101–3, 110, 112, 116–17, 120, 125–26, 132, 141, 164, 169–71, 173, 175, 178, 184–86, 188–89, 191–93, 196–97, 199–200, 202, 212
"Spiritual Civilization," campaign to build, 5, 114–38, 197

Spring 1989 Democracy Movement, 1, 3–4, 6, 27, 46, 59–61, 76, 119, 154, 165–66, 190, 192–93, 200–2, 211–12
Stalin, Joseph, 15, 46, 77, 90–91, 94, 96, 103, 110, 120, 141, 164, 178, 196
Stone Company and Institute for Research on Social Development, 51, 59–60, 188
Su Shaozhi, 40, 43, 52, 58, 60, 65, 96, 173, 185–86, 190
Sun Changjiang, 53, 60, 65

Taiwanese influence on Chinese mainland, 43, 62, 73, 120, 125, 127, 137, 147, 149, 151, 159, 165, 167, 181–84, 186, 191–93, 199–200, 203. *See also* East Asian model
technical intellectual (TI), 44, 49–52, 65–66, 145, 150, 193. *See also* counterelite; intellectual and professional
tongren kanwu (cliquish journal), 27, 64, 66, 69–70, 131
"Toward the Future" series, 67–69, 145–46
transition from communism, 5, 9, 10, 26–27, 32, 35, 194–97, 202–3. *See also* revolutions of 1989

university students, 13, 36–37, 70, 131, 133–34, 154, 160, 175, 187, 190–93, 209, 211. *See also* counterelite; intellectual and professional
unofficial publication, 54–55, 60, 70, 99, 101–9, 198. *See also* campus magazine

voluntary organization, 27–28, 54–55, 57, 59, 62–64, 66–67, 72–78, 80, 145–46, 162, 188, 193–96, 203

Wan Runnan, 51, 150
Wang Dongxing, 85, 88, 90–91
Wang Juntao, 51, 74–76, 100, 182, 190, 209
Wang Ruoshui, 43, 52, 60, 64, 93–94, 98, 190
Wang Yuanhua, 64–65, 145
Wang Zhen, 40, 65, 90, 98, 143–44, 160, 164, 173, 189
Wei Jingsheng, 43, 54, 99–102
Wen Yuankai, 51, 118–19, 188–90